126355

D1420390

THE COMPLETE ENCYCLOPEDIA OF

BORDER PLANTS

Informative text with hundreds of photographs

HANNEKE VAN DIJK

REBO PUBLISHERS

The symbols:

ⵊ = annual

ⵛ = biennial

❀ = perennial

◌ = bulbous and tuberous plants

⊶ = sub-shrub

♨ = shrub

⥉ = tree

☼ = prefers sun

○ = prefers light-shade

◑ = prefers half-shade

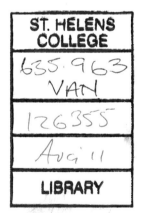
© 1997 Rebo International b.v., Lisse, The Netherlands

Text: Hanneke van Dijk
Cover design: Minkowsky Graphics, The Netherlands
Photography: Gerge M. Otter
Editor: Ireen Niessen
Production: TextCase, The Netherlands
Typesetting: Hof&Land Typografie, The Netherlands

ISBN 90 366 1585 2

Contents

Preface

Yesterday's cottage garden made way for the border as we know it today. Various plants together soon make a border, but variety is the spice of life.Show me your garden and I will tell you who you are. A formal, English border could belong to Gertrude Jekyll. A border with tall plants intertwining happily could be Ton ter Linden's*. A dream of a border with assorted grasses and natural perennials could belong to Piet Oudolf* and a rather exotic border in flaming colours suggests Christopher Lloyd. A border in which shapes and forms of flowers alternate with patches of colour reminds me of Mien Ruys*. All are artists when it comes to creating borders; plants seem to do their bidding without any effort.

Annuals, perennials, bulbs and tubers, shrubs and small trees together become the unique blend which we call a border. Plants blending into the limitations of space, possibilities and knowledge - and the last, a sound knowledge of plants, their characteristics and the demands they make on their environment, is the most important. We come across many of the traditional border plants, but there are also plenty of new ones in our present-day borders. New plants, even stronger, more beautiful and natural thanks to our devoted growers. This book is dedicated to them and to all gardeners. An up-to-date reference book for makers, lovers and users of borders with information on hundreds of border plants.

This encyclopaedia of border plants was compiled with great pleasure and the lavish photographs are by George.M.Otter. Many thanks are due to Brian Kabbes for his valuable comments and for going through the whole manuscript. Thanks also to Wim Snoeyer for checking the Agapanthus and Clematis, David Way for his advice on Penstemon and Pieter Zwijnenburg for his advice on shrubs. Thanks to Liesbeth Kappelhof for correcting this work and to Mineke Kurpershoek for the introduction.

Great care was taken in naming the plants. Synonyms have been given where necessary to avoid confusion.

Hanneke van Dijk

---

* Dutch growers and garden designers

Introduction

Borders

The sight of magnificent borders in full bloom when visiting an open garden, or one of the numerous model gardens on show at home and abroad can make many a gardener feel slightly jealous. What is the secret of such a splendid border?

We have to realise that a visit of this kind is a fleeting moment; the same border will look completely different a month later. A well-appointed border will have something to offer in every season and making one is a work of art.

There is much to be learned from visiting gardens; the pleasing combinations and the contrasting shapes of flowers and foliage. But try not to fall into the trap of copying a border which you admire in your own garden, or choosing only those plants which catch the eye. Just as with clothing, if you only buy showy things and forget the basics then nothing will match.

A border is more than a collection of plants

English double border (Culzean Castle)

Double border in a vegetable garden (Threave Garden)

Border combined with topiary (Mertoun Gardens)

and there is more to it than the plants alone. They are dependent on the type of soil, the light, the wind, the environment and last but not least, on our taking good care of them.

The soil

First of all you have to know what kind of soil you have. If your garden is new it is advisable to have a sample of the soil taken because it may look good and rich in humus, when it is in fact deficient in nutrients.

Old gardens may not have been manured for years. There may also be an impenetrable layer of hard clay under a part of the garden so that rainwater seeps into the subsoil very slowly. That spot could be suitable for a little marsh, covered with moisture-loving plants.

The first requirement for a beautiful garden and border is to put thought and money into the cultivation and improvement of the soil. Later on, once the garden has been laid out and planted it will be much more difficult and costly to correct any defects and you will be sorry that you did not pay more attention to the cultivation of the soil.

In a large garden it may be wise to install a sprinkler installation where the soil is sandy and dry. If this is too expensive, allow for water points at various places in the garden where the hose can be used for watering.

The light

The second important point is the light. With a south-facing garden and no trees or buildings to cast a shadow on your border for part of the day, you are free to choose sun-loving plants. These sun lovers will make do with less sun, but they must have at least five hours a day.

If your border only gets one or two hours of sun a day then shade-loving plants will be suitable. Between two and four hours will be ideal for the group of plants preferring partial shade. We all hope for plenty of sun and only at night some gentle rain. But we hardly ever have such ideal weather conditions in summer - so the hours of sun mentioned here merely indicate the needs of the plants.

The wind

The wind can cause severe damage to plants. Try to avoid putting tall, spindly plants in a windy area, unless you make a point of tying them up firmly, or placing them between other sturdier plants. For instance, you fancy one of the tall meadow rues/*Thalictrum* so much that you decide to have one like it in your border. See that it is in a sheltered position, supported by other, stronger hardy plants, or

low bushes so that its fluffy clusters wave elegantly over their crowns. If your garden is prone to fall winds and hard gusts of wind from between buildings then you should take sturdy, compact plants for preference.

In any case it is necessary to support plants in flat, windy country so that they do not fall apart. There are all kinds of supports on the market for this purpose, including plastic rings which are attached to a stake at the required height. The rings are applied early on so that the plants grow through them naturally. Unfortunately their unnatural green colour clashes with the plants.

The dark-green iron staves, which can be linked to form a web between and around perennials, are much better. But this system is quite expensive, as are the dark-green hoops which give all-round support to collapsed plants.Both these metal systems, which are driven into the ground, are available in varying heights.
Brushwood sticks are much cheaper but less durable. This branched pruning wood is best staked around the plant while its stalks are still fairly young. The plant then weaves itself between the branches, completely overgrowing the supporting branch within a few weeks, and hiding it from view.

Plants (*Baptisia australis*) supported by sticks (Blickling Hall)

Plants supported by sticks

Mixed border with white willow-herb, geraniums, phlox and elderberry. (Catforth Gardens)

Border of perennial plants combined with *Pirus salicifolia* 'Pendula' (Chomondeley Castle)

Brushwood sticks are usually only good for one or two seasons. Bamboo lasts much longer, many years will have passed before it rots. Tonkin canes are available in various thicknesses and lengths. These are straight stems of bamboo without sideshoots and very useful if applied properly. Instead of placing one cane against the plant and tying with string, wire or raffia, tie up each flower stem separately, or a few at a time. Tonkin canes are most suitable for tying up hollyhocks, delphiniums or monkshood, all of which have upright stems with little support from their own foliage. If you have a large clump of bamboo you can cut your own stems. Trim the leaves away from the sideshoots and you have a sturdy bamboo cane with sideshoots which are cut to size and staked around the plant for firm support. It has many advantages over the materials mentioned above. It is cheap and durable and it looks so natural that it does not spoil the overall effect of the border.
At the same time it is best to cut back many of the perennials by half before the longest day. The plants will be bushier with stronger growth, not so tall and still flowering (often later). Asters, monardas heleniums and eupatoriums benefit by this treatment.

Use

The way a garden is used is equally as important, even though it takes fourth place here. It is always a pity when the neighbours remark how lovely the garden looked while you were away on holiday. This can easily be taken into account when choosing plants, timing the holiday before or after they are in full bloom.

The same tactics were used by head gardeners of large estates in the old days, to ensure that the borders were at their best when the family was at home.

Choose easy-care plants if you are often away for the weekend, instead of plants which need to be tied up or deadheaded regularly.

Basic structure

Shrubs and trees form the bones of every garden and border, along with paths, a terrace, pond, pergola and other constructions.

A garden without shrubs is most unattractive and bare in winter as most perennials die off aboveground.
It is most important in a small garden to select trees and shrubs which do not grow too tall or

Smyrnium perfoliatum provides a colourful note (Piet Oudolf)

bushy and which look attractive for a longer period. The flowers which they produce are not the only consideration in this case, but the foliage and overall appearance or habit of the shrub. A *Forsythia* or a *Ribes* may look wonderful, but what will it look like for the rest of the year, after its exuberant flowering is over? This can be a very disappointing sight in summer, when its shape is out of place among the other plants. Why was this particular plant on the list? For its early blooms? See if you can find other shrubs which bloom during the same period but with a more pleasing appearance.

Perhaps the bright yellow hazel/*Corylopsis* is a better choice, or one of the fragrant viburnums. Another idea is the winter-flowering ornamental cherry/*Prunus subhirtella*, a real beauty, with tiny scented pale-pink flowers, sometimes as early as Christmas. It is a small tree or a sturdy shrub.

While on the subject of scent, put fragrant plants where you can enjoy them to the full; for instance beside the terrace or sitting area, under a bedroom window or by the front door to welcome visitors.

Animals in the garden

Twittering birds, fluttering butterflies and humming bees are lively accessories to all the flowering beauty in the garden and border. When compiling the list it would be friendly to cater for their needs by adding shrubs such as a serviceberry/*Amalanchier*, a butterfly bush/*Budleia*, *Caryopteris*, *Deutzia*, ivy/*Hedera helix* 'Arborescens' and *Hedera Colchica* 'Arborescens', *Kolkwitzia*, lavender, roses, lilacs,

Achillea, Delphinium and *Galega* with a clipped hedge as background (Newby Hall)

Salvia nemorosa 'Ostfriesland' is prominent in many borders

blackthorn/*Prunus spinosa* and viburnum to attract butterflies. Many hardy plants attract butterflies, bees and bumblebees, including the Mexican giant hyssop/*Agastache* and butterflyweed/ *Asclepias tuberosa*, masterwort/*Astrantia*, cone flower/*Echinacea*, globe thistle/*Echinops*, varieties of fleabane/*Erigeron*, eryngo /*Eryngium*, boneset/*Eupatorium*, sunflowers/*Helianthus* and *Heliopsis*, varieties of loosestrife, particularly the *Lysimachia clethroides*, bergamot plant/*Monarda*, ox-eye/ *Telekia*, *Verbena bonariensis*, also herbs including basil, chives, hyssop, marjoram, sage and thyme. Butterflies also love to sip from some of the annuals.

Butterflies are not alone in favouring serviceberry bushes and ivy; many birds visit them to feast on their berries in autumn and winter. Other berried trees and shrubs which tempt our feathered friends are holly, elderberry and the hips of some roses. When butterfly plants are included in a border, the butterflies will often lay their eggs there. These grow into caterpillars which can cause some damage.

The caterpillar stage is quite short and the plant singled out to feed on will soon recover, so please do not spray, but leave nature to restore the balance. There is no pleasure (butterflies) without pain (some damage).

Another point is that the caterpillars form a delicious meal for the birds which also have to feed their young during this period.

It would be disastrous for them to eat poisoned caterpillars. Fortunately organic pesticides have been developed in recent years for use in case of serious plagues, and these are not unduly harmful to nature.

The border in winter

Evergreens are indispensable when planning the lay-out of planting. Especially in winter they ensure that the garden is not dull and bare, giving it attractive focal points just when you need them.

Make a selection from the many evergreen shrubs and perennials and include a few lovely ferns. Bamboo also keeps its foliage in winter.

Grasses look stunning in winter and summer with their elegant silhouette, as long as they have not been cut back. There are also some evergreen ornamental grasses.

Leave the stalks with faded flower heads and seeds when possible to create lively, glistening forms in winter, frosty or snow-covered. Seeds also form the winter diet of many interesting birds. What could be prettier than a goldfinch eating seeds out of a teazel head?

How to continue

With the information given above you can now make a list of plants suitable for the soil and sun afforded in the border, using your favourite colours, naturally. Select plants from each group for separate lists; trees and shrubs first, then the perennials, annuals and bulbs. Note the height and spread of every plant, including their ultimate size, when they flower, the colour and perhaps the number of the page in the book where you saw the photograph of that very plant or combination of plants which appealed to you.

Planting

Now that you have made your lists you can begin to plan the lay-out for planting. Use squared paper and cover it with a sheet of transparent paper. Secure both with tape to a firm, smooth base such as a piece of hardboard. Draw the shape of the border to scale on the transparent paper. A scale of 1:100 is best, 1cm is then 1m (approx. 1/2in = 3ft). Of course you can use another scale, but this can be very confusing.

Verbascum, Campanula and roses (Cawdor Castle)

The squared paper (divided into centimetres and millimetres) gives something to go on for a sense of dimension.

Trees and shrubs

We will assume that there is an entirely new border to be made which is completely empty as yet. When planting a tree, consider that it may deprive the neighbours of sunlight. There are laws to prevent unpleasantness of this kind and trees should be planted at least 2 metres (6ft)from the boundary.

Shrubs and hedges can only be planted on the boundary between two gardens if there is mutual agreement on the subject. It is advisable to plant shrubs at least 50cm (20in) from the boundary as the friendly neighbours may move away, to be replaced by occupants with other ideas.

The number of trees and shrubs in the border will depend on the size of your garden and the space these plants will take up over the years. Another point to decide is whether the border is to consist mainly of shrubs with ground-cover and a few clumps of plants, or of many flowering perennials and annuals, with room for only a few shrubs besides.

Draw the shrubs in their fully-grown state and resist the temptation to plant them nearer together as you will regret this after a few years, when they encroach on each other and lose their individual character. It is best to plant more than one of each of a favourite variety, if you have room for them. The same applies to shrubs of medium height and spread. This promotes restful areas in the border and highlights the shrub when in flower.

A selection could include hydrangeas, the hardy *Fuschia*, lavender and other low shrubs which are often hardy, the lowest of which are *Deutzia*, genista, small rhododendrons, azalias and also *Caryopteris* and *Ceanothus*. Do not place them in a row against the background, let a group or a single shrub reach out to the foreground of the border and leave some space between shrubs. This creates depth and the plants look more vigorous and more interesting as a result.

Hedges

A hedge often forms an excellent backdrop for the lush growth of shrubs and colourful hardy plants. The emphasis is on the planting of the border which has to stand out against the background.

For this reason a green background is a better choice than a variegated one. An evergreen hedge is usually chosen as a screen between adjoining houses.

On new housing estates with small gardens, every street has its conifer hedge of Leyland cypress/ *Cupressocyparis leylandii*, which are cheap and evergreen, true enough. But they need regular attention which is usually overlooked and within a few years the problem arises that the hedge has become so wide that there is only a narrow strip of garden left where nothing will grow. Think ahead and plant a hedge which is easy to prune.

A gigantic border with a high beech hedge as background (Royal Botanic Garden Edinburgh)

Border against a partly free-growing hedge (Catforth Gardens)

Border enclosed between hedges (Levens Hall)

The cherry laurel/*Prunus laurocerasus* is another hedge which is only suitable for larger gardens. The loveliest conifer hedge is the yew, a beautiful dark green and easy to prune but it is expensive and poisonous (children, pets).

To be economical, the good old-fashioned privet, almost evergreen and unobtrusive, is a good choice. Deciduous hedges are fascinating because they change colour with every season: a lovely fresh green in spring, turning a darker green, to cheerful yellow in the autumn.
Among these are *Acer campestre*, the hornbeam/*Carpinus betulus*, and the beech/*Fagus sylvatica*. The last two hedges retain their leaves for most of the winter, turning brown in the meanwhile. Hedges of this kind are stunning with snow on them or hoary frost.

A well-kept hedge which is pruned will grow to a width of 30 to 50 cm (12-20in). Remember to plan a space between the hedge and the border for clipping.

Alternative backgrounds for the border

The hedge is not the only kind of background for a border. An old wall gives the garden a special atmosphere, but these are scarce and it is costly to have a wall built, particularly on loose peaty soil. A firm foundation is needed and it may be necessary to sink piles into the ground. A fence is a good alternative and less expensive.

Nowadays garden centres have all kinds of panels which simplify the job of putting up a fence.The fence should be as plain as possible in order to set off the flowers and shrubs well and preferably made of upright panel parts. As plants also grow vertically, the verticle lines of shade thrown on the fence will not be so noticeable.

The trellis or lattice work which is so popular at present is too transparent for a screen between neighbouring gardens. Lattice work is most suitable against a wall to train climbing plants, or as a screen between two parts of the garden.

A border in pastel colours in front of a clipped yew hedge (Kinross House)

A mixed border against an old wall as background (Chenies Manor)

Rush-mats are also suitable, but remember that they will only last for a few years. Wire-netting covered with climbing ivy forms a splendid green backdrop after some years, remaining quite narrow if cut back every year.

A closed background is not ideal in windy parts. The wind will rebound off a wall or fence, causing much damage to the plants positioned against it. This is not the case with a hedge or trellis as background because the wind is not broken, but able to blow straight through them.

A lupin border (Chatsworth)

The shrub border

It is really important in a shrub border not to plant one of each kind, as this will become chaotic. What applies to all planting is certainly true of the shrub border, that it should not be without a good basic structure. Look for clear contrasts in foliage and growth. For instance, a tall, specimen shrub with decorative overhanging branches and lovely

A split-level border (Culzean Castle)

racemes of flowers, or a small tree, is planted among a group of ivy or hydrangeas. It could be a serviceberry or a hortensia, a fine Japanese maple, a witch hazel *Hamamelis*, or a winter flowering *Viburnum bodnantese* or *Prunus subhirtella*.

One of the many crab apples are also worth considering with their spring blossom and attractive fruit later on. For interest in winter there should be some evergreens or groups of them.

My personal preference is for rhododendrons and holly rather than conifers and their golden-yellow cultivars; there are the familiar high varieties and *Ilex crenata* resembling box.

The *Skimmia* and the ivy/*Hedera helix* 'Arborescens' mentioned above are beautiful; and for a sunny spot the grey-green *Elaeagnes x ebbingei*, very fragrant when in bloom. Another evergreen is mahonia, but it is not a popular shrub, perhaps because it is often planted in public parks. The *Mahonia bealei*, which grows taller than the other varieties,

A peony border (Helmingham Hall)

woodland planting of rhododendrons, for instance, will also require woodland ground cover: evergreen ivy, periwinkle/*Vinca*, and *Pachysandra* could form the basis, interspersed with smaller groups of low, hardy plants for contrast. Add a group of contrasting ferns, astilbe, large-leaved hosta or rodgersia. Foxglove/*Digitalis* provides a striking vertical note. In spring you can enliven the shrub border with various flowering bulbs and tubers, particularly those which will naturalize, like narcissus, crocus, snowdrop, winter aconite and for later the bluebell/*Hyacinthoides hispanica* syn. *Scilla hispanica*, or the tall and magnificent *Camassia*.

has a splendid habit which comes out best in low, even ground cover.

Box/*Buxus*, can be clipped formally, or it can be left to grow; depending on the variety it will stay compact, but not quite so formal. Ground cover will be needed as the link between all these different shrubs, to create a unified whole. Choose one or more varieties according to the size of the border and plant lovely big patches of them. There are many varieties and the choice is also determined by its position in relation to the sun and the character of the shrub border. A border with

Contrasts

It makes no difference whether the border is in the sun or the shade, but it is important that the planting looks vigorous at all times. As perennial plants often bloom only once, (but then for several weeks), with a lighter second flowering later in the season, the structure of the leaves deserves attention. See that delicate foliage is set off against coarse or even very large leaves.

As moisture evaporates more readily from large leaves than feathery leaves, we usually

An astilbe border (Ness Botanic Gardens)

Alstroemeria and *Salvia sclarea* (Hill of Tarvit)

find large-leaved plants in light shade and shaded spots.

Hosta, rodgersia, *Kirengeshoma*, the light green foliage of the *Astilboides* and the shiny leaves of the *Darmera* are their strong features. The latter tolerates more sun as long as the soil is moist and this also applies to other large-leaved plants including the sea kale/ *Crambe cordifolia*, the yellow flowering ligularia, the plume poppy/*Macleaya* and the ornamental rhubarb/*Rheum palmatum* var.

Lilies and *Ruta* in an unexpected combination (Holker Hall)

tanguticum. The *Bergenia* should stand in the foreground with its sturdy evergreen, glossy leaves. Lady's mantle/ *Alchemilla mollis* has beautiful foliage and is found in almost every garden. The *Brunnera* also remains decorative after the glorious forget-me-not-blue flowers in spring, thanks to its large round leaves: an excellent plant for a lightly shaded spot.

Contrasting splendidly with all these large to very large leaves are the delicate green foliage of the fern, the low *Corydalis lutea, C. ochroleuca* and the bleeding heart/ *Dicentra*.

Varieties of rue/*Thalictrum* have the same leaf structure; the height of these plants varies from 80cm (32in) to over 2m (6ft), depending on the sort and the cultivar. Another contrasting note is a different type of leaf found in the blades of various grasses which combine well with all the other types of foliage. Like the ornamental grasses, the iris, the spiderwort/*Tradescantia* and the day lily/ *Hemerocallis* also have long, slender leaves. Plant a group of these shapely types of foliage for a pleasing effect between the perennials with less conspicuous or feathery leaves.

You should also take note of the various ways of flowering.

Alternate strong, vertical spiky leaves with the pronounced flower shapes of various composites, including Michaelmas daisies/*Aster*, marguerites, fleabane/*Erigeron*, sneezeweed/*Helenium*, *Heliopsis* and the coneflowers/*Rudbeckia* and *Echinacea*.

The image of the border is often determined by these plants with pronounced flowers such as the Japanese anemone, poppy and peony, and plants which bloom profusely in a riot of colour while they do so, for instance the phlox; all are striking features in the border. Plant them in several groups to show them off or make the group larger than those of fine-leaved plants. Plants with domed clusters of flowers provide a horizontal splash of colour when they flower; among these are the yarrow *Achillea* and the late flowering succulents *Sedum telephium*, *S. spectabile* and their cultivars and hybrid cultivars.

Strong, upright blooms contrast well with other plants, whether fine-boned, or dome-shaped clusters or big. Mexican giant hyssop/*Agastache*, foxglove/*Digitalis* purpurea and other varieties *D. ferruginea* and *D. grandiflora* and monkshood/*Aconitum* in light shade, *Delphinium*, several salvias, *Dictamnus*, purple loosestrife/*Lythrum*, mullein/*Verbascum* and above all, the high varieties of veronica now known as *Veronicastrum virginicum*, and the lower *V. longifolia*, to name some examples. Bear's breeches/*Acanthus* has sturdy, upright, spiky flowers, together with magnificent large, dark -green leaves.

Grey-leaved plants love the sun, lending the border a distinctive character if several varieties are arranged in large groups. You can try

A contrasting combination of *Campanula, Phlox* and *Astilbe* (Castle Kennedy)

Campanula and Hemerocallis - contrast in colour and shape (Newby Hall)

Roses, grasses and perennials provide diversity (Newby hall)

out combinations of these strong, distinctive plants, with all kinds of flowering plants with a delicate or feathery habit.

As long as you arrange groups with clear-cut outlines in the border, the design can hardly fail.

Planting

The number of plants you use in a group naturally depends on the variety of plant and the type of soil. Plants will grow bigger on clay than on sandy soil. No definite answer can be given to this question. Most plants are arranged in groups of seven to the square metre (3ft2), or there may be nine smaller plants, or five or sometimes only three of the larger plants. For instance, if you buy periwinkle/*Vinca*, as ground cover and plant seven plants to the square metre (3ft2) as some books advise, the long horizontal shoots will soon begin to climb upwards against each other, resulting in a rolling green landscape instead of an even ground cover.

Mark on your planting plan how big the patch of any particular plant is to be and work out how many plants you will need. The more you know about plants, the better this will be. When visiting a garden it would be wise to take note of the size and above all the spread of a plant, in addition to the flowers and combination of plants.

A good grower will never part with his plants without giving you advice and he will not sell you more plants than you need in your garden. It is essential that you buy the plants from a really good nursery so that your border gets off to a good start. Then at least you know the plants are named correctly and that they are of good quality, because one plant is not always as good as another. Beware of bargains at the counter and giveaways and plant the border according to plan.

Now that plants and shrubs are grown in containers it has become possible to plant them all the year round. But whether it is such a good idea to plant a border at the height of summer, when the sun is high in the sky is another matter. It is still preferable to plant in spring or autumn. Sensitive plants are best planted in spring. See to it that the border is well-dug and manured and lay the plants out before planting them. If the plants are in pots, you can safely lay out the whole border at

This photograph shows how the entire front garden was made into a border

once. But if they have bare roots it will be better not to do this or the roots will dry out. Plant the shrubs first in a mixed border and only then the perennials.

Make the planting holes deep enough and press the soil firmly into place and around the roots so that they are in close contact with the soil. When the border is planted, water it well and keep this up until the plants have struck root.

Roses, *Delphinium, Eremurus, Geum* and *Nepeta* (Newby Hall)

Grasses give the border an unexpected dimension
(Coen Jansen)

Box hedges separate the border from the path
(The Crossing House)

Colours

Every border contains the colours of both flowers and foliage. In a shady border green will be dominant. Provide varying leaf structures and contrasting shades of green.
For instance, the dark-green of the hazelwort/*Asarum europaeum* is a perfect foil for light-green ferns. A *Hosta* with variegated foliage makes a stunning accent in a dark corner. But do not put a holly with variegated leaves beside it as this will diminish the strength of both. Put the variegated holly some distance away and never bring too many different species of variegated foliage together in a small space.

A self-coloured border is very popular these days. The colour is not important, but the greenish-yellow flowering plants such as lady's mantle/*Alchemilla* and spurge /*Euphorbia* can be combined with every colour forming attractive, restful areas. There are many splendid combinations imaginable with grey-leaved plants, especially together

with various pastel shades. Red-leaved shrubs and perennials often provide beautiful accents. In order to find the right colour combination it will be worthwhile to study many of them and to write down your preferences. A variety of gardening books with magnificent photographs can be a source of inspiration. The choice of colour is a personal matter and that is a good thing too, otherwise all gardens would look alike.

Annuals and biennials

In recent years growers and seed merchants have been giving more thought to the assortment of annuals and biennials.In addition to an extensive range of seeds there is an increasing number of unusual and attractive plants to be found which lend colour to the border all through the summer. It is a joy to see how some garden-owners enrich their borders with these plants.

Flowering bulbs and tubers

There are many splendid varieties of bulbs, corms and tubers which are suitable for the border. Not only the familiar spring-flowering snowdrop, crocus and narcissus, but also a fantastic array of summer flowering varieties including the little known hyacinth *Galtonia*, the *Gladiolus callicanthus* 'Murielae' and not forgetting the beauty of allium, eremurus, dahlias, tuberous begonias and of course the magnificence of lilies.
The disadvantage of bulbous plants is often that their dying foliage becomes untidy and

Nepeta edging along the border (The Old Rectory)

yellow as it dies off soon after, or even while the plant is flowering. This foliage ensures that the bulb absorbs enough nutrients to regain its strength and reproduce itself in order to produce flowers again next year. For this reason it has to die off slowly and may not be cut off. As this may take several weeks, many a gardener will think twice before planting bulbs. If you plant the bulbs behind other plants, these will hide the fading foliage from view.

Low, early-flowering bulbs can be put between *Tiarella*, periwinkle/*Vinca*, low campanulas or low varieties of geranium. The grassy foliage of narcissus remains a pleasing accent for a while after flowering, until it turns yellow when it looks ugly against the fresh green of shrubs and perennials. In order to be rid of this blemish you can plait the leaves and lay them between the perennials, so giving them a chance to die off. Secure the plait to the ground with a stick or piece of wire if necessary. It is also quite simple to knot the leaves together and smuggle them away between plants.

The high growth of various plants which flower in summer, such as the *Eremurus* and the highest allium, is shown off well behind a group of asters about 50cm (20in) high. The ugly leaves are then completely hidden behind a group of perennials.

Care of the border

The border is made up of living things, which makes the planting a movable feast. However much thought you put into the selection of species which, according to the books, are suited to the soil and the hours of sun in the garden, there are always some plants which die, and others which thrive so well that they fill the open places, or try to oust their neighbour. You will have to intervene continually to keep the border as lovely and harmonious as possible. You can experiment freely with annuals in the vacant spots. There may be some plants which remain smaller or grow taller than was indicated. It helps to make notes and perhaps photographs of plants

The borders spill over the path, softening the hard outline (Capesthorne Hall)

A white border (Ton ter Linden)

which you want to transplant in the autumn. However good your memory is, keep a note of the places where bulbs are planted to avoid damaging them when transplanting perennials, as it often turns out that they are just to the right or behind the spot where you thought they were.

Staking plants was mentioned above under the heading of 'The wind'. Place the supports early on so that the plants can grow through them naturally. If you wait too long, until the plant is mature and falling over, the supporting material will be visible and the flower stems will have grown crooked. Supporting the stems at this stage with the crooked stems bent over inwards will be an ugly sight and it will take them some time to resume their natural upward growth.

It is best not to clear away all the fallen leaves and faded flowers in the autumn; this makes for a pleasing sight in winter, especially when there is snow or white frost to enliven the branches and flowers with a delicate crystal lace edge. This is not only pretty, but it is also much better for the plants. Where plants have been cut off, water can collect in the hollow stalks and this will damage the plant, when it freezes. Remove the fallen leaves of plants which were diseased, for instance from roses. There are some disorders which will otherwise recur the following year. Healthy leaves are best left in the border where possible. All kinds of beetles and other insects find shelter there and they eat the rotting leaves which are turned into compost in this way. Bear in mind that all those tiny creatures make a meal for hungry birds. The fallen leaves also form a thick blanket, protecting the roots of plants from the cold and above all from severe frost. When spring comes, first remove the thick layer from the place where the bulbs are beginning to show their noses, starting with the smallest bulbs which would otherwise be stifled. Clear the rest of the border later, raking the leaves away carefully from between the plants and bushes and cut off last year's stems from the perennials.

Remove faded heads regularly from plants which flower early as this stimulates a second flowering. Autumn-flowering phlox/*Phlox paniculata* and cultivars are often topped when they are about 30cm (1ft) high to stimulate the growth of sideshoots, so that the plant develops bushier growth. This can be done with the hedge-clippers.

Put delphiniums behind a group of hardy plants of medium height as there is very little left of a delphinium when it has finished flowering and the stalk has been cut off.

A final word

This book will be a great help in making a satisfactory selection of plants with which to create a border. A border is never really finished. There will always be plants which do not survive the winter, or which have so many offspring that they overgrow other plants. There will also be plants which refuse to grow in your garden, although you have taken all its requirements into consideration. A plant may turn out smaller, or much taller than was indicated.

The various border plants are described in detail and the conditions which they prefer have been carefully considered. Annuals, biennials, perennials, summer-flowering bulbs, tubers and shrubs which are suitable for a border are discussed in alphabetical order. It is an excellent and up-to-date reference book. I wish you great pleasure and success with your border.

Mineke Kurpershoek

Acanthus pattern

Acanthus

BEAR'S BREECHES

❀ ☼

An impressive plant, not one to lose itself in a crowd. At home in a border or as a specimen when it can take on great dimensions. The magnificent leaves are deeply cut with more or less finely-divided leaves according to the variety. It grows from a rosette at ground level, with spectacular blooms which tower above it in July and August. The plant dislikes wet soil and must never be planted in the autumn. It is hardy but it is best to protect it from frost, particularly during the first winter. The foliage of *Acanthus* was used in ornamental patterns by the ancient Greeks.

Acanthus mollis

Acanthus spinosus

Left: *Acer palmatum* ' Ornatum'

The splendid dark-green spiny foliage of *Acanthus spinosus* was their model, a plant which can reach a height of 1,5m (5ft) including its lilac-pink flowers. There is much confusion over its names and it appears that *Acanthus spinosus* 'spinosissimus' (a cross between *A. mollis* and *A. longifolius*) with more deeply cut leaves, is often sold under the generic name. *Acanthus hungaricus* (syn. *A. balcanicus* and A. *longifolius)*; it has deeply-cut, toothed leaves, but without sharp spines. The reddish-purple bracts are spinous.

Acanthus mollis remains smaller, 1m (3ft) and has huge, less deeply-cut leaves. The higher cultivar *A. mollis* 'Latifolius' is usually sold because it is a stronger variety, able to withstand severe frost, like the *A. hungaricus* and *A. spinosus*. The flowers on their long stems can be dried after flowering.

Acer palmatum 'Bloodgood'

Achillea miilefolium 'LachsschÜnheit'

low shrub with bronze foliage turning a splendid orange-brown in autumn. Maples thrive on soil rich in humus; of course, there are other Japanese maples suitable for a mixed border, with their beautiful habit and remarkable leaf-shape and colour. They form a good foil for perennials with their deeply-cut foliage, sometimes with finely divided fronds.

Acer

MAPLE

Acer palmatum, the Japanese maple tree with green, digital, deeply-lobed, star-like leaves, has several cultivars of great beauty. The cultivar 'Bloodgood' has lovely black-red foliage turning a flaming crimson in autumn. This shrub with reddish-purple flowers, followed by winged red fruits, blooms in spring; it can grow up to 3m (9ft). It is a cultivar from America, an improved 'Atropurpureum' which retains its remarkably dark leaves the whole summer. *Acer palmatum* 'Nicholsonii' grows as wide as it is high, 2-3m(6-9ft) with big green leaves tinged with brilliant red in spring and turning a deep red in the autumn. *Acer palmatum* 'Ornatum' is a

Achillea

YARROW

Someone ought to write a book about the achillea. This familiar plant likes a dry and sunny border and it always used to be planted to contrast with long, spiky flowers. Most of the long stems bear broad, flat clusters of tiny flowers and the leaves are so cut as to resemble ferns. The best-known achillea are cultivars of the *A. filipendulina*, A.*f* . 'Parker's Variety' and 'Cloth of Gold', with large yellow clusters of flowers which can be dried. Both grow to a height of 1,2m (4ft) and have that distinctive *Achillea* aroma. These

Acer palmatum 'Atropurpureum'

Achillea millefolium 'Peardrops'

Achillea ptarmica 'The Pearl'

Aconitum × cammarum 'Bicolor'

plants may be considered common, but there are enough cultivars of *A. millefolium*, the common yarrow growing in the wild, to choose from.

Every nurseryman grows the plants which he prefers, for instance, the pale-yellow 'Martina', the wine-red 'Summerwine', the crimson 'Fanal', the apricot-coloured 'Lachssch Ünheit', the pink 'Peardrops', the pale mauve 'Lilac Beauty', the white 'Schneetaler' and 'White Beauty', 'Wesersandstein', with the colour of flagstones, the yellow 'Credo' and the red 'Petra' - we could go on and on. There are hybrid-cultivars including the familiar light-yellow 'Moonshine' and the less well-known red 'Walter Funcke'. German growers in particular are working on the development of new cultivars.

There are more varieties, such as *Achillea grandifolia*, a very high plant, 1,5m (5ft) with clusters of white flowers and *Achillea ptarmica*, including 'The Pearl'. Achilleas are rewarding plants, but they dislike wet feet. The yarrow especially is not long-lived and has to be regenerated regularly. The new 'Summer Pastels', a mixture of pastel shades, can bloom in its first year and is at its best if sown every year.

Aconitum septentrionale 'Ivorine'

Aconitum

MONKSHOOD

✿ ○ ◕ ☼

The beautiful monkshood is extremely poisonous. Some varieties can be seen in Scandinavian woods. They need a spot with some shade and moist, fertile soil. But the pale-yellow *A. lamarckii*, 1m (3ft) from southern Europe which blooms in June and July and some of the cultivars love the sun. The elegant ivory-white *A. septentrionale* 'Ivorine' , 70cm (28in) high, begins to flower in May and continues for some time, even in the

Aconitum henryi 'Spark's Variety'

September with 1m (3ft)-high spikes of brilliant blue flowers and glossy green foliage. 'Arendsii' 80cm (32in) and 'Barker's Variety', 1,5m (5ft) make their dark-blue and amethyst contribution to the border in late summer. Early-flowering monkshood needs a successor in the border because it disappears after flowering. If the plants decline, they should be replanted: select the largest tubers.

Actaea

BANEBERRY

⊛ ○ ◕

Sturdy, shade-loving plants which need moist soil. They are more like a small shrub than a perennial and that is due to their berries. After the white flowers have faded they produce a dessert of conspicuous berries. The true *Actaea* with white flowers and black berries is so rare that it is an endangered species. There are some varieties with white and red berries. *Actaea pachypoda*, 1m (3ft) has beautiful white berries on red stalks; *Actaea rubra*, or Red baneberry, 50cm (20in) resembles it but has red berries on thin red stalks. The berries are poisonous.

Adenophora

GLAND BELLFLOWER

⊛ ☼

These vigorous plants can hardly be distinguished from campanulas. But Adenophora has a raised ring at the base of the flower which Campanula has not. *Adenophora liliifolia* grows to a height of 50cm (20in) and flowers in July and August with violet-blue, bell-shaped flowers on lightly bending stems. *Adenophora aurita*, 50cm, has blue-grey foliage and porcelain blue flowers.

sun. Many monkshoods will grow in the sun, but they flower longer if they are in a shady position. Other early-flowering monkshoods are *A. napellus*, the common dark blue and its cultivars: the white 'Album', 80cm (32in); 'Grandiflorum Album', 1ß2m (4ft) and the off-white 'Carneum' ('Roseum'). *A. x cammarum* 'Bicolor' is an early-flowering blue monkshood with a white edge and 'Franz Marc' is a bright blue cultivar which blooms a little later. *Aconitum henryi* 'Spark's Variety', 1,2m (4ft) produces deep blue flowers in July and August. *A. carmichaelii* is one of the monkshoods which flowers late, in August and

Actaea rubra (red berry) + *Actaea pachypoda* (white berry)

Adonis aestivalis

28

Adonis aestivalis

Adenophora takedae 'Alba', 40cm (16in) has pendent white flowers. These are not difficult plants to grow as long as they have well-drained, fairly dry soil and a sunny position.

Adonis

♀ ☼

Adonis aestivalis resembles a piece of burning coal, with firy red flowers and a dark centre, like the anemone, contrasting well with the delicate foliage. These are easy plants to sow in the garden where they flower from July to September.

Sow them outdoors in good soil in a sunny position as they have a tap root and do not like being transplanted.

Agapanthus in pot

Agapanthus africanus 'Albus'

Agapanthus

AFRICAN LILY

❀ ☼

Often seen in tubs, as most of them are not hardy. The Headbourne-hybrids changed this; they can be grown outdoors if protected in winter by a covering of mulch and conifer branches. The plants grow much bigger outdoors and flower more profusely than in a tub. They need a sunny spot and fertile, well-drained soil, especially in winter. It is said that the width of the leaves affects their hardiness, but growers deny this. The dark blue 'Bressingham Blue', the 'Bressingham White', the blue 'Bressingham Triumphator', the white 'Umbellatus Albus', and the smaller, 50cm

Agapanthus in pots can be placed in the border

Agastache rugosa 'Alabaster'

Agastache foeniculum

(20in) dark blue 'Liliput' are fairly hardy. We can always smuggle an Agapanthus which is not hardy, such as the 'Albus', between the other borderplants, pot and all.

Agastache

MEXICAN GIANT HYSSOP

These hardy plants suddenly became popular, perhaps because they are so attractive to butterflies. They are short-lived, but seed themselves with such enthusiasm that this is

Agastache rugosa

no problem. They love the sun and well-drained soil and they need some light cover against frost. The leaves have a strong aroma (not always pleasant).

A. rugosa is the most common species, a bushy, rather coarse plant with violet-blue flowers and a scent of aniseed and mint. 'Alabaster' 1m (3ft), a cultivar with light-green foliage and white flowers, looks splendid in a border. *A. cana* is not so coarse, 50cm (20in) high with mauve plumes, but less hardy, as also *A. barberi* 'Firebird', with orange flowers. This cultivar stems from *A. rupestris*. *A. mexicana*, a rose-red flowering plant is beautiful but not hardy, with a deep pink cultivar, 'Mauve Beauty'. The plant which is sold under this name is not a cultivar of *A. mexicana*, but of the wild *A. barberi*. 'Champagne' is a true cultivar of *A. mexicana*. *A.* 'Blue Fortune' is a new hybrid-cultivar with long bluish-purple spikes of flowers. This cross between *A. rugosa* and *A. scrophulariifolia* is not self-seeding as it is sterile. *Agastache scrophulariifolia*, 1m (3ft) flowers from July into September with violet-blue spikes of flowers. The names given to these plants are confusing to say the least. *A. foeniculum*, which is often available, usually turns out to be *A. rugosa* or *A. scrophulariifolia*. The genuine A. foeniculum, 1m (3ft) which is seldom grown, has dark-green, glossy foliage, with white undersides, short leaf stalks and a penetrating aroma of aniseed. *A. rugosa* has longer leaf stalks, mid-green foliage with inconspicuous undersides and a minty, aniseed aroma. *A. scrophulariifolia* is less distinctive and has no noticeable scent.

Ageratum

FLOSS FLOWER
↕ ☀

This annual edging plant has some higher, less compact cultivars which are excellent for use in the border. They can be sown and brought on indoors, but they are also available as small plants from specialised growers.

Make sure that you have the right cultivar as any *Ageratum* will usually be a low one. *Ageratum houstonianum* 'Kwekersblauw' grows to 60cm (2ft) , the purple-blue 'Dondoschnittperle' 70cm (28in), the mid-blue 'Blue Horizon' also 70cm, the deep-blue 'Dondo Blue' 80cm (32in)and 'Old Grey', 50cm (20in) is a powder-blue colour. These high cultivars are good border plants and excellent for cutting.

Ageratum 'Summit' remains low, good edging plant

Ageratum in the border

A group of *Agrostemma githago*

Agropyron

❀ ☀

Agropyron pubiflorum is one of the grasses which are grown for their foliage instead of the flowers. The long, slender leaves are a blue-grey colour which goes well with flowering perennials. Many of the *Agropyron* species belong to the *Elymus* genus. Most notorious of these is the *Elymus repens* or couch grass. Even the most tolerant gardener dislikes this type of grass with unbelievably rampant growth by means of its long stolons. There is no fear of this with *Agropyron pubiflorum* as it does not spread, but unfortunately it is not quite hardy.

Agrostemma

CORNCOCKLE
↕ ☀

Who would have thought that this weed of the cornfield, *Agrostemma Githago*, would ever come to grace our borders? Of course the word weed is only relative and the corncockle is seldom seen in fields, and then only in mild areas. This annual plant can be sown outdoors in autumn or early spring. Once it has settled down in the border it will seed itself every year after which it will be a matter of weeding to keep it within limits.

The corncockle will be at home in a cottage garden where plants grow profusely, interweaving of their own accord. 'Milas' is a deep-pink cultivar and there is a selection of this, 'Purple Queen", with larger, purple flowers. This branched plant grows to a height of 60 to 80 cm (2-2¹/₂ft) and is also excellent for cutting. The seeds are poisonous, so take care with children.

Agrostemma and *Linaria*

Agrostemma githago

Ajuga

✳ ○ ☀

This rewarding ground-cover plant has a part to play in the border. For instance, it is useful at the edge of the border to fill in bare spaces, or in an alternative border where high plants rise up from the ground cover, as the edging of island beds and in the favoured English border without a background. There are many different varieties, all flowering in May and June: *Ajuga reptans* 'Alba', with the best evergreen foliage and white flowers; *Ajuga reptans* 'Grey Lady' with light greenish-grey

Ajuga reptans 'Catlin's Grant'

leaves like flecks of light in the shade; 'Boromir', 30cm (1ft), with deep blue flowers; 'Ivoren Toren', a white cultivar of the same height; 'silver Shadow' with grey-blue spikes of flowers and hairy, light green foliage; 'Catlin's Giant', with larger flowers and big purple leaves; 'Jungle Beauty', with large dark green leaves and indigo-blue flowers; 'Rosea', with pink flowers and 'Pink Surprise', with lilac-pink flowers toning beautifully with the purple of the foliage. There are plants with variegated leaves: 'Multicolor', with brown-red foliage, flecked with pink and white; 'Variegata', with white-flecked leaves and 'Burgundy Glow', with three-coloured foliage. These plants need more light to retain their colours. It is odd that all these cultivars stem from the creeping *Ajuga reptans* which still grows in the wild.

Ajuga reptans 'Rosea'

Ajuga reptans 'Burgundy Glow'

Alcea rosea

Alcea against a wall

Albizia

🌱 ☼

Trees are not often planted in a border, but *Albizia julibrissin*, the Silk tree is sometimes given a place for its decorative foliage. This small deciduous tree, 6m (18ft) has lovely feathery foliage; it flowers in late summer and autumn with striking clusters of pink flowers. *Albizia julibrissin* var. *rosea*, a smaller tree with candy-pink clusters of flowers, is hardier. The trees grow in the wild from Iran to Japan, but they are not fully hardy and will need a sheltered position, preferably against a wall.They love the sun and well-drained soil.

Alcea

HOLLYHOCK

🌱 🌿 ☼

There is something magical about hollyhocks, perhaps to do with Andersen's fairy tales or pretty cottages with hollyhocks against their walls, at least as high as the house. It is difficult to see the difference between the annual, biennial and even the short-lived hardy plants. The modern cultivars of *Alcea rosea* will often flower in the same year if sown early. The packets of seed usually contain an assortment of hollyhocks in various colours. Sometimes they are sorted into singles, doubles, (Chater's Doubles) or fringed. But self-coloured hollyhocks are more

attractive in the border. *Alcea rosea* 'Nigra' is a single hollyhock, almost black; A. rosea 'Negrita' has double flowers, just as dark. A. *rosea* 'Icycle' is a double white, A. *rosea* 'Newport Pink' a double pink; A. *rosea* 'Chamois' and 'Double Apricot' have double, apricot-coloured flowers. 'Chamois Cockade' is a distinctive shade of orange-yellow and 'Chestnut Mare' has chestnut-brown flowers.

Alcea, white hollyhocks

Alcea ficifolia, a branched plant with pale-yellow, single flowers and deeply cut, fig-like foliage. These hollyhocks are also available in other colours and they can return for three or four consecutive years. All hollyhocks love a position in the sun, a warm spot and fertile soil.

Alchemilla

LADY'S MANTLE
✿ ☀

Alchemilla mollis is a bestseller which we see in many gardens. The leaves are almost round, lobed, hairy and a grey-green colour, holding a drop of water in their centres after dew or rain. They are very useful in flower arrangements. The pale green sprays of tiny flowers are ideal to give body to bouquets - and to the border. The species grows to a height of 40 cm (16in).

The cultivar 'Robustica' exactly resembles the species; the cultivar-name 'Senior' is often

Alchemilla mollis - foliage

Alchemilla mollis as border edging

Alchemilla erythropoda

used for cuttings or separated plants. Lady's mantle seeds itself so successfully that it is advisable to remove the flower heads after blooming, to avoid endless weeding.

Alchemilla venosa sometimes called *Alchemilla mollis* ' Mr. Poland's Variety' is smaller than A. mollis and rarely seeds itself. Added to this, it is not sensitive to mildew, which is more than can be said of other alchemillas.

Lady's mantle feels at home between the stones as well as in the border, adorning Gertrude Jekyll's terraces in her time. *A. erythropoda* does not seed itself and remains much lower than *A. mollis*. According to some growers *A. epipsila* is superior to *A. mollis* as regards foliage and flowers.

Alchemilla laperousii is a healthy species, with grey-green leaves, silvery-green and hairy on the underside. Lady's mantle often begins to bloom in May, continuing until September.

Allium

ONION
✿ ◇ ☀

Onions, chives, garlic and many more are all called Allium. Some are most suitable for the border, if they can be forgiven for their yellowing foliage as the flowers of the *Allium* last much longer than the leaves. *Allium* 'Purple Sensation' (*A. aflatunense* 'Purple Sensation') towers above perennial plants in May and June, with its grand, deep-purple globes.

The globes, on their 70 cm (28in)-tall stems, continue to play a part in the border after flowering. *Allium caeruleum* (*A. azureum*)

Allium 'Purple Sensation'

Alstroemeria in a conifer

Allium caeruleum

sphaerocephalon, the familiar drumsticks, have 5 cm (2in)-wide, very compact globe-shaped blooms on 70cm (28in)-tall stems. A large group of this allium belongs in every garden, in combination with *Hosta*, *Artemisia* and grasses. *Allium* with small globes can hold its own very well in the border, but the species with larger globes should be cleared after flowering and stored at a temperature of 23-25 °C, (70-75°F) to be replanted in another place in November.

Allium likes well-drained soil and a wet winter could be fatal. There is an incredible number of them, besides those mentioned above, so it is worth considering allium with a view to planting some in the border.

Alstroemeria

PERUVIAN LILY
 ☼

We all know these as cut flowers which do very well in mixed bouquets. Peruvian lilies are grown in a hothouse because they are not hardy. There are some cultivars which can stand up to 10°C of frost, (14°F) not quite hardy, but they can survive a winter if it is not too severe, given protective covering. *Alstroemeria aurea* 'Lutea' is yellow, growing to 80 cm (32in) tall, *Alstroemeria aurea* 'Orange King' is bright orange. This colour is rare in perennials and can bring a cheerful note to a yellow border.

flowers in June with globe-shaped blue blooms on 40cm (16in)-tall stems. This *Allium* is not usually recognised as such and is sometimes mistaken for an *Agapanthus*. The mauve blooms of *Allium sphaerocephalon* top the shorter stems of 40cm (16in) in July. *Allium*

Allium sphaerocephalon

Alstroemerias flower from June until August. Peruvian lilies need a sunny position in the border and well-drained soil.They prefer dry conditions to wet and may sometimes disappear after a wet winter.

Alstroemeria aurea 'Orange King'

Amaranthus caudatus and *Cosmos*

Amaranthus

AMARANTH

♀ ☼

The old-fashioned annual amaranth loves the sun and soil that is not too rich. This plant, with arched or upright plumes was out of favour for years, but it is now fairly popular again.

Amaranthus caudatus 'Viridis' needs its height of one metre (3ft) for its lovely green tails to hang down elegantly. *Amaranthus caudatus*, also 1m high, with the beautiful name 'love-lies-bleeding', has dark-red hanging plumes. A. tricolor 'Joseph's Coat' is difficult to combine as its leaves are flecked with cream, red and green. Upright -growing amaranths are the *A. hypochondriacus* 'Green Thumb' with yellowish-green plumes, 40cm (16in) high, and A. h. 'Pigmy Torch', with red plumes. *Amaranthus hybridus* subsp. *paniculatus* 'Oeschberg', which grows up to 1m (3ft), has upright plumes and exceptionally beautiful dark-red foliage. It lends a little extra something to the border and it has a new name, *Amaranthus cruentus*, which is easier to remember than the old name.

Amaranthus caudatus

Amaranthus in autmn colours

'Pumila' are good cultivars of the *Amelanchier rotundifolia*. The serviceberry grows in all kinds of soil and prefers a sunny position.

Amelanchier

SERVICEBERRY

These pleasant, airy, deciduous shrubs and small trees harmonise well in the border. *Amelanchier lamarckii* grows up to 6m (18ft), but it can be pruned if necessary. A pruned, round serviceberry is still attractive. The charm of the *Amelanchier lamarckii* lies in the fact that it blooms abundantly with clusters of white flowers at the same time as its bronze foliage is sprouting. The leaves turn dark green later, changing again into bright red and orange in the autumn. The serviceberry also bears purple-black berries or currants, sought after by the birds. The cultivar 'Ballerina' has large, pure white flowers and currants appearing at the beginning of July which we humans also like to eat. The leaves are greener in summer than those of the species and the autumn colouring is less spectacular. *Amalanchier ovalis* remains lower at 3m (9ft) with less abundant growth. The leaves are smaller than of *A. lamarckii*, but this serviceberry also has clusters of white flowers which last longer before fading. 'Edelweiss', 'Helvetia' and

Ammi

This beautiful annual with white umbels of flowers is well suited to mingle with other border plants. The plants are not intrusive and adapt themselves to their neighbours.They can be brought on indoors but it is better to sow them directly outdoors. *Ammi majus* grows up to 80cm (32in) and is often sold with

Ammi majus flower

Ammi visnaga 'Green Mist'

Ammi majus

the cultivar name 'Snowflake'. 'Snowflake' is identical to the species in every way. The plants are well branched and tend to use their neighbours to lean on. *Ammi visnaga* has more finely-divided leaves so that it looks slightly fuller. The flowers are compacter and a little flatter. *Ammi visnaga* 'Green Mist' has greenish- white flowers which, like the other varieties, look lovely in a bouquet. Sow them generously so that there will be plenty for cutting.

Ammobium

♀ ☼

The annual strawflower is not often associated with a border, but the ammobium does not

Ammobium alatum 'Bikini'

look at all out of place there. The taller *Ammobium alatum* 'Grandiflorum', 70cm (28in) and the lower *A. alatum* 'Bikini' are useful plants. The modest white flower with a yellow centre, rustling like straw, is true to strawflowers in preferring a sunny spot in dry soil which is not too rich. The flowers are

Amsonia tabernaemontana

Amsonia tabernaemontana var. *salicifolia*

borne on sturdy, winged stems. They are suitable for cutting and drying. The flowers should be picked before opening altogether as they continue to ripen while drying. This is not in fact a true annual and it tends to survive a mild winter.

Amorpha

🌿 ☼ ○

This deciduous shrub with pea-like flowers remains low enough to be planted in the border, mainly for its lovely foliage and spikes of flowers. *Amorpha canescens*, the Lead plant is a beautiful shrub 1m (3ft), bearing violet-blue flowers with contrasting orange stamens from August to September.

The grey, downy foliage consists of many tiny leaves. *Amorpha fruticosa* grows up to 2.5m (8ft) bearing clusters of purple flowers with contrasting yellow stamens in July. These shrubs are hardy and like a sunny position.

Amsonia

BLUE STAR
🌸 ☼ ○

A little-known hardy plant with blue flowers. The most common is *Amsonia tabernaemontana*, 1m (3ft)-high, with oval, lance-shaped leaves, variable in shape and with funnel-shaped flowers of an exceptional light-blue colour. Due to this colour the plant is not easy to combine in a border with perennial plants, but in a shrub border it looks pleasant. The plant needs well-drained, moist soil. *A. ciliata*, with smaller leaves requires drier soil. *Amsonia tabernaemontana* var. *salicifolia* also has smaller leaves than the species, but it

is not an official variety. *Amsonia tabernaemontana* is in fact an extremely variable species. The young stalks of this plant are a reddish brown. *Amsonia hubrechtii* deviates clearly from all the other species in its needle-like, narrow foliage with beautiful colours in the autumn. *Amsonia illustris* flowers earlier than *A. tabernaemontana* and has much wider leaves. This hardy plant flowers in early spring with sky-blue flowers and grows up to one metre (3ft). *Amsonia* species resemble each other strongly and their names are sometimes confusing. But anyone who has seen an *Amsonia* in flower will always remember it, whatever the species.

Anaphalis

PEARL EVERLASTING
🌸 ☼

This plant has become so common that it no longer figures in the catalogues of growers specialising in hardy plants. The plant prefers a sunny position in dry soil and complements more colourful perennials very well. Its disadvantage is a tendency to untidy and spreading growth. It is rewarding as it flowers for a long period with grey foliage and white, strawflower-like small flowers which can also be dried. *Anaphalis margaritacea* can grow up to between 40 and 100cm (16 and 40in), depending on its shape and the variety *A. margaritacea* var. *yedoensis* has shorter foliage. The species *A. triplinervis* remains lower, but the snow-white cultivar 'Sommerschnee' is a little taller, a beautiful, compact plant. The yellow-flowering cultivar 'Schwefellicht' has changed its name to

Anaphalis margaritacea var. *yedoensis*

Anaphalis triplinervis

Anchusa azurea 'Dropmore'

Anaphalis triplinervis 'Schwefellicht' (*Helichrysum* 'Schwefellicht')

Helichrysum 'Schwefellicht'. These long-flowering plants are not demanding and will even grow in moist soil in a shady position if need be.

Anchusa

The name and the appearance of anchusa may be familiar to those who like to walk in the dunes; the common *Anchusa officinalis* with its deep-blue to purple flowers is at home there.

The plant which we usually grow in the border is the perennial *Anchusa azurea* which can grow up to 1.5m (5ft). It has several cultivars; the azure 'Dropmore' grows as high as the species; the gentian-blue 'Loddon Royalist' 1m (3ft) is branched, with royal-blue flowers in large plumes; 'Little John' (45cm) is true to its name and is only half as tall as the other two cultivars. The flowers are dark blue and the plants go on flowering for a very long period.

They are hardy plants, but not long-lived and have to be regenerated regularly. They like humus-rich soil and need some protection in winter.

The biennial *Anchusa capensis* is grown as an annual; 'Blue Angel' is 25cm high and sky blue; 'Blue Bird' is twice as high and a deeper bluish purple; 'Pink Bird' is a lovely pink colour and 'Dawn' is a mixture of pink, white, blue and lavender shades. The bees love them.

Anchusa officinalis

40

Anchusa azurea 'Loddon Royalist'

Anemone

JAPANESE ANEMONE

There are far more anemones, but the Japanese anemone is especially suitable as a border plant. There are four species of Japanese anemone: *Anemone hupehensis*, *Anemone x hybrida*, *Anemone vitifolia* and *Anemone tomentosa*. *Anemone hupehensis* and *A. vitifolia* originally came from moist, open woodland and *Anemone tomentosa* is found above the tree line. *Anemone x hybrida* has no natural origins as it includes all the products of crossbreeding. Anemone vitifolia is a compact plant with dark-green foliage and white flowers with yellow stamens; it can grow up to 1m (3ft). Anemone *tomentosa* 'Robustissima' (syn. *A. vitifolia* var. *tomentosa*), over 1m high, blooms earlier than the other anemones, with bright red flowers. Most of these autumnal anemones lend colour to the border form August until October. They prefer humus-rich soil, not too dry and they like a place in the sun or light shade. When there is frost before snowfall, which is usually the case, they will need a covering of mulch, straw, or conifer branches (not peat). The cultivars of *Anemone hupehensis* and *Anemone x hybrida* are really wonderful border plants and good for cutting. *Anemone hupehensis* 'Praecox' is a deep pink and grows to 70cm (28in); A. h. 'Prinz Heinrich' has dark maroon single flowers and grows up to 80cm (32in); 'September Charm' is as tall in a bright pink colour. *Anenome x hybrida* 'Hadspen Abundance' is low for an anemone, 60cm (2ft) and its flowers have the most

Anemone hupehensis 'Prinz Heinrich'

Anemone × hybrida 'Königin Charlotte'

Anemone × *hybrida* 'Richard Ahrends'

Anethum graveolens

delicate colours. The petals are deep pink alternating with pale pink, as though two cultivars were planted together. *A. x hybrida* 'Honorine Jobert' is still one of the loveliest white Japanese anemones. This cultivar grows to 1m (3ft) or taller and was found in the garden of M. Jobert in France, in 1858. The famous French grower Lemoine introduced it to the market in 1863. *Anemone x hybrida* 'Königin Charlotte' has single pink flowers and grows to 80cm, (32in), no more. *Anemone x hybrida* 'Pamina' has dark-red double flowers, stiffer growth, up to 1m (3ft). *Anemone x hybrida* 'Richard Ahrends', has pale-pink blooms and grows the tallest of all, 1.5m (5ft). There are enough Japanese anemones to choose from and they flower when many other perennials have finished flowering.

Anethum

DILL
☷ ☼

Dill, *Anethum graveolens* is so common as an annual herb in the vegetable garden that we almost forget to use the plant in the border.

Anethum graveolens

Anethum graveolens 'Vierling'

The greenish-yellow umbels of dill look well in bouquets and in a mixed border. Dill goes just as well in a yellow border as in a blue or red colour scheme, with its modest colouring. The plant tends to soften the bright colours around it and adapts itself to its neighbours. It will also attract the bees and you can still use the plant as a herb. A few leaves of dill in a fish dish, or some clusters of dill in the bud when pickling gherkins will not be missed. You can sow the herb or buy plants from a specialised grower or a nursery. *Anethum graveolens* 'Vierling' is a special selection with bluish-green foliage and very large heads of flowers.

Angelica

🛈 ❀ ☼ ○

The common angelica, Angelica sylvestris is found by the waterside and on wet grassland. The pink variety is sometimes available from a specialised grower. The wild angelica, *Angelica archangelica* is an imposing plant with dome-shaped clusters which grows in the wild in some regions. It can grow up to several metres on fertile soil. The young stems of this angelica are candied for use on cakes; it also makes delicious bitters. The leaves can be used in herb teas and in potpourri as they even retain their aroma when dried. Both the common and the wild angelica are host plants

Angelica sylvestris

Angelica archangelica

to the caterpillars of the swallowtail butterfly. This makes them useful, as well as decorative, besides which the flowers attract numerous insects with their nectar. *Angelica* is usually biennial, but if you remove the flower clusters before they set seed, the plant sometimes lives longer.

There is no reason why wild angelica should not seed itself in a wild botanical garden, but this could be a nuisance in a border. *Angelica gigas* is an unusual sort from Korea. It is a biennial plant with striking maroon stems and flower clusters of the same colour. There is no point in collecting the seeds for the following

spring if you want to keep the plant. It has to be sown at once as it is only capable of germinating for a short period. *Angelica atropurpurea*, which comes from the United States, has deep-purple stems and unusual reddish-brown and green foliage.

Angelica taiwaniana is a large plant growing up to 2.5m (8ft) easily, with red or grey-green stems and umbels of white flowers.

Anthemis

CHAMOMILE

These plants go on flowering so profusely, for so long, that they are only short-lived as hardy plants. If you cut them back just above the ground in September, they will have a greater chance of surviving the winter. Do not wait with this until they have finished flowering altogether, or they will not have time to form new foliage before the winter.

The flowers look lovely in a vase anyway as they are good for cutting. The higher cultivars are very suitable for the border, flowering in shades of yellow, from lemon yellow to canary yellow, or white. Here, too, the names lead to some confusion among the experts. Some say that almost all the cultivars stem from *Anthemis tinctoria*, others hold that many cultivars stem from *Anthemis x hybrida*. The best-known cultivar is 'E.C. Buxton', a sturdy plant with dark-green foliage and pale-yellow flowers like the marguerite, 60cm (2ft) tall.

'Wargrave' is a deeper yellow and grows much higher and sturdier. 'Sauce Hollandaise' is true to its name, with creamy pale-yellow flowers. 'Kelwayi' grows up to 80cm (32in)

Anthemis tinctoria

Anthemis × hybrida 'E.C. Buxton'

Anthriscus sylvestris

Antirrhinum majus 'Coronette Crimson'

with golden-yellow flowers. 'Alba' has white flowers with a yellow centre. All cultivars have finely divided fern-like foliage; they like well-drained soil and a sunny position.

Anthriscus

COW PARSLEY

 ☼

You would never dream of planting cow parsley, *Anthriscus sylvestris*, in the border. Magnificent plants, but only really for the banks of the ditch. If you were to plant it in the border, you would be inundated with its

Anthriscus sylvestris

progeny in no time, having to dig it out from between the other border plants. But now there are more modest cultivars which are worth having. *Anthriscus sylvestris* 'Ravens-wing' has the same finely divided, fern-like foliage as the common cow parsley, in a dark brown-red. This plant grows up to 1m (3ft), with finer heads of white flowers in beautiful contrast with the dark-red foliage. If you want to keep the dark-leaved cow parsley you can remove the green seedlings and leave the dark ones.

This plant seeds itself, but not so fast and its colour is worth the trouble. Bear in mind that cow parsley withdraws into the soil after flowering, leaving open spaces in the border which have to be filled by neighbouring plants.

Antirrhinum

SNAPDRAGON

 ☼

Tall or medium-height snapdragons are very suitable for a border. A mixture is difficult to combine and it is better to sow them or to buy them self coloured. These annuals can even be brought on indoors. They like fertile soil and a sunny position and they flower longer if you cut out the faded flowers. Snapdragons are not true annuals but short-lived perennials. They

Antirrhinum majus nanum 'Tahiti Yellow'

Aquilegia chrysantha 'Yellow Queen'

Antirrhinum with *Ageratum*

come in all colours except blue, so the choice will not be difficult to make. 'Coral Rose' is a bright pink and grows up to 40cm (16in). 'Black Prince' is as tall, with dark-red flowers and dark foliage. 'Scarlet Giant' is bright red and grows tall. 'Orange Glow' is a soft shade of orange, 'Canary Bird' is yellow and grows up to 60cm (2ft)and 'Snowflake' can only be white. There are snapdragons in the Coronette series, of medium height, which are also available in one colour. The Tahiti series remains low and is only suitable for the edge of the border. Unusual annuals are available from specialised growers if you have neither the room nor the time to sow snapdragons and other annuals yourself.

Aquilegia

COLUMBINE
✿ ☼ ○

Aquilegia is an easy plant to have in the border, with something old-fashioned about it. It blooms in May, one of the first plants to flower. The fresh green foliage appears above ground when other perennials are still nowhere to be seen. Aquilegia is a short-lived perennial, but this is hardly noticeable because it seeds itself copiously. Very few aquilegia are stable in returning from seed true

Aquilegia with variegated *Euonymus*

Aguilegia 'Nora Barlow'

Akelei with roses and *Euphorbia*

to the species, as they crossbreed among themselves ('Nora Barlow' is stable). The only way to make sure of a true cultivar is to avoid planting other aquilegias anywhere near it.This plant is not demanding, but it does not like clay soil. *Aquilegia alpina* can grow to 50cm (20in) with true blue flowers; 'Alba' is a white cultivar. *Aquilegia caerulea* 'Clematiflora', 60cm (2ft) has erect flowers without spurs in white, pink and blue. *Aquilegia caerulea* 'Red Hobbit', 40cm (16in) has red flowers with a yellow centre. *Aquilegia canadensis*, 60cm (2ft) is an asset for a red border with its red and yellow colouring.

White aquilegia with variegated honesty

Aquilegia chrysantha, 90cm (3ft) with pale-yellow flowers, blooms in May, June and July, a month longer than most aquilegia. The cultivar 'Silver Queen' has pure white flowers and 'Yellow Queen' is bright yellow. Aquilegia vulgaris 'Adelaide Addison' has dark blue and white flowers; 'Nora Barlow', is an ancient aquilegia, with double flowers in red, pink and green; the double flowers of 'Ruby Port' are dark red all-over and both grow up to 80cm (32in). 'Nora Barlow' is called after the granddaughter of Charles Darwin even though he did not like this cultivar at all.

Aralia

Aralia is more familiar as the shrub *Aralia elata*, the Japanese angelica tree, than as a perennial, but there are some hardy aralias. They take up so much space and are so impressive that you could not squeeze them into a small border. Some of the species of *Aralia* are so enormous that they would make good specimens. *Aralia californica* can grow up to 3m tall (9ft), with the same spread and it has large feathered foliage. The arching branches bear plumes of small green fowers in July and August, turning a reddish-brown. The plant is covered with black berries in the autumn. This perennial is a match for any small shrub and fits in a large, mixed border. *Aralia cordata* is only half as big and *Aralia*

Aralia californica

racemosa grows over 2m (6ft), but both bear berries in the autumn. The true Aralia cordata grows to a height of 2.5m (8ft) tall and the lower *Aralia continentalis* is often sold as *A. cordata*. But the shrub *Aralia elata* could have a carefully-chosen place in the border, serving as a canopy to filter the light. This deciduous shrub with spiny branches has fairly open growth and other shrubs or shade-loving perennials can grow beneath it. It lends the shrub border an exotic touch, with its large leaves. The roots of this species have an irritating habit of growing suckers and will

need to be kept in check. The leaves of *Aralia elata* are edged with a creamy white and this lovely aralia has less vigorous growth than the type, as also the cultivar 'Aureo-variegata' with golden-yellow -edged leaves. They flower at the end of summer and early autumn with large plumes of flowers. Even in winter, without its leaves, the aralia is still a handsome presence. All aralias prefer a spot in the sun or partial shade, in fertile, well-drained soil.

Arctostaphylos

BEARBERRY

It is said that bears eat the berries of these plants, hence the name. A*rctostaphylos uva-ursi* is an evergreen, low-growing shrub, 10cm (4in) with oval, dark-green foliage. Pinky-white flowers appear in summer, followed by red berries. It forms excellent ground cover in a shrub border and grows well in the sun and also in light shade. 'Vancouver Jade' is a beautiful new cultivar from Canada; the sprouting leaves of 'Woods Red' are tinged with red and it has big berries. They need well-drained, slightly acid soil.

Argyranthemum

Argyranthemum frutescens, the Marguerite, is a small shrub, not hardy and grown as an annual for that reason. We can ensure its continuity by taking cuttings before the winter. It is often seen in pots, sometimes even grown as a standard plant, but the daisy-like

Arctostaphylos uva-ursi

Argyranthemum frutescens subsp. *canariae*

Argyranthemum frutescens

Argyranthemum – hybride-cultivars

flowers can also brighten the border. They like a sunny position and well-drained soil. The true argyranthemum naturally has white flowers with a yellow centre, but there are also cultivars with coloured flowers. The hybrid-cultivar 'Yellow Star' has larger pale-yellow flowers, 'Rosalinde' has pink flowers and 'Vancouver' has double pink flowers. *Argyranthemum frutescens* subsp. *canariae* has larger flowers. *Argyranthemum maderense* 'Sissinghurst' has yellow flowers; there is one argyranthemum, 'Silver Queen', which is grown for its silver-green foliage.

Armeria

THRIFT

These mat-forming, evergreen plants cover themselves with rounded flower heads in every shade of pink and in white, from May into July; some cultivars even bloom in August. They are more familiar as rock plants, but the higher varieties fit into the front of the border very well. They are ideal edging plants with modest requirements, especially suitable for coastal gardens as they love salt. Their need of salt is so great that they settle beside motorways where salt is strewn, of their own accord. The genus is found in salty areas, in dry, grassy meadows and on some islands, but rarely in other areas. Cultivars of *Armeria maritima* are usually planted in the garden including the white 'Alba', the crimson 'Düsseldorfer Stolz', the pink 'Rosea', the dark red 'Splendens' and 'Splendens Perfecta'. These cultivars all grow to between 20 and 25cm (8 and 10in). *Armeria pseudoarmeria* grows higher, with pink flowers; its cultivar 'Bees Ruby' is a bright maroon growing up to 40cm (16in) high. This higher variety of thrift

Armeria maritima 'Rosea'

Armeria pseudoarmeria

Armeria maritima 'Alba'

Aronia melanocarpa – berry

is very useful in the border. The stiff little globules on straight stems are good cutting flowers which keep their freshness for a long time in water. All armerias prefer full sun and well-drained soil.

Aronia

CHOKEBERRY
✿ ☀ ○

Aronia – autumn

Aronia arbutifolia and *Aronia melanocarpa* are two deciduous shrubs with brilliant autumn colours. The sunnier its position, the more glowing the flaming red autumn colour of *Aronia arbutifolia* will be, and the reddish brown of *Aronia melanocarpa*.

A. arbutifolia does well in good, rich, well-drained soil, growing up to 2m (6ft) and flowering in late spring with small white flowers with red stamens, followed by bright red berries which it retains until the middle of winter. The cultivar 'Brilliant' has many berries and the most beautiful autumn foliage. *Aronia melanocarpa* is lower, 1m (3ft), flowering in late spring and early summer with

Artemisia 'Powis Castle'

Aronia arbutifolia

Artemisia absinthium 'Lambrook Silver'

white flowers, followed by black berries. These modest shrubs combine well in both a shrub border and a mixed border, but bear in mind that their roots tend to spread.

Artemisia

WORMWOOD

Many herbs belong to this genus, including the lemon plant (*Artemisia abrotanum*), common wormwood (*A. absinthium*) and tarragon (*A. dracuculus*). Artemisia is an excellent border plant, not for the flowers, but for the foliage

Artemisia ludoviciana 'Silver Queen'

which varies according to the species and cultivar, from deeply divided and fern-like, to coarsely toothed. The colour of the foliage varies from silvery aluminium via shining silver to a pale pewter. There are low, clump-forming, tall and very tall artemisias, to suit all tastes. These restful plants should play their part in every border. Artemisia absinthium 'Lambrook Silver' always used to be planted until the hybrid-cultivar 'Powis Castle' (or *A. arborescens* 'Powis' or A. a. 'Powis Castle', or even 'Powis') came on the scene. 'Powis Castle' is bushier than 'Lambrook Silver' and is lower at 60cm (2ft). The flowers of both are negligible; 'Powis Castle' often fails to flower at all. *Artemisia* 'Canescens' has grey, very finely-divided irregular foliage and elegant flower stems. There are some very tall cultivars, 1.5m (5ft) of *Artemisia lactiflora* called 'Guizhou' (syn. 'Dark Form'). The plants grow with purple shoots in spring and the stems and veins of the leaves are the same colour; the plume-shaped flowers are a creamy white. *Artemisia ludoviciana* 'Silver Queen' has finely-divided, silvery leaves and grows to 60cm (2ft) high. 'Valerie Finnis' is less unruly than the silver queen. *Artemisia mandshurica* is an almost unknown species which grows up to 1.4m.(4½ft). This sub-shrub has silver-green foliage and the overblown flowers give the plant something special until late in the season. Prune the artemisia from time to time, but not too early, nor too hard, or it will not survive. Do not prune until it is growing well.

Arum

CUCKOO PINT LORDS AND LADIES

The mottled arum, *Arum maculatum*, and the

Arum italicum

stalks between the other plants. The leaves of the Italian arum appear in autumn and survive the winter, labelling the plant as evergreen. The flowers bloom at the end of spring, followed by striking orange-red and poisonous berries in the autumn. *Arum italicum* 'Marmoratum' has beautifully-marked dark-green foliage with cream-coloured or white veins. This arum is more sensitive to frost than the type and needs a protective mulch or old manure. Arum likes moist, well-drained soil during its period of growth and prefers dry conditions while the berries ripen and when it is dormant.

Aruncus

MEADOWSWEET

❁ ○ ◐

There are tall and low varieties of meadowsweet . The smallest is *Aruncus aethusifolius*, a plant that grows 30cm (1ft) high with a green compound leaf, turning red in autumn.

Aruncus dioicus 'Kneiffii'

Italian arum, *Arum italicum*, are both plants which are found on old country estates. They are tuberous plants which prefer a shady border. Woodland plants by nature, they require good soil, rich in humus and moisture retentive. The mottled arum, cuckoopint or lords-and-ladies, can survive dry conditions in summer as the foliage dies off. The dark-green, arrow-shaped leaves, usually flecked with black, reappear in January or February. The greenish-white bracts appear in April/May. The plant is still decorative in autumn with its orange-red, poisonous berries attracting attention, like colourful surprises on stiff

Aruncus dioicus

Asarum caudatum

Asarum europaeum and tongue fern

The white plumes of flowers also turn red. *Aruncus dioicus* is much growing up to 1.5m (5ft). This is a good, strong plant which is elegant in spite of its size, flowering with large, creamy-white plumes. The cultivar 'Kneiffii' is lower, 60cm, (2ft) and has deeply dissected foliage, more fern-like than the type. 'Glasnevin', slightly taller than the species, has broad, light-green foliage and is very strong, like the type. *Aruncus sinensis* 'Zweiweltenkind' (Child of Two Worlds) has large bronze leaves in spring. This 1.5m (5ft)-high cultivar, has denser growth and it is a strong plant. Tall meadowsweet also does well as a specimen.

Asarum

WILD GINGER
❀ ○ ◓

Asarum is a ground-cover plant which grows well in the shade. It is useful as an edging plant in a shady border. There are about seventy varieites of *Asarum* in the world of which three are most often grown: *Asarum caudatum*, with large, heart-shaped, dark-green foliage, not glossy; *Asarum europaeum*, with glossy evergreen foliage and *Asarum canadese*, with its flowers appearing before the light-green leaves. The modest, brownish flowers are hidden away underneath the foliage and they have a distinctive scent. Its seeds are distributed by ants. This true native of woodland loves the shade and loose, humus-rich soil. The plants should not be too far apart: fifteen plants per square metre (3ft2) of *Asarum europaeum* and eleven of *Asarum caudatum*. They will take some time to establish themselves and cover the ground. There are so few plants which thrive in the shade and wild ginger is one of them. The heart-shaped leaves are useful in small posies.

Asclepias

SILK WEED
❀ ☀

The flowers of this plant are more often seen in a flower shop than in the border, but some of them are good border plants, if handled with care. *Asclepias syriaca* is one of these, 1.5m (5ft) tall , flowering from June into August with pale-pink flowers, if only it did not grow so rampantly. Not for the lazy gardener, but for those who do not mind weeding for a beautiful plant. Take care with these and other asclepias as they contain a highly poisonous milky juice. If this milk comes into contact with the skin in sunny weather it will cause the same unpleasant reaction as the giant hogweed and rue.

Asclepias incarnata

Asclepias tuberosa

Asperula taurina

Asclepias incarnata, 1m (3ft) has pink, vanil-la-scented flowers. *Asclepias incarnata* 'Ice Ballet' is a wonderful white-flowering cultivar.

Asclepias tuberosa, 50cm (20in) has orange flowers and looks daring in the red border. *A. tuberosa* 'Gay Butterflies' is a cheerful mixture of orange shades. Both type and cultivar

Asperula orientalis

Asperula orientalis with Papaver commutatum 'Ladybird'

are only half hardy. Silk weed likes full sun and dislikes over-rich soil. They are all firm favourites with bees and butterflies.

Asperula

WOODRUFF

♀ ✿ ☘ ☼ ○

There are several different asperulas: annuals, perennials and small shrubs. Sweet woodruff used to be called *Asperula odorata* and is now *Galium odoratum*. Some asperulas are low-growing and suitable for the rock garden. *Asperula taurina* resembles a strapping version of sweet woodruff, but grows to 40cm (16in), with coarser foliage. The white flowers of the type are bunched together in little plumes. *Asperula taurina* var. *caucasica* has pale mauve flowers. Both flower from April into July and interweave well with other shade-loving plants. There is one more annual woodruff for the border, the blue *Asperula orientalis*. The plant grows in the cornfields of the Lebanon and Syria, but it originally came from southwest Asia. This pleasing little flower with its distinctive shade of blue was only recently rediscovered.

Asphodeline lutea

Asplenium scolopendrium 'Cristatum'

Asplenium scolopendrium

Asphodeline

ASPHODEL

Asphodels are plants not often seen in the border. But *Asphodeline liburnica* and *As-*

phodeline lutea, the Yellow asphodel, both growing to 1m (3ft) are valuable assets. They both produce yellow flowers with grassy leaves. *A. lutea* is an evergreen with spiky clusters of fragrant flowers. These starry flowers are 2 or 3cm (1-2in) long, flowering from below upwards. The seedpods are also interesting after flowering is over. The plant flowers in April, May and June. *A. liburnica* flowers a little later.

These plants prefer dry soil and a sunny position. They are not really hardy and need protective covering in winter.

Asphodeline lutea

Aster ericoides 'Golden Spray'

Aster novae-angliae 'Purple Dome'

Aster × frikartii 'Mönch'

Asplenium

Aspleniums are usually small ferns such as the wall rue, which like to grow on old walls rather than the border. But the Hart's tongue fern is another matter. This fern was always called *Phyllitis scolopendrium* and is still listed under that name in most of the catalogues. According to the latest trend the tongue fern is now called *Asplenium scolopendrium*. The long, slender fronds which give the fern its name, are evergreen making it an attractive plant for the shadow border. The old foliage is replaced in spring by fresh, light-green fronds to give it a glossy look for the summer. The cultivar 'Angustatum' ('Angustifolium') remains lower and has ribbed edges; 'Crispum Nobile' grows up to 50cm (20in) with lovely frilled fronds; 'Cristatum' has strongly waved edges; 'Muricatum' 25cm (10in) has crinkled fronds; 'Undulatum', 30cm (12in) also has waved edges. Tongue ferns will grow in a sheltered position on either limy or humus-rich, acid soil.

Aster

MICHAELMAS DAISY

This incredibly extensive genus deserves a book for itself alone. We can describe the best examples of each type. The old-fashioned asters have a reputation for grey, mildewed leaves, or for plants which take possession of the whole garden, cropping up everywhere uninvited. Nowadays there are so many asters which are not prone to mildew that we can plant them in the border with every confidence. Many asters start flowering in July or August, continuing into October. The name 'Michaelmas daisy' is very apt for them. The cultivars of *Aster amellus*, which flower from July until the end of September, have single flowers, do not need staking and are not sensitive to mildew. 'Jacqueline Genebrier' has deep-pink flowers and grows up to 70cm (28in); 'King George' is a beautiful blue aster, 60cm (2ft)-high; 'Lady Hindlip' is as tall, but with bright- pink flowers; 'Lac de GenÅve has lavender-blue flowers and is 60cm-high; 'Joseph Lakin' is a lovely violet colour and 50cm (20in)-high; 'Sonora' is also violet and 60cm (2ft)-high; 'VeilchenkÜnigin' ('Violet Queen') has fairly small flowers for an *A. amellus*, in a dark-violet colour. The cultivars of *Aster cordifolius* have a cloud of tiny flowers on loose, elegant clusters. 'Little Carlow' is a violet colour and grows up to 1.2m (4ft); 'Elegans' has small white flowers and grows up to 1m (3ft)and 'Silver Spray' is true to its name with silvery bluish-white flowers. The cultivars of *Aster novi-belgii* and *Aster dumosus* are sensitive to mildew so we will pass on to the cultivars of other types. *Aster ericoides* forms small, compact shrubs. 'Blue Star' has pale-blue flowers and is 60cm (2ft)-high; 'Brimstone' grows to 50cm (20in) and has white flowers with a yellow centre; 'Esther' grows up to 60cm with pale-pink flowers which keep their looks after flowering; 'Golden Spray ' has creamy-white flowers and is 1m (3ft)high; and 'Pink Cloud' is 80cm (32in)high with pale-pink flowers. *Aster x frikartii* is a cross between *A. amellus* and *A. thomsonii*, with some beautiful cultivars:

Astilbe chinensis 'Pumila'

Astilbe 'Fanal'

'Jungfrau' and 'Wunder von Stèfa resemble each other; they are both blue, but the flowers of the first are smaller. *Aster x frikartii* 'Mönch', is a topper with large lavender-blue flowers, but it is not fully hardy. 'Lady in Black' is an unusual cultivar of *Aster latiflorus*; it has purple foliage throughout the growing season and its white flowers with a reddish centre grow on a splendid, shrub-shaped plant which can grow up to 1.2m (4ft). This Michaelmas daisy can even be used to form a hedge. *A. lateriflorus* 'Horizontalis', a plant which spreads wide, 1m (3ft)high, has dark-green foliage and small, white to pale-mauve flowers.

Aster novae-angliae, from New England, is a dependable plant with rough leaves. The many cultivars in wonderful colours need some support. 'Andenken an Alma PÜtschke', in a striking shade of pinky-red, grows up to 1.4m (41/2ft); 'Herbstschnee', the only white cultivar, 1.2m (4ft) is sadly susceptible to mildew; 'Purple Dome' is only 50cm (20in) high and has purple flowers; 'September Rubin' grows up to 1.2m (4ft) with crimson flowers. Two more lovely Michaelmas daisies with small flowers are *Aster pringlei*, the white 'Monte Cassino' and 'Pink Star'.

Astilbe

✿ ○ ●

Astilbes have been cross-bred so often that it is almost impossible to classify them in groups. It really makes no difference to the border whether an astilbe belongs to the Arendsii-hybrids or the Japonica-hybrids. The only thing that is useful to know is that the Crispa-hybrids and some Simplicifolia-hybrids

Astilbe 'Washington'

Astilbe 'Washington'

remain fairly low, making them less suitable for the border. The familiar *Astilbe chinensis* 'Pumila' is only 30cm (12in)-high and is better used as ground cover. Slightly higher cultivars of *Astilbe chinensis* are 'Finale', pale-pink and 50cm (20in) high; 'Spètsommer', pinky-red, 50cm and 'Veronica Klose', purple and 40cm (16in) high. It is all a matter of taste and some astilbes have looser growth than others.

The colours range from white via cream and all shades of pink to red, purple and violet. The sturdy foliage is attractively cut, usually green and sometimes bronze-coloured. Astilbes need moisture-retaining soil and prefer a position in partial shade. They will grow in the sun if the soil is moist enough, but they will not flower as long. Most astilbes flower late, from July into September; some cultivars already bloom in June. *Astilbe rivularis* is very like meadowsweet (*Aruncus dioicus*), with the same lovely foliage and lighter growth. *Astilbe grandis*, 1.4m (4½ft) fits into a natural, shaded border very well, with airy, white plumes. These are just a few of the many cultivars. Some borders consist entirely of astilbes and they look most impressive. 'Amerika', pale pink and 70cm (28in); 'Aphrodite', pink and 40cm (16in); 'Dunkellachs', deep pink and 50cm (20in); 'Erika, pink and 70cm (28in); 'Europa, bright pink and 50cm; 'Fanal', garnet-red and 60cm (2ft); 'Feuer', blood-red and 80cm (32in); 'Irrlicht', pale-pink and 60cm; 'Koblenz', crimson and 50cm; 'Peach Blossom', salmon-pink and 40cm (16in); 'Prof. van der Wielen', white and 1.2m (4ft); 'Snowdrift', white and 60cm (2ft); 'Washington', white and 50cm (20in).

Astilboides

🏵 ○ ◖

Astilboides tabularis was formerly called *Rodgersia tabularis*. Not all rodgersias are now Astilboides, as this applies to the one species, the only one to belong to this genus. The plant comes from northern China and has spectacular shield-shaped leaves.

The branched plumes of white flowers which appear in June and July play a minor part, as with the rodgersia. Not a plant for any flower border, but it has an impressive habit fit for a shadow border, where it is at its best; it also needs moist soil to cater for its large foliage. *Astilboides tabularis*, which can grow to 1m (3ft) or higher, will grow by the waterside as a specimen, but not too near the water as it likes its feet moist, not wet.

Astrantia

MASTERWORT

🏵 ☼ ○

These are fantastic border plants. They combine well in a colourful border in spite of (or perhaps because of) the fact that their flowers are not brightly coloured but subdued. Their pretty 'flowers' are also good for cutting. Every bloom which we call a flower consists of bracts which fit like a collar around the global bunches of flowers. The bracts of *Astrantia major* subsp. *involucrata* are fairly big, so that they enclose the flowers completely. This bract is slightly smaller in the *Astrantia major* species. The colour of the flower, which comes mostly from the bracts, is light green with pink. There are several beautiful cultivars

Astrantia carniolica 'Rubra'

Astrantia major 'Shaggy' ('Margery Fish')

of this species which also have fresh green compound foliage. Some cultivars are propagated by division, others from seed. When weeding near astrantias in spring, look out for seedlings with strong, glossy green foliage. 'Canneman' is grown from seed and may be variable. The first flowers are dark red, turning green or white. The flowers of the second flowering later in the year are white with green. The plant grows up to 70cm (28in) and the flowers are fairly big. 'Green Star' has bracts tipped with green. 'Claret' has dark-red flowers, like 'Ruby Wedding' - no wonder as it is one of its (variable) seedlings. 'Ruby Wedding' is splendid and goes on flowering for a long time. 'Lars' is maroon coloured and flowers for some time, but according to some growers 'Rubra' is much better, because 'Lars' soon loses its colour. 'Rosea' is pink with a light-green centre; 'Rosensinfonie' is an improved version of 'Rosea'; 'Shaggy' used to be called 'Margery Fish' and has white, green-tipped bracts.

Not everyone likes 'Sunningdale Variegated'. This *Astrantia* has yellow variegated foliage in spring, turning green in summer. *Astrantia carniolica* 'Rubra' remains low, 40cm (16in), for an astrantia and has red flowers. *Astrantia maxima* has old-rose coloured flowers and is more demanding than other astrantias as to the soil; it dislikes sandy soil.

Astrantia maxima

Athyrium filix-femina

Athyrium

LADY FERN
🕸 ○ ◐

Many species and cultivars of this deciduous fern do well in a shaded border. It is always a surprise in spring to see the natural inhabitant of moist woodlands, the Lady fern, *Athyrium filix-femina*,1m (3ft) coming up with its lovely light-green foliage. This fern can grow in deep shade and it needs moist soil. A few of the cultivars are: 'Cristatum' with fan-shaped-foliage, 'Frizelliae' with very narrow foliage and 'Minutissimum', a dwarf variety. *A. distentifolium* 'Kupferstiel', 60cm (2ft) resembles the native fern, but the foliage is lighter with striking reddish-brown stems. *A. niponicum* 'Metallicum' (now *A. niponicum* 'Pictum'), 50 cm (20in), a most unusual fern with its variegated silvery grey-green foliage and purple stems. *A. othophorum* 'Okonum', 50cm has light-green, yellowish leaves and purple stems and needs a sheltered spot. *A. vidalii*, 60cm (2ft) is a graceful fern with darker stems. It prefers moist soil rich in humus, and shade.

Athyrium filix-femina 'Minutissimum'

Atriplex, red orach, with *Campanula*

Atriplex, red orach, with *Calendula*

Atriplex

ORACH
⚲ ☀

Atriplex is not a spectacular plant, but the foliage of the various cultivars has beautiful colours which combine well with other plants in the border. This is an annual, but once you have sown it you will never have to do so again, it will seed itself. Then you have to weed it away where the plant is not welcome. These weeds make a tasty salad - atriplex is a versatile plant. The red atriplex is the most popular. The cultivars 'Rubra', 'Purpurea', 'Red Plume' and 'Cupreata' all have red foliage and resemble each other - because they are in fact all the same plant ('Rubra'). These cultivar synonyms were created as a result of different gradations in colour. You can select your favourites by removing the plants which are not to your taste. The best ones are allowed to seed themselves in this way.

Atriplex hortensis 'Rubra'

Aucuba japonica 'Rozannie'

In addition to the red-leaved atriplex there is the 'Gold Plume' with yellow foliage and 'Green Plume' which is in fact the species *Atriplex hortensis* or Red orach. The plant can grow up to 2m (6ft) and is at home in any situation.

Aucuba

An old-fashioned and unusual evergreen shrub which goes on forever. Perhaps that is why this typical Victorian plant was out of favour for so long. But where would you find an evergreen with decorative, often variegated foliage which also bears red berries and grows in both sun and shade? The leathery foliage is coarsely toothed. The plants are unisexual, only producing berries if separate male and female specimens are planted, although there are some bisexual cultivars. The male cultivars are for those who prefer their *aucuba* without berries. *Aucuba japonica* 'Variegata' with yellow-spotted leaves and red berries is the best-known aucuba. 'Crotonifolia is the best variegated golden cultivar without red fruits. 'Picturata' (a male form) has dark-green foliage with one or two golden-yellow spots in the centre. 'Rozannie' remains fairly low, 1m (3ft), with shiny-green, coarsely-toothed foliage and many bright-red berries which always appear as this is a bisexual version. 'Sulphurea Marginata' has fairly slender green foliage with a pale-yellow margin. If the plant is in the shade its leaves may turn green. Aucuba tolerates quite hard pruning. The plant grows in any soil, as long as it is not waterlogged.

Aucuba japonica 'Variegata'

Aucuba japonica 'Sulphurea Marginata'

Baptisia australis

Baptisia tinctoria

Baptisia bracteata (*B. leucophaea*) grows less tall, 50cm, than *B. australis*; it has arching grey-green foliage and flat clusters of pale-yellow flowers. *Baptisia lactea* (synonym B. *leucantha*) has beautiful upright clusters of white flowers.
Baptisia pendula has arching plumes of white flowers. These pea-like flowering plants like full sun and well-drained soil. They are excellent for cutting.

Baptisia lactea

Baptisia

FALSE INDIGO

 ☼

The names are very confusing, but all agree on one of them, namely, *Baptisia australis*, or False indigo, which is also the most common *Baptisia*. This tall plant (upwards of 1m, 3ft) has bluish-green compound foliage and indigo-blue spikes of flowers resembling lupins. The pea-like flowers are not so close together as those of the lupin.
The seed boxes are left to decorate the border after flowering. *B. tinctoria* is used to make dyes in North America, its native land.

Left: Forms of pruning in the border

Bergenia

❀ ☼ ○

Gertrude Jekyll (1843-1932) loved bergenias. She preferred to use them as a thick edge between the border and the path. *Bergenia* is not always appreciated these days. Most people think of it as a coarse plant with large, leathery foliage which never flowers. But those who buy the right plants will have no such problems. It is best not to buy any plant labelled *Bergenia*, as this will usually have been sown, which does not promote good flowering. Select plants which have been grown from root slips by a good grower; these will certainly flower.

The plant retains its large and usually leathery foliage in winter, changing colour beautifully, according to the cultivar. Bergenias can be used in the same way as hostas but they tolerate drier soil and a more open situation. Both flowers and foliage keep well in a vase.

The following are lovely cultivars: 'Baby Doll', 30cm (12in), with fairly small, round leaves and pale-pink flowers, turning darker; 'Bach', 40cm (16in), with white clusters of flowers and dark-green foliage; 'Bressingham White', 30cm (12in), pure white; 'Britten', 40cm (16in), pale pink with a white eye; 'Morgenröte', 30cm (12in), red, with smaller leaves; 'Schneeglocke', 50cm (20in) with large flowers, pure white; 'Schneekönigin', 50cm (20in), a very pale pink, with beautiful foliage;

Bergenia 'Morgenröte'

Bergenia 'Wintermärchen'

and finally 'Wintermèrchen, 30cm (12in), rose-red the foliage turning dark red; this bergenia has the loveliest colours in winter.

Bidens

The free-flowering annual *Bidens* fits well in a yellow border. *Bidens ferulifolia* grows up to 50cm (20in) and the cultivar 'Golden God-

Bidens aurea

dess' to 70cm (28in). Both have 4-5cm (1-2in) bright-yellow flowers and go on flowering until late autumn. The foliage is finely divided and the plants stand up to all weather conditions. Bees love them. *Bidens aurea* is a perennial which grows up to 1m (3ft), with the same characteristics.

Blechnum

HARD FERN

Blechnum spicant grows in the wild in damp woods, beside ditches and wooded banks. It has horizontal, infertile leaves and upright leaves bearing spores on the back. The horizontal leaves are evergreen, the upright leaves die off. It is suitable for a damp situation in deep shade.

Boltonia

Boltonias are very like Michaelmas daisies. They grow in the wild in North America. Bees

Blechnum spicant

love these unruly plants which grow to some height and will need support. *Boltonia asteroides* var. *latisquama* has small white flowers and grows up to 1.5 to 2m (5-6ft). *Boltonia asteroides* 'Pink Beauty' has pale-pink flowers and is lower; the cultivar 'Snowbank' has white flowers. These plants flower in late summer and autumn.

Brachyscome

This little annual flowers long and profusely from July into September and is 30cm (12in) high. The plants need a dry position in the full sun. They are often seen in flower tubs but they also combine in a border. The following cultivars of the Swan River daisy *Brachycome iberidifolia* are especially useful in combination with perennials: 'Blue Splendour', 'Purple Splendour', 'White Splendour' and even 'Special Mixture', of blue, pink and purple colours.

Brachyscome iberidifolia

Boltonia asteroides 'Pink Beauty'

Boltonia asteroides 'Snow Bank'

Briza

QUAKING GRASS

There are many varieties of quaking grass and *Briza maxima* is the most suitable for the border. This most delicate grass grows up to 50cm (20in) with branched clusters of drooping ears which tremble like aspen leaves in the lightest breeze. This makes a rustling sound, so that quaking grass is often planted in gardens for the blind and visually impaired. It needs good loam and full sun. It is better not to plant it next to coarse plants as the contrast

Brachyscome iberidifolia 'Special Mixture'

Briza media

would be so great that its effect would be lost. Quaking grass weaves the flowers together when combined with the tobacco plant, low cosmos and other more modest plants. The grass can also be dried well, in which case it is best to pick it before it is fully grown. *Briza minor* is at home among even finer plants. This delicate grass grows as high as *Briza maxima*, but the ears are much smaller. These two varieties of quaking grass are annuals, while *Briza media* is a short-lived perennial, sometimes seen in the wild and between the two in size.

Brunnera

KAUKASISCHE VERGEET-MIJ-NIET
🕸 ○ ◖

These plants are often taken for forget-me-nots as the flowers resemble them strongly,

but the leaves do not, as the common forget-me-not has oval to round foliage. The heart-shaped foliage of brunneras speads out after flowering to form a good ground cover. The leaves enhance the plant, so that they continue to please in the border after its early flowering in April and May. The plants prefer moist soil in shade or half shade and they are also at home by the waterside. They will even grow in the sun, as long as the soil is damp. This species has some exceptional cultivars: 'Betty Bowring' is a fairly rare and correspondingly expensive white-flowering

Brunnera macrophylla

Briza maxima with California poppies

Brunnera macrophylla

Brunnera macrophylla 'Variegata'

Brunnera. 'Hadspen Cream' has spiky foliage with an irregular creamy-white edge; 'Variegata', which is said to be a synonym for 'Dawson's White', has more rounded, cream-flecked foliage. 'Langtrees' has small silvery-white mottled leaves. All these variegated brunneras have forget-me-not-blue flowers which are shown off best against the plain green foliage of *B. macrophylla*, or *Siberian bugloss*.

Buddleja

BUTTERFLY BUSH

Budleia davidii 2.5m (8ft) the butterfly bush, has many cultivars fit for a shrub border, including *Buddleia alternifolia*, 4m (12ft). This heavily arching shrub with narrow, grey-green foliage has mauve flower clusters close together on overhanging branches. The cultivar 'Argentea' has silvery-green, hairy leaves, combining well with its mauve flowers. *Buddleia alternifolia* flowers on last year's growth and the only pruning consists of removing old wood. If this *Buddleia* were to be pruned like *Buddleia davidii*, it would have a drastic effect on its flowering. This deciduous shrub is not always recognised as a *Buddleia* because *Buddleia davidii* is the one and only butterfly bush. This bush flowers with striking, 15 - 35 cm (6-14in)-long clusters of flowers which attract butterflies such as the red admiral, the tortoiseshell- great and small, the brimstone and cabbage-white butterflies. If you prune this shrub back hard in spring,

Buddleja alternifolia

Delight' has many deep pink, very long plumes. 'Royal Red' has crimson, fairly small clusters and spreads in width and 'White Bouquet' is true to its name. Butterfly bushes are extremely strong, even tolerating pollution and sea winds, to the delight of butterflies and gardeners alike.

Bupthalmum salicifolium

strong, new shoots will grow which will flower richly in August. The colours of the various cultivars range from all shades of violet, purple and blue to red, pink and white. One of the darkest cultivars is 'Black Knight' with dark-violet plumes of flowers. 'Border Beauty' is a real beauty in the border and flowers profusely with violet-purple plumes. 'Dart's Ornamental White' has white plumes of flowers, remaining fairly low, like the bluish-purple 'Dart's Papillon Bleu' and the purple 'Dart's Purple Rain'. 'Nanho Blue' is a low, 1.5m (5ft) wide, blue-flowering shrub. 'Pink

Buddleja davidii 'White Bouquet'

Bupthalmum salicifolium 'Dora'

Bupleurum rotundifolium

Bupleurum longifolium

Buphthalmum

 ☼ ○

These plants bloom freely in July and August with cheerful, golden-yellow daisy-like flowers growing to a height of 50cm (20in) or more. If you remove faded flowers they will go on flowering longer. The soil should not be too rich as they then tend to grow strongly, forgetting to flower. The plants will benefit if they are divided regularly. The name of the genus, *Bupthalmum salicifolium*, the Yellow

Buxus in the border

ox-eye, suggests that the plants resemble the willow. They thank the name to their narrow leaves which are like those of the willow. 'Sun Wheel' has larger ox-eyes in a lovelier colour than 'Dora' and grows up to 75 cm (2¹/2ft). *Buphtalmum speciosum* is now called *Telekia speciosa*.

Bupleurum

The annual *Bupleurum* is presented in seed catalogues as filling for bouquets, and this is how it is used by the florist. There are few mixed bunches of flowers without some Bupleurum. Instead of 'bouquet filling' we could also call it 'border filling'. The plant can interweave among other plants in the border without intruding - this is hardly likely with such subdued, lime-coloured flowering, resembling the euphorbia. *Bupleurum rotundifolium* 'Green Gold' is most often grown, with light-green foliage and golden-yellow flowers.
Bupleurum longifolium is a perennial which grows taller than the annual, but it can be used in the same way.

Buxus

BOX

Buxus sempervirens is the species of box most often grown.
Box can be used in the border as an evergreen shrub growing freely, but it is usually clipped. It is so rewarding to clip box that globes, squares and animals or birds can be fashioned out of it in the border.

A slightly harder, green line sometimes works wonders in a perennial border. Neatly clipped box catches the eye among a maze of colours and the contrast will set off the colours all the better. Box is usually planted to form a small, clipped hedge; this can be also be effective in a border.

A low hedge at the front of the border will frame it like a picture and here again box performs a restful function.

Box may only be clipped when the sky is overcast and this is done twice a year, in May and August. Topiary work in box should be allowed to stand out from other plants.

Calamintha nepeta subsp. *nepeta*

Calamintha nepeta 'White Cloud'

Calamagrostis

RATTAN

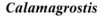

Calamagrostis x acutiflora has some very lovely cultivars. 'Karl Foerster' is an imposing figure, 1.5m (5ft) high with glossy-green, elegantly arched narrow leaves and long brown plumes which are retained until mid-winter. This grass is most suitable as a specimen or in an extremely large border. The cultivar 'Overdam' is lower 1.4m (4½ft) with light-brown flower heads and white-flecked foliage tinged with purple.

Only the hybrid *Calamagrostis x acutiflora* and its cultivars are mentioned here because it is the only *Calamagrostis* of which the roots do not grow rampant. Almost all the others (and there are over 250 varieties) are most unsuitable for the border as they are too invasive. This type of grass will grow in any soil, even if it is heavy and wet or infertile and sandy.

Calamintha

A difficult plant as regards the various names; there is a synonym for every species. But the

Campanula latifolia 'Alba'

plant is no less beautiful for that, and it does not put the bees off as they love it. The leaves are aromatic with mint or thyme and the plant needs dry soil and full sun.

Calamintha nepeta subsp. *nepeta* was a prize-winning perennial some years ago. This plant is 30cm (1ft) high and flowers all summer and longer with a host of lavender-blue flowers. 'White Cloud', 'Blue Cloud' and 'Lilac Cloud' are splendid cultivars. *Calamintha grandiflora* flowers profusely from June into September in a beautiful shade of pink. The plant is 40 cm (16in) high and forms pleasing clumps. *Calamintha grandiflora* 'Variegata' has variegated leaves.

Calamintha grandiflora

Calceolaria mexicana 'Goldarin'

Calceolaria

SLIPPERWORT

ℹ ✿ ☀

The familiar slipperwort with its large flowers in every colour under the sun does not really fit into a border. But the annual *Calceolaria* mexicana, with more modest, bright- yellow slippers, makes a cheerful diversion in the border. The cultivar 'Goldarin' has slightly bigger flowers. There are some biennial slipperworts grown as annuals, such as *Calceolaria integrifolia* 'Goudboeket'.

Calendula

MARIGOLD

ℹ ☀

This is an annual which is so familiar that we tend to forget it. But the common orange marigold, *Calendula officinalis* can cause some surprises in the border. Put it next to *Ruta graveolens* with its lovely bluish-green foliage, or plant a bright-orange marigold in a red border. *Calendula officinalis* is the true, single marigold. The seed of the double marigold is usually the only kind available,

Calceolaria mexicana

Calceolaria integrifolia 'Goudboeket'

and occasionally some of the single varieties. If we are looking for a cultivar for the border then it ought to be a tall one. There are marigolds which remain short and stocky permanently. When you sow them yourself or buy them from a specialised grower there will be no danger of this; otherwise you have to be careful what you buy. Marigolds are not always orange; 'Apricot Beauty', 'Lemon Beauty' and 'Cream Beauty' are proof of this. *Calendula muselli* has yellow to orange-yellow single flowers and grey-green foliage.

This marigold could be synonymous with *Calendula arvensis*, which grows in the wild in southern Europe (and casually in western parts); it would be quite at home in a natural border.

Callicarpa

Callicarpa bodinieri var. *giraldii* is one of the best known. This 2m (6ft)-tall shrub flowers

Calendula officinalis

Calendula arvensis

Callicarpa bodinieri 'Profusion'

best to soften. There are various cultivars besides this familiar variety. In contrast with the dull-green of the latter, 'Mood Indigo' has dark-green foliage turning lilac-pink in autumn, with many indigo-purple berries. 'Profusion' lives up to its name with a mass of large, violet-purple berries. Discretion is needed when planting *Callicarpa* in a perennial border or shrub border as the berries have such a distinctive colour that they do not combine well with every plant at close quarters. They need rich, well-drained soil.

Callistephus

CHINA ASTER

♀ ☼

There are many different kinds of annual asters. They can be high or low, single, double or extra double, in one colour or two, or mixed. We usually choose the high asters for a border, preferably self-coloured. This can be awkward as many asters are available in a mixture.

Callistephus chinensis 'Miss Europa' is a pink aster, 60cm (2ft) high. And for those who like to sow their own there is seed of the 'Light Blue Andrella', a powder blue one, 80cm (32in) high. The striking 'Hino-Maru' is red with a white edge, 60cm (2ft) tall. 'Blue Moon'

from June until August with insignificant little purple flowers. The dark-lilac berries appear in October and November like clusters of beads along the branches. The plant has a stiff, unbending habit which the berries do their

Callistephus chinensis 'Pompon Formule Mix'

Callistephus chinensis with kale

Calycanthus floridus

people recognise the aroma of cloves. The leaves are large and oval; the brownish-red flowers appear in June and are most unusual. They have a fruity fragrance very much like strawberries. It is a fairly coarse shrub which feels perfectly at home in the shrub border - in fertile soil and a sunny position.

Camassia

INDIANENLELIE

○ ☼

You will not find camassia at a nursery for perennials. This is a bulbous plant, but it combines well in a border. It prefers fertile soil in a sunny spot where it is not too dry but well-drained and shaded from the midday sun.

The plant is not fully hardy and needs protection during a long period of severe frost. Camassias flower in June and July. *Camassia cusickii* grows up to 60cm (2ft) and is pale blue. The cultivar 'Zwanenburg' has larger flowers, as blue as wistaria. *Camassia leichtlinii* has the most cultivars. 'Blauwe Donau' is deep blue; 'Plena' has greenish-white, semi-double flowers; 'Alba' is 80cm (32in) high with bluish-white flowers.

The latter is usually classed as a cultivar of *Camassia leichtlinii*, but in fact it belongs with the blue to violet flowering *C. leichtlinii* subsp. *suksdorfii*. *Camassia quamash*, with pale violet flowers remains lower at 40cm (16in). 'Orion' is its beautiful cultivar with slightly larger, steel-blue flowers.

Camassia in a flower meadow

is blue with a white edge, also 60cm (2ft)high. These last two are more difficult to combine than asters in one colour. They bloom longer if the faded flowers are removed. Asters need a different position every year to avoid wilt.

Calycanthus

⚘ ☼

Calycanthus floridus, or *Carolina allspice* is the most often grown of this genus. The shrub grows up to 3m (9ft) and is not called allspice in vain. The whole shrub smells spicy - most

Camassia leichtlinii subsp. *suksdorffii*

Camassia, white and blue

Camellia

🌿 ○ ●

Camellia is no ordinary shrub. Usually planted as a single specimen, with its glossy leaves and large, showy flowers, it is a little aloof. However, with some persuasion it can take its place in a shrub border, as long as it has a sheltered spot, in the shade of small trees in light, slightly acid, woodland soil rich in humus. It is important when buying a *Camellia* to make sure that it is hardy. Many camellias are sensitive to frost, but the following cultivars of *Camellia japonica* are

generally hardy: 'Adolphe Audusson', with semi-double red blooms; 'Brushfield's Yellow with peony-like yellow flowers; 'Kramer's Supreme', with big, peony-like red flowers; 'Shirobotan', with semi-double white flowers.

Cultivars of *Camellia x williamsii* including 'Anticipation', with peony-shaped crimson blooms; 'Golden Spangles', with single, cherry-coloured flowers; and 'Water Lily', with double, pink flowers are all hardened off in England and sold on the European market as camellias from New Zealand. The degree of hardiness of camellias depends very much on

Camellia 'Anticipation'

Camellia japonica, white, against a wall

the circumstances. The shrub may be hardy in itself, but its flowers may be nipped in the bud by frost when almost open. It is better able to withstand frost when the temperature changes gradually, than when there is a sudden drop in temperature.

Swift fluctuations in temperature are not good for camellias. They like a sheltered spot, but on no account in the morning sun as the buds would thaw out too quickly in winter. Young plants especially need protective covering in winter.

Campanula

BELLFLOWER
♀ ♀ ✿ ☀ ○

The number of campanulas is astonishing. The taller ones are the most suitable for the border, but here too, there is endless variety. The cultivars of *Campanula lactiflora* are much-loved high border plants which combine well with roses. 'Alba' with white flowers grows up to 1.5m (5ft); 'Blue Lady' is as tall with bright-blue flowers; 'Loddon Anna' is a lilac-pink long-time bestseller, 1.5m (5ft) high; 'Pouffe' is lower, 40cm (16in), has lilac-blue bells and a white variety called 'White Pouffe'; 'Pritchard's Variety', 50cm (20in), is supposed to be amethyst blue, but

Campanula glomerata 'Superba'

Campanula lactiflora 'Pouffe'

light- blue plants are also sold by this name. It is best to buy this last cultivar from a good nursery. *Campanula latifolia* 'Alba' has lovely white bells on 80cm (32in)- stems. 'Brantwood', another cultivar of this species, has violet-purple blooms. *Campanula persificolia*, with peach-like leaves, has some splendid cultivars with elegant bells.

'George Chiswell' has white flowers tinged with lilac at the edges. 'Hampstead White' has a double row of petals so that the flowers resemble cups and saucers. *Campanula glomerata* 'Superba' is a dashing focal point of colour with its dark-purple, close-set clusters of flowers topping the stems. There are also some wonderful biennial campanulas, such as the Canterbury bells, *Campanula medium* and the *Campanula pyramidalis*. Canterbury bells have large flowers in various shades of pink, white and blue and they can grow up to 1m (3ft). 'Calycanthema' has big cup -and - saucer flowers. 'Russian Pink' is an annual campanula which can bloom within sixteen weeks of sowing.

Campanula pyramidalis, although a hardy plant, still has to be sown every year and can grow up to 2m (6ft). These biennial and annual bellflowers love full sun while the perennial plants tolerate light shade. They need fertile, well-drained soil and almost all of them like lime.

Carex

SEDGE

Carex grows in the wild where the soil is wet enough and its cultivated relatives also prefer moist soil. *Carex elata* 'Aurea', 50cm (20in), also available under the name of 'Bowles' Golden Sedge', has long, narrow, golden-yellow blades with a fine green edge. *Carex morrowii* 'Variegata' 30cm (12in) is a familiar sedge with white-flecked leaves. *Carex muskingumensis* has lance-shaped leaves wrapped around the stem, like an umbrella. *Carex siderosticta* 'Variegata', only 20cm (8in) high, has wide leaves striped with white. The leaves of this *Carex* are sensitive to burning sunlight. Sedge grows very well around a pool, or in a moist border.

Caryopteris

This low shrub, 1.5m (5ft) is sometimes touched by frost in winter but always sprouts again, flowering in the autumn on year-old shoots. *Caryopteris x clandonensis* has many cultivars which all bloom during late summer and early autumn in various shades of blue.

The cultivar 'Arthur Simmonds' is usually sold as *C. x clandonensis* . 'Dark Knight' has large, coarsely toothed foliage and dark violet-purple flowers, is hardy and remains lower. 'Ferndown' has deep violet-blue flowers; 'Heavenly Blue' has the truest blue flowers; 'Kew Blue' produces many navy-blue flowers, but is not fully hardy. 'Longwood Blue' is a new cultivar, 60cm (2ft)-high, with violet-purple flowers; 'Worcester Gold' has greenish-yellow foliage and dark-blue flowers. *Caryopteris incana* has broader leaves and flowers later; 'Cary', a new cultivar from Denmark, has deep-blue flowers and is hardy. *Caryopteris* is more like a sturdy perennial in its habit than a shrub and for this reason - and for its lovely shades of blue - it is useful in a mixed border.

Catalpa

This tree can grow up to 10m (30ft), which seems tall for a border, but if it is pruned back almost to the ground every year it will sprout with splendid, exceptionally large foliage every year. In this way the tree becomes a shrub suitable for a mixed border. Two of

Caryopteris

Catalpa bignonioides 'Aurea'

Catalpa erubescens × ™Purpurea'

Catalpa bignonioides 'Aurea'

sowing and is also grown as an annual. The reason for this is that the plant suffers from wet winters. *Catananche* has a large rosette of grassy leaves from which thin, strong, branched-stalks topped by lovely papery flowers grow from July until September. The species is purplish-blue, the cultivar 'Major' is lavender-blue with a darker centre; 'Alba' is white and 'Bicolor' is white with a blue centre. They grow up to 70cm (28in), are fairly hardy on dry soil but will need protective covering in wet ground during severe frost.

Catanache caerulea

these trees are particularly suitable here, namely the Indian bean tree, *Catalpa bignonioides* 'Aurea', with magnificent golden-yellow sprouting foliage, turning greenish-yellow later, and *Catalpa x erubescens* 'Purpurea', with dark, black and brown foliage, turning green later.

Catananche

BLUE CUPIDONE

Catananche coerulea is a pleasing perennial which already flowers during the first year of

81

Ceanothus

These low shrubs combine very well with perennials in the border, but unfortunately they are not fully hardy. Given a sheltered position and hard pruning in spring they will flower on year-old shoots. *Ceanothus x delianus* 'Gloire de Versailles' is the most common. The plant grows up to 1m (3ft), flowering profusely from July until October with large clusters of deep-blue flowers. 'Topaze' is a strong cultivar with pale-blue flowers. *Ceanothus x pallidus* 'Marie Simon' grows up to 70cm (28in) with pure-pink flowers. Plant them in a warm, sheltered spot in good soil which must not be wet.

Centaurea

KNAPWEED

The most familiar knapweed is naturally the common blue weed which used to grow in the cornfields. This is the Cornflower, *Centaurea cyanus* with single (floret) flowers of true, cornflower-blue. Many of the annual cornflowers are double, ranging in colour from white, pink, red and purple to every shade of blue. It is best to use them self-coloured in the border. 'Victoria Blue' is an early variety, like 'King Size Pink'; 'Blue Diadem' flowers later. 'Black Boy' is deep purple and cultivars with 'Frosted' in the name are two-coloured for those who like them. There is a great variety in perennial cornflowers. The best-known is certainly *Centaurea macrocephala*, a large, 1.2m (4ft) high, fairly coarse plant with big, golden-yellow flowers, excellent for drying. Centaurea

Ceanothus × pallidus 'Marie Simon'

Centaurea macrocephala

Centaurea hypoleuca 'John Coutts'

hypoleuca 'John Coutts' 50cm (20in) has slender branched stalks with large pink flowers and leaves with grey-green undersides. *Centaurea montana* of the mountains has many lovely cultivars, none higher than 50cm (20in). The flowers are more delicate than those of *C. macrocephala*. The species itself is blue, 'Alba' has white flowers and 'Carnea' a pale lilac pink; ' Lady Florence Hastings' has large white flowers; 'Parham' ('Parham Variety') has lilac-purple flowers and 'Grandiflora' has big violet-blue flowers. *Centaurea bella* has large pink flowers, about 40cm (16in) high and resembling *Centaurea simplicicaulis*, with elegant lilac-pink flowers and grey-green foliage which forms good ground cover even in winter. *Centaurea* 'Pulchra Major' (synonym for *Leuzea centaurides*) is an impressive plant, 1.5m (5ft) tall with large, grey-green leaves and lilac-pink flowers. The flower buds are most decorative,

Centaurea montana 'Alba'

flowering is brief, but still lovely when the flowers have faded. Cornflowers like the sun and dry soil, but this must contain some nutrients. Many cornflowers are excellent for cutting and they can also be dried.

Centranthus

 ☼

The flowers of centranthus have long spores and together with the little flowers they form plume-like branched clusters with a light and delicate habit. These plants will grow on poor, dry soil, even making do with a place in an old wall. They do this with a reason, namely that they like chalk. Not many growers have taken the trouble to 'improve' these plants, as the species *Centranthus ruber* has only a handful of cultivars. 'Coccineus' is the best-known of these. This red valerian, which flowers from May into July, is a beautiful red, matching its smooth, bluish-green foliage very well. 'Albus' has white flowers, 'Rosenrot' has pink flowers. These plants require a sunny position and will grow in any well-drained soil. They flower early and go on for months, especially if they are cut back after the first flowering. This prevents the plant from collapsing and promotes a second flowering. It is a short-lived plant, not always hardy, which will need replacing every three or four years. Given enough freedom it will see to this by seeding

Centranthus ruber 'Coccineus'

itself. The plants grow up to 60cm (2ft) tall and are as much at home in the border as the flowers are in a vase.

Centranthus ruber

Cephalaria

This plant is sometimes wrongly called scabious and that is no wonder because the flowers are very like those of the scabious. For instance, the robust *Cephalaria gigantea* is also known as the Giant scabious and is most often grown and - true to its name - it can reach the gigantic height of 2.5m (8ft).

The flowers which appear from May into August, are pale yellow with a greenish centre. These plants are not at all suitable for a small border, but they are indispensable in a large border. In spite of its height the plant needs hardly any support and it is graceful rather than coarse.

The colour is subdued so that the plant combines well with other perennials. *Cephalaria alpina* flowers earlier, remains slightly lower 1.5m (5ft) and is a paler colour. *C. dipsacoides* has less deeply- dissected foliage and cream-coloured flowers. All cephalarias attract bees and butterflies. They like their flower heads to be in the sun and

Centranthus ruber 'Albus'

Cephalaria gigantea

their roots in well-drained, moist soil, although they will also grow in dry soil.

Ceratostigma

🌸 ⚘ ☼

Ceratostigma plumbaginoides is a perennial plant which begins to flower when most others are fading. The dark, gentian-blue flowers appear in September and October. The plant combines its blue flowers with foliage turning a reddish-brown colour. It is 20 cm (8in)-high and makes a useful edging plant for

Ceratostigma plumbaginoides – flower

Ceratostigma plumbaginoides

the perennial border, or as ground cover under shrubs in the shrub border. The plant needs protection from frost for the first few years. The shrubs *C. griffithii* and *C. willmottianum* are not much hardier than the perennial *C. plumbaginoides*. *C. willmottianum* grows up to 1.5m (5ft) and like *C. plumbaginoides*, its leaves turn red as it flowers well into autumn with deep-blue flowers. These shrubs are too temperamental and vulnerable for use in a border, but they do very well in large pots, spending the winter indoors, frost-free. The perennial C. plumbaginoides loves a sunny spot and well-drained, good soil and will also grow in a dry position.

Cercis

JUDAS TREE

Cercis siliquastrum is a small tree, or a big shrub, growing from 3m to 10m (9-30ft)-tall eventually. It blooms with pinkish-purple, pea-like flowers in April and May, before the foliage appears.

The tree is then covered with a cloud of pink flowers which are followed by pod-shaped fruits. The flowers and foliage are both splendid. The rounded, kidney-shaped leaves are like coins, or the pieces of silver which gave the tree its name.

Cercis canadensis 'Forest Pansy'

Cercis siliquastrum

Chaenomeles × superba 'Cameo'

Cercis siliquastrum 'Alba' has white flowers. *Cercis canadensis* 'Forest Pansy' is a very beautiful cultivar from America, with purple-black foliage when sprouting, turning from crimson to dark green later. The pale-pink flowers appear before the foliage. It makes a wonderful specimen, but the trees or shrubs are also lovely as a background.

Chaenomeles

FLOWERING QUINCE JAPONICA

These thorny shrubs with large flowers bear sweetly-scented quinces in the autumn. The golden quinces keep so well that they can be used to give the car or the linen cupboard a lovely fragrance, or you can make jam with them.

They do not need pruning, but you can do so if they take up too much space . They also grow well against a wall, when the shrub becomes a wall covering by means of pruning.

The shrubs have white, pink, apricot, red and orange flowers. Cultivars of Chaenomeles speciosa are: 'Geisha Girl' 1.5m (5ft), with apricot, double flowers; 'Nivalis' 2m (6ft), with white flowers; 'Simonii' 50cm (20in), with dark red flowers; 'Umbilicata' with pinkish-red flowers. 'Yukigoten' has unusual, pale-yellow flowers. *Chaenomeles x superba* also has many cultivars, which generally remain lower: 'Cameo' has double, salmon-pink flowers; 'Clementine' 1.5m (5ft) has orange-red flowers; 'Fascination' 1m (3ft) has scarlet flowers; 'Jet Trail' is a low ground cover with white flowers; 'Nicoline' 1m (3ft) has deep-scarlet flowers. These shrubs are easy to grow, but they need fertile and well-drained soil.

Chaerophyllum

CHERVIL

According to the experts there is some kinship between this plant and *C. temulum* or rough chervil, and *C. bulbosum* or chervil. 'Rough chervil' does not sound so good, in any case. *Chaerophyllum hirsutum* 'Roseum' flowers with pink clusters and like the wild varieties it has finely divided, fern-like foliage tinged with green, like the stems.

These plants flower early, in May and June, growing up to 1m (3ft). They need good, moist soil in sun or light shade.

Chaerophyllum hirsutum 'Roseum'

Chamerion

ROSEBAY WILLOW HERB

Rosebay willow herb, *Chamerion angusti-folium*, grows rampantly and there is nothing

Chamerion angustifolium

against this in wild, open places, on the contrary. It is another matter in the border, but that is no reason to do without willow herb because you can always plant a cultivar. The white 'Album' is the most popular, with less rampant growth. The plants which flower in June grow to a height of 1.5m (5ft) if they like their environment. 'Stahl Rose', with lovely, pale-pink flowers is forgiven for spreading by some and also grows to 1.5m (5ft). *C. dodonaei*, with lavender-pink flowers, is lower, 80cm (32in), does not grow rampant but needs very well-drained soil as it will otherwise not be hardy. The plant may still be called *Epilobium* by many growers as this was the old name for willow herb. All except *C. dodonaei* prefer good, moisture-retentive soil and sun.

Chelone

TURTLE-HEAD

Chelone is a rigid plant growing upright, straight as a die and not to be blown over in a storm. A very reliable plant; some would call it rather dull, others value it highly. The flowers resemble a turtle's head, or a shell, and they are also good for cutting. The plants are easy to grow, as long as they are not in dry soil. They are at their best in a moist spot in half

Chamerion angustifolium 'Album'

Chamerion angustifolium 'Stahl Rose'

Chelone obliqua

shade. *Chelone obliqua* bears lilac-pink flowers in August and September and its cultivar 'Alba' has white flowers.

The cultivar 'Parelmoer' 1m (3ft) has apple blossom-pink flowers. There are also *Chelone glabra* with pinkish-white flowers and *C. lyonii*, differing from *C. obliqua* in foliage with longer stems and paler flowers, with clearly ribbed upper lips. After flowering from July until September the plant is still attractive because of its seed capsules. Take care if you collect the seeds of this plant as they may cause skin trouble.

Chimonanthus

Chimonanthus praecox or Wintersweet is a shrub, 3m (9ft)-tall, flowering in March with fragrant, yellow flowers, wine-red on the inside and sensitive to frost. The species does not flower as a young plant, but the two cultivars 'Grandiflorus' and 'Luteus' do so. The flowers of 'Luteus' are fairly big and a uniform waxy yellow on the inside without the red. The flowers of 'Grandiflorus' are a darker yellow and red on the inside. The shrub flowers particularly well after a long, hot summer and needs a sheltered spot as it is not fully hardy. It tolerates limy soil.

Chrysanthemum

The *Chrysanthemum* genus has been treated badly. The 'true' *chrysanthemum* (now *Dendranthema*), the marguerite (now *Leucanthemum*), and many more used to belong to the genus. There are only really five species left of which three matter to the garden: *Chrysanthemum carinatum*, *C. coronarium* and *C. segetum*. Various seed mixtures of the cheerful *Chrysanthemum carinatum* are available: 'Court Jesters' exists in every possible colour except blue. The flowers are 50cm (20in)-high and bloom in white, red, brown, pink, orange and yellow; as though this was not enough, there is also a yellow one with a red band around its centre. But the odd thing is that all these colours go well together. 'Flame Shades', in different shades of red, is more subdued. 'John Bright' has single, yellow flowers with a dark ring and 'Poolster' or

Chrysanthemum segetum

Cichorium intybus

'Polar Star' has large, white flowers with a yellow ring around a dark centre. They are excellent for cutting and so colourful that some would prefer to plant them in the border for cutting flowers. *Chrysanthemum coronarium* resembles the above in height and flowers, except for a less pronounced ring around the heart, if any. 'Golden Gem' has semi-double, yellow-ochre flowers and 'Primrose Gem' is pale yellow. *Chrysanthemum segetum*, the corn marigold seen in the wild, is often used in combination with corncockle, cornflowers and poppies for wildflower mixtures. The species is colourful enough, but some of the cultivars are even more cheerful. "Eldorado' has large, canary-yellow flowers with a darker ring and a dark centre; 'German Flag' is red and yellow with a black centre; 'Prado' is lemon yellow with a chocolate-brown centre. We see many *chrysanthemums* going by another name, but the familiar, cheerful ones are still with us.

Cichorium

CHICORY

❀ ☼

Few people will associate the vegetable chicory on their plate, with the tall plants with sky-blue flowers, usually growing wild in the verges and in dry meadows.

The neat heads of chicory are not grown from the species *Cichorium intybus*, but from one of its many cultivars. In spite of its bright blue flowers, chicory is not usually planted in a neat and tidy border. Neither are the cultivars, 'Roseum' or the white 'Albus'. But for slightly more casual planting they deserve to be given a chance.

The plants always flower with a few blooms at a time. They are over a metre (3ft) tall and bees love them. There are many more chicory

Chrysanthemum carinatum

Cichorium intybus 'Albus'

Cimicifuga racemosa

cultivars, possibly including some with a beautiful flowering habit, but chicory is naturally selected to produce good roots for the table.

Cimicifuga

BUGBANE

 ☼ ○

No border should be without this plant! It needs good, humus-rich soil that is not too dry. It flowers in late summer and autumn with arched or upright spikes. The plants are sturdy and uncomplicated and do not need

Cimicifuga simplex 'White Pearl'

supporting in spite of their height, which is always over 1m (3ft). They combine well with Japanese anemones. Many plants have been renamed and not all experts are in agreement so we will rely on the names of perennials as listed in 1995.

Most of the cultivars stem from *Cimicifuga simplex* , the last to flower at the end of

Cimicifuga ramosa 'Atropurpurea'

Cirsium rivulare

Cirsium rivulare 'Atropurpureum'

Cirsium rivulare 'Atropurpureum' in the border

September and in October. The species can grow up to 1.5m (5ft) with beautiful arching spikes of flowers. 'White Pearl' grows up to 1.3m (4¹/2ft) and there are also various brown-leaved cultivars, such as 'Braunlaub'. The name *Cimicifuga foetida* reveals that these plants do not always smell good.

The arched stems bear little creamy-white flowers which are really yellow, but look lighter beside the white stamens. *C. racemosa* var. *cordifolia* (syn. *C. cordifolia*) grows up to 1.5m (5ft) with upright stems branching at the top to bear creamy-yellow flowers. The species, *C. racemosa* flowers early in July and grows up to 2m (6ft) tall.

C. ramosa 'Atropurpurea' flowers from August until October, resembling *C. simplex*, but with longer flower stems. The leaves and buds are purple. The expert on *Cimicifuga*, James Compton, has classified this cultivar as belonging to the *C. simplex Atropurpurea* Group.

Cirsium

 ☼

No one really wants thistles in the border, but an exception ought to be made for *Cirsium rivulare* 'Atropurpureum'. This plumed thistle has none of the mean spines for which other thistles are notorious. The species is a native of northern Spain and the Pyrenees, where it grows in moist meadows. The cultivar will make do with less moisture. The lovely dark-red flowers top branched stalks with a height of 1.5m (5ft); as they flower a second time, they flower almost continuously from May into September. It is obvious where the biennial, sometimes hardy plant *Cirsium japonicum* originated and there this plumed thistle is known as 'No-Azami'. The flowers range from pink to purple; the cultivar 'Pink Beauty' is pale pink, 'Lilac Beauty' is purple, 'Snow Beauty' is white and 'Rose Beauty' is carmine. These cultivars are sown and grown as annuals.

Clarkia

GODETIA

Clarkia is an old-fashioned annual which turns up from time to time. The 30 cm (12in)-high *Clarkia concinna* 'Pink Ribbons' has deep-pink, single, scented flowers and it is a cultivar deriving its name from the species called 'Red Ribbons'. *C. pulchella* has larger flowers, grows a little taller and flowers throughout the summer. The seed mixtures contain all shades of pink, red and white, but seed in a single colour is also available. *C. pulchella* 'Snowflake' is white. Several of the cultivars of *C. unguiculata*, growing to a

Clarkia pulchella – a mixture

Clematis recta 'Purpurea'

height of 60cm (2ft), are available self-coloured: 'Albatross' is double and white, 'Apple Blossom' is pale pink, 'Chieftain' is double and lilac-purple, 'Enchantress' is salmon-pink and 'Glorious' is red. Like most annuals, clarkias thrive in full sun, which they need to flower profusely and to set seed, because one year is all they have.

Clematis

OLD MAN'S BEARD   TRAVELLER'S JOY

Not all species of clematis are climbers. Some of them are perennials which do not climb, but they die off in winter. They look well in the border with some support. *Clematis x bonstedtii* ' Crépuscule' grows to between 1 and 1.5m (3-5ft) and needs supporting. The bluish flowers are delicate, drooping little bells with their tips curling cheerfully outwards. *Clematis heracleifolia* is a semi-shrub, 1m (3ft) tall which will even grow in the shade, but this means fewer flowers. This species has pale-blue flowers. The flowers of cultivar 'China Purple' are a deep purple and 'Wyevale' flowers are deep blue. *Clematis integrifolia* grows to 1m (3ft) and needs some support. It has lovely blue, pendent flowers of which the entire petals are reflexed, not only the tips. *C. integrifolia* 'Alba' has white flowers, 'Olgae' has blue flowers and 'Rosea' has pink flowers. The best-known herbaceous clematis is *Clematis recta*, between 1 and 1.5m-high (3-5ft), a plant with white flowers needing some support. It is a strong plant which can reach a ripe old age. Its best-known cultivar is *C. recta* 'Purpurea', not with purple flowers as you would expect from the name, but sprouting brownish-red shoots in spring.

Cleome serrulata

Cleome serrulata 'Orchid Festival'

Clematis stans resembles *C. heracleifolia*, but it has smaller blue flowers and grows higher, 1.8m (5^1/2ft).

Excepting *C. heracleifolia*, which will grow in light shade, all these species of clematis need full sun and fertile soil. They appreciate some rotted manure at the end of the winter.

Cleome

SPIDER FLOWER
⚲ ☼

Cleome hassleriana 'Colour Fountain'

If there is one plant which deserves a prize for the best annual border plant, then this is the one (but not in a cold summer). The high cultivars 1m (3ft) of *Cleome hassleriana* are especially good. Both seeds and plants are available in shades of white, pink and violet colours which blend very well, such as 'Colour Fountain', but there are also single colours. 'Cherry Queen' is bright pink; 'Violet Queen' is purple; 'White Queen' or 'Helen Campbell' is white.

The flowers have long stamens like cats' whiskers. The flowers open from below upwards forming long, slender seed pods when they have finished flowering. Given a position in the sun and good soil they will flower well into the autumn. They do not need staking in spite of their height. Some lower and less striking examples are *Cleome marshalli* 'White Spider' and *Cleome serrulata* 'Orchid Festival'. The plants have thorns which may cause inflammation in people with sensitive skin.

Clerodendrum

⚘ ⚘ ☼

Clerodendron bungei, a shrub which can grow up to 2m (6ft), with heart-shape foliage like that of hydrangea, flowers at the end of summer with globe -like clusters of small maroon flowers. This shrub is not fully hardy; it is grown for the lovely fragrance of the flowers. The foliage smells different - of peanut butter. The larger *Clerodendron trichotomum* produces white flowers with a red calyx. The fruits are blue-grey at first,

Clerodendrum trichotomum

Collomia grandiflora

turning black later. This shrub 3m (9ft) is not fully hardy either. The *fargesii* variety is hardier and slightly smaller than the type, with purple-brown young leaves.

Clethra

ஃ ☼ ○

The Sweet pepper bush, *Clethra alnifolia*, a shrub 2m (6ft)-tall, flowers from July until September with upright clusters of creamy-

Clethra alnifolia

white, fragrant flowers. The fruits, or their remains are retained by the shrub during the whole winter. The leaves turn golden yellow in autumn. It has some beautiful cultivars including 'Clea', a new and lower cultivar from Denmark; 'Paniculata' with very long clusters; 'Pink Spire', flowering first with long, pale-pink clusters, turning white later and 'Rosea' in the same colours. *Clethra* prefers moist soil and tolerates coastal wind.

Collinsia

ↀ ☼ ○

This almost unknown annual flowers briefly so that it can be sown a few times. It can even be sown in September to ensure early flowering. If you sow in spring this can be repeated every six weeks. *Collinsia* is one of the few annuals which tolerates shade. It needs staking with sticks in the border. The plant can grow up to 60cm (2ft) and bears large butterfly-shaped flowers with a pale-purple underlip and a white upperlip. 'Alba' has a greenish-white upperlip; 'Candidissima' is all white; 'Blushing Rose', a new cultivar, has a white upperlip and a pale-pink underlip. The flowers are good for cutting.

Collomia

ↀ ☼

This unusual annual is not often seen, but it is a good border plant, with foliage playing an important part. *Collomia grandiflora* originally came from Canada and the USA. The small apricot-coloured flowers are clustered at the top of the stems. The cultivar 'Palinka' has slightly larger flowers. *Collomia cavanillesii* (sometimes with the unnecessary addition of 'Neon') has lovely little scarlet flowers and rich foliage.

Consolida

LARKSPUR
☀ ☼

Larkspur is the name for the annual variety of the *perennial* 'delphinium'. *Consolida ambigua* (*Delphinium ajacis*) is a larkspur from the Mediterranean Sea area. The plant always has unbranched stalks, flowering in much the same way as a hyacinth which is why it is also called the 'hyacinth-flowered' larkspur. It is available in pink, blue, white and assorted. 'Frosted Skies' has semi-double white flowers edged with blue. *Consolida regalis* (*Delphinium consolida*) has many cultivars and these larkspurs are excellent for cutting and drying. They also make good border plants. Both the larkspurs are better sown in October than in spring. These plants will flower in June, while those sown in spring will not flower until July. The advantage of sowing in the autumn is that the germination temperature must not be too high and the

Consolida regalis 'Blue Cloud'

Convallaria majalis 'Variegata'

germinative capacity of the seed decreases strongly if it is stored. If larkspurs feel at home in the garden, they will seed themselves. The seedlings will not survive severe frost without snow and they should be protected by a tunnel, or sown under glass, to be on the safe side. Cultivars are available in one colour.

'Blue Cloud' is as blue as a delphinium ought to be, 'Snow Cloud' is white and both grow to 90 cm (3ft). 'Miss Carolina' is white with a blue edge and 'Blue Picotee' is pale blue edged with white. These larkspurs make very good border plants and they are also excellent for cutting.

The best moment for picking is when the first flowers open. If they are picked in full flower they will soon lose their petals.

They flower briefly in comparison with other border plants, so this has to be taken into account. If you plant the higher cultivars in small groups at the back of the border it will not be noticed when they drop out, or you can plant other annuals to fill the empty spaces. You could also plant them in combination with longer-flowering annuals straight away, to ensure that these will take the place of the faded larkspurs.

Convallaria

LILY-OF-THE-VALLEY
❀ ○ ◕

This is not something you can plant in the border as a clump which then stays where it is.

Lilies of the valley, *Convollaria majalis*, go places and grow rampant, in an amiable way. You can never really have enough of these friendly plants. They often inhabit old estates and are most suitable as ground cover in a shrub border, but not in a border for perennials. The pleasant, drooping, white bell-shaped flowers appear in May, clustered together; they stay fresh in a vase for some time.

The ground must be moisture-retentive. There are cultivars now with pink or off-white and double flowers and with white or yellow-striped or edged foliage, *Convollaria majalis* 'Variegata'. They are unusual, certainly, but it is not really possible to improve on the species. It is a very strong plant.

Convolvulus

ⵀ ✿ ☼

Convolvulus tricolor is a pleasant annual plant, 30cm (1ft)-high, with large flowers in all shades of blue depending on the cultivar. The flowers have more colours as they have a white centre and a yellow eye. The seed is available in an assortment, or self-coloured. 'Blue Ensign' is a bright blue; 'Cambridge Blue' is pale blue; 'Blue Tilt', 'Dark Blue' and 'Royal Ensign' are all dark blue; 'Rose Ensign' is pink; 'Lavender Rosette' and 'White Ensign' are true to their names. These are really short-lived perennial plants but they are always

Convallaria majalis

Convolvulus tricolor 'Dark Blue'

Convolvulus sabaticus

grown as annuals because they are only half-hardy. They are not demanding but they need a sunny position. *Convolvulus sabaticus* is often grown in a pot, but it can also be grown as light ground cover in a sunny part of the border.

Coreopsis

TICKSEED
ⵀ ✿ ☼

The seed of the annual *Coreopsis tinctoria* is available in various assortments but also in a self-coloured. 'Carmen' has brownish-red flowers growing to 50cm (20in). 'Gold Star' and 'Mahogany Mixed' are only half as high and so less suitable for the border. There are also perennial species of coreopsis. *Coreopsis verticillata* is the best known, with bright yellow flowers and delicate, fern-like leaves. The cultivar 'Grandiflora' has larger flowers, but 'Moonbeam' is easily the favourite. The 'eyes' of this plant are lemon yellow, less bright than the type, and it flowers throughout the summer.

Coreopsis grandiflora 'Badengold'

Coreopsis verticillata 'Grandiflora'

Coreopsis verticillata 'Moonbeam'

Coreopsis grandiflora 'Badengold' is 1m (3ft)-high, with warm-yellow flowers and 'Sunray' has double, yellow flowers. *Coreopsis rosea* 'American Dream' was a prize-winning perennial in 1993, with its deep pink flowers. *Coreopsis rosea* 'Alba' has splendid creamy-white flowers. There are many more, but the last is *Coreopsis tripteris*, with yellow flowers and a darker centre. A robust plant for a large border.

Cornus

DOGWOOD

There are so many different types of dogwood, varying from low ground cover to tall shrubs. *Cornus canadensis* and *Cornus suecica* are ground cover plants. *Cornus canadensis* has green flowers with large white bracts followed by red berries. An ideal ground-cover plant for a shrub border on acid, peaty soil which retains moisture. *Cornus suecica* grows less vigorously and has black and red flowers with big white bracts and a smaller whorl of leaves directly under the flower than *Cornus canadensis*. This is why *C. canadensis* is more often used, as the dense whorls of leaves cover the ground more efficiently. *Cornus alba* 'Aurea' and *Cornus alba* 'Elegantissima' are valuable assets to the shrub border, with

Cornus suecica

Cornus alba 'Elegantissima'

Coronilla varia

Cornus alba 'Sibirica'

their lovely yellow -green and silvery-white margined foliage. The coral stalks of *Cornus alba* 'Sibirica' are most striking in winter; if the shrub grows too big for the border it can be pruned. The best time for this is just before Christmas as the brilliant red wood can be used for lovely decorations.

The young shoots of *Cornus sanguinea* 'Midwinter Fire' are yellow in winter. Cornus generally prefers moist soil and light shade, but most of them are not particular and will grow anywhere.

Coronilla

Coronilla emurus, 1m (3ft) tall, flowers from May into July with yellow clusters and can be found growing wild in the open woodlands of Italy and the French Riviera. *Coronilla varia* is a perennial of the same height, flowering from June into September with a cloud of pinky-white flowers. This vigorous plant weaves itself among other sturdier plants but may need some additional staking. Bees love it. Though not suitable for a neat border, coronilla will feel at home in a wild border.

Corydalis lutea

Corydalis is delightful in having both unusual flowers and foliage. The flowers have long spurs, the leaves are finely lobed. Most varieties grow well in half shade and well-drained, preferably woodland soil. There are always exceptions to nature's rule. *Corydalis ochroleuca* with pale-yellow flowers is in its element in the cracks of a warm wall or between the flagstones of a terrace. Gertrude Jekyll loved them and we can see this species in many of her gardens. *Corydalis lutea* is as strong with golden-yellow flowers. These plants are short-lived perennials, but they seed themselves liberally to make up for this. Both types flower exceptionally long, from May to

Corydalis ochroleuca

Corydalis cheilanthifolia

Corydalis flexuosa

September, with a height of 30cm (12in). The strangest of them, *Corydalis cheilanthifolia*, has leaves which do not seem to belong to the flowers.

If you do not know the plant, you assume it is a fern which has somehow produced a flower. *Corydalis* has yellow blooms, but its leaves are arranged in a rosette exactly like a fern. *Corydalis cava* (*C. bulbosa*), with flowers ranging in colour from maroon to white, also has some cultivars. But these plants are better off in the woods than in the border.

A plant which has become very popular in recent years is *Corydalis flexuosa*. Its attraction lies in its blue flowers rather than its strength. Variable in hardiness, it does not always survive the winter.

If you once lose your heart to the heavenly-blue flowers, you will not hesitate to provide the plant with protective covering in winter. This blue resembles the curious blue tint of Meconopsis. 'China Blue', 'Père David', and 'Purple Leaf' are cultivars.

Corylopsis

These pleasant shrubs flower before the foliage appears and are useful in mixed or shrub borders. *Corylopsis pauciflora* is one of the smallest types, only 1-1.5m (3-5ft). The pale-yellow, bell-shaped flowers appear in March and April.

Corylopsis spicata grows taller and wider than *C. pauciflora*, with slightly longer clusters of flowers and it blooms later. These shrubs are hardy, but a late frost can damage the flowers. They need moist, well-drained, acid soil.

Cosmos

The tuberous cosmos, *Cosmos atrosanguineus*, has dark-red, almost black, chocolate-scented flowers.

A plant for connoisseurs and not suitable for a border as it is far from hardy and will disappear at the end of the year. It is better to grow the plant in a pot and to store the tubers in a frost-free place during the winter. The

Corylopsis spicata

Cosmos en *Nicotiana*

Cosmos bipinnatus

Cosmos bipinnatus 'Sea Shells'

Cotinus

SMOKE TREE

🌿 ☼ ○

The smoke tree, *Cotinus coggygria* is essential in a shrub border and it is not out of place in a mixed border. It has everything - the colour of the feathery flower plumes and the foliage, its lovely growth and overall habit. The species has large plumes of flowers and green foliage turning yellow and red in the autumn. The stems grow larger as the fruits ripen and the effect is of a wig. The name 'smoke tree' also describes the appearance of the tree well, as though under a loud of smoke. The cultivar 'Nordine' has purple foliage with large,

Cotinus coggygria 'Purpureus' in the border

Cotinus coggygria 'Royal Purple'

annual cosmos is far more useful in the border as it combines well with perennial plants. *Cosmos bipinnatus* has some beautiful cultivars, all growing to 1m (3ft). There are even striped and two-colour varieties. But the self-coloured are still the best. 'Purity' is white; 'Gloria' is deep pink; 'Dazzler' is carmine red. The 'Sonata' cosmos are only 60cm (2ft)-high, but they are lovely in a border. 'Sea Shells' is an unusual cosmos with petals furled like tubes. They grow more vigorously, up to 1.5m (5ft), robust and shrubby.

The sea shells come in all shades of pink, red and white. Cosmos will grow in any soil, but they grow taller in fertile soil.

purplish-brown pappi; 'Royal Purple'has very dark-red foliage. 'Purpureus' has maroon foliage and flower plumes a shade lighter. 'Velvet Cloak has dark-purple foliage sprouting reddish-purple in spring.

The smoke tree prefers good garden soil, not too rch. It needs full sun to achieve its splendid autumn colouring. The crushed leaves release a strong scent of ripe angos, to which they are related.

Crambe

There are twenty types of crambe, but we usually only find two kinds in the garden as the other eighteen are uninteresting annuals.

Crambe maritima, 0r Sea kale, belongs in the vegetable garden. The true sea kale used to be blanched and eaten as a vegetable. This was done by placing a special pot over the kale similar to those used for blanching rhubarb. The 50cm (20in)-high plant has beautiful grey-green foliage and clusters of white flowers. The plant thrives in a border with sandy soil and is sometimes seen in coastal parts of Kent. *Crambe cordifolia* makes a magnificent specimen, very impressive with enormous foliage and finely branched clusters of white flowers.

Crambe maritima in the vegetable garden

Crambe maritima

Crambe cordifolia

This plant is only suitable for a large border and then with some reservations as it has good years and bad years. It may flower one year and not the next.

It is not a good idea to plant it near the terrace as its odour is not very pleasant.

Crepis

DANDELION

 ☼

Crepis rubra has such ordinary little flowers that the plant is hardly ever grown. But this pink dandelion is worth having. It is a very easy plant to grow, flowering throughout the summer with pink flowers, if sown often enough. The plant grows to 40cm (16in) and is good for cutting. There is a cultivar, 'Snow White'.

Crocosmia

MONTBRETIA

◊

Many people dislike montbretias. They find them pushy and loud. Perhaps their flowers look too much like freesias. These old-fashioned flowers have made a comeback since the red border became popular once more and they have always been a feature in large borders, providing brilliant colours in the autumn.

Crepis rubra

Crocosmia with *Campanula*

Crocosmia masonorum

The plants' main need is well-drained soil. Plant them in spring and cover them in winter. The best-known hybrid-cultivar is 'Lucifer', an apt name for the fiery-red flowers which rise up like cockscombs from the lance-shaped leaves. 'Emberglow' has orange-red flowers and 'Rheingold' has surprising golden-yellow flowers. The cultivars vary in height from 70cm (28in) to over 1m (3ft) .

Crocosmia masonorum has large, tawny to flaming orange-red flowers.

Crocosmia 'Lucifer'

Cynara

GLOBE ARTICHOKE, CARDOON

Two familiar kitchen-garden plants belong to
this genus, namely *Cynara cardunculus*,
cardoon, and *Cynara scolymus*, the globe
artichoke. Cardoon is an asset to a large
border. It has grey-green, deeply serrated
leaves. It used to be grown as a vegetable,
when its rosette of leaves was tied up and
blanched. These tied leaves are still often seen
in France, covered with a brown paper bag.
The flowers of cardoon resemble small
artichokes and are very attractive to bees.
These are big, impressive plants which take up
a great deal of room. The leafstalks of *Cynara
scolymus*, the globe artichoke, are not eaten,
but the flower heads are a delicacy when

Cynara scolymus

Cynara cardunculus

Cynoglossum amabile 'Pink Shower' in the border

cooked and served with a dressing. The bracts
are enjoyed first, followed by the best part, the
base, which appears when the stamens have
been removed. The artichoke is so decorative
that it deserves a place in your border. There
are several cultivars of the globe artichoke, all
cultivated to achieve the best possible flower
heads. The cardoon and the globe artichoke
are not fully hardy.

Cynoglossum

HOUND'S TONGUE

The annual, *Cynoglossum amabile* and its
cultivars resemble the forget- me-not.
They flower profusely and are firm favourites
with garden lovers and insects. 'Blue Shower'
and 'Pink Shower', 70 cm (28in) are taller
than 'Firmament' and 'Blue Bird', 40cm
(16in).
'Mystery Rose' is a white 'forget- me- not'
which blushes, 70cm (28in) and 'Avalanche' is
true to its name, with white flowers.
Cynoglossum wallichii is a biennial which
can grow to over 1m (3ft) and becomes
perennial by seeding itself freely. It has lighter-
blue flowers and blooms later than the
annuals.
Cynoglossum nervosum is a perennial, growing up to 70cm (28in). Like the annual types,

it has blue flowers. All cynoglossums are easy to grow and flower freely.

Cytisus

BROOM

The common broom has numerous cultivars, hybrid-cultivars and other relatives, so there are enough to choose from for the border. *Cytisus x praecox* 'Allgold' is the one which really succeeds in coming up to our expectations of broom. This strong cultivar flowers in the middle of May in a beautiful shade of yellow. The species, which is not grown as often, has creamy-yellow flowers. The broom which grows in the wild is *Cytisus scoparius* which can be seen on a heath, on verges and sand dunes, on railway embankments and at the edge of the woods. The pods which appear after flowering is over, pop open audibly in the warm summer sunshine to release their seeds. There are some hybrid-cultivars of broom in other colours. The familiar 'Boskoop Ruby' has dark -carmine

flowers and 'Criterion' is pinkish-white with orange-red; 'Dukaat' is in two shades of yellow; 'Golden Sunlight' is golden-yellow; 'Hollandia' is pale yellow with cherry-red; 'Roter Favorit' is dark red. *Cytisus nigricans*, formerly called *Lembotropis*, is another type of shrub altogether, 1.5m (5ft)-tall and with 10-30cm (4-12in)-long, bright yellow clusters in July and August. This plant needs well-drained, fairly poor soil in a warm and sunny spot.

Cynoglossum amabile 'Blue Shower'

Cynoglossum in the border

Dahlia with box edging

Dahlia

⬠ ☀

Many people are apprehensive about planting dahlias in their borders. They are often associated with garish colours and large flowers dominating other plants. But with a little discretion dahlias can be used in the border with effect. Make a prudent start with 'Bishop of Llandaff' and you will soon learn to appreciate dahlias. The bishop has single, bright-red flowers, dark foliage and grows to 90cm (3ft). This dahlia is also an excellent plant for a tub. 'Moonfire' also has dark foliage, here in combination with single yellow flowers and red centres. 'Roxy' is single flowered, but lavender-purple and lower.

Dahlia merckii is a tall species with pale-pink, single flowers, toning subtly with the darker foliage. 'Gerrie Hoek' is a hybrid cultivar, 1m (3ft)-high with pale-pink flowers - a decorative dahlia which even Penelope Hobhouse grows in her borders. There is such an abundance of dahlia cultivars that there must be one suitable for the border. The only features to watch out for are the colour and the size of the flowers. A big red-and-white dahlia will be an eyesore in any border. Dahlias grow from tubers which have to be planted in the middle of May after the last frost. They do not tolerate any frost at all and the tubers must be stored frost-free during the winter. Dahlias can also be sown, but they are nearly always only available as a mixture. You can remedy this by sowing them and saving your favourites after they have flowered. They will have formed tubers which can be stored for the winter. If there are some single dahlias with good colours you can go on growing these and give the rest away or compost them. Taller dahlias usually need staking.

Dahlia 'Bishop of Llandaff'

Dahlia 'Moonfire'

Daphne

🌿 ☀ ○

An extensive genus of slow-growing, ever-green deciduous bushes of which the smallest species are destined for the rock garden. Most daphnes have beautiful, scented flowers followed by berries. *Daphne x burkwoodii* has several splendid cultivars for the shrub border, or a mixed border. 'Somerset' has purple-pink flowers. *Daphne laureola* is an evergreen bush with lime-coloured flowers which are fragrant in the evening but malodorous by day. *Daphne mezereum*, the red mezereon, has almost disappeared in the wild.
The violet-coloured flowers of this species are sweet-scented, followed by red (poisonous)

Daphne laureola

large, green shield-shaped leaves appear later. The genus has only one species, *Darmera peltata (Peltiphyllum peltatum)*. It has a beautiful cultivar, 'Nana', 40cm (16in)-high, which flowers with star-shaped, pale pink flowers appearing - as with the species - in clusters on tall stalks before the foliage. The plant is more sensitive to frost, especially the flower stalks can be damaged by a late frost, but the plant itself will survive this.

Decaisnea

Decaisnea fargesii grows into a shrub with a wide spread, up to 2.5m (8ft) tall with thick branches and very large foliage. The arched plumes of lime-coloured flowers are followed by peculiar blue fruits, 10cm (4in)-long and resembling gherkins. They need a sheltered and sunny position.

Delphinium

This is the hardy perennial delphinium. The annual larkspur has been relegated to the genus *Consolida*, but it is still found under *Delphinium* in most seed catalogues.

Delphinium ajacis is now called *Consolida ambigua* and *Delphinium consolida* is now called *Consolida regalis*. In this encyclopaedia the annual larkspurs are to be found under their new name.

Only the *perennial delphinium* is given here. Some order has been brought into the huge quantities of *delphiniums* available by dividing them into three groups. The first group is of *Delphinium* elatum-hybrids, also known as hybrid-cultivars - D. elatum was one of the parents, but not the only one. The large

berries. Daphne mezereum 'Alba' (*D. meze-reum f. alba*) has white flowers and 'Ruby Glow' is true to its name. Daphnes prefer full sun and well-drained soil.

Darmera

UMBRELLA PLANT

This is an unusual perennial with root runners. It is at its best by the waterside where it also serves a purpose by supporting the banks. The plant would be useful in a moist border, for instance adjacent to water. The pale-pink flowers on stiff stalks rise up first, like flowering trees, in April and May. The

Darmera

Darmera in the bud, with borrowed foliage

Decaisnea – fruit

delphiniums which are grown from cuttings belong to this group, which consists of two different types, one English and one German. The English type has large, heavy clusters of flowers which need support in the border,

such as 'Blue Triumphator', violet blue, 'Blue Nile', blue with a white eye, 'Stawberry Fair', deep pink, and 'Lord Butler', pale blue with a white eye. Many of the German type were developed by Karl Foerster in Germany; these have lighter clusters of flowers not so likely to collapse, but this does not mean that they need no support at all. 'Berghimmel' has light-blue flowers with a white eye; 'Finsteraarhorn' is dark blue; 'Ouvertüre' is blue tinged with pink; 'Perlmutterbaum' is pale blue with pink. The second group, also grown from cuttings, is of the Belladonna-hybrids. These are lower than the former group and branched, with smaller, less dense clusters. 'Atlantis' grows up to 1.2m (4ft), and is a deep violet; 'Piccolo' grows to 1m (3ft) with gentian-blue flowers; 'Völkerfrieden' has deep-blue flowers with a white eye.

The third group is made up of the Pacific Giants which are grown from seed. This makes them cheaper than delphiniums in the other two groups. 'Astolat' is lavender pink; 'Black Knight' has dark violet flowers with a black eye; 'King Arthur' is dark violet with a white eye. There are so many different delphiniums that it would not be possible to give a complete survey here.

The flowers are of such beauty, enriching the border so much that we are glad to tie them up when necessary. They prefer fertile soil, not

Delphinium 'Strawberry Fair'

Delphinium 'Lord Butler'

wet, especially in winter. Watch over them in spring when the plants are sprouting as snails and slugs love to eat the tender young leaves. If the stalks are cut back after the first flowering the plants will flower a second time. Alternatively the 'Jekyll model' can be applied. The famous garden designer Gertrude Jekyll (1843 - 1932) planted some sweet peas - *Lathyrus latifolius* - behind the delphinium. When it had finished flowering, the sweet peas were high enough to climb up the fading stalks of the delphinium. A good idea.

Dendranthema

CHRYSANTHEMUM

A chrysanthemum by any other name does not seem possible, but officially it is now called *Dendranthema*. It is still listed under *Chrysanthemum* in many seed catalogues. These are extremely popular cut flowers recognizable by the spicy tang of their foliage. The chrysanthemum always used to herald the autumn, but now it is grown all the year round. The florists' chrysanthemums grown for exhibitions, especially the 'plucked' varieties (of which only one bud is allowed to grow into a flower on each stem) with their compact, global flowers are great favourites. Just before the show all the petals are arranged neatly with tweezers. Naturally these are not

Dendranthema 'Mary Stoker'

the chrysanthemums we want in our border, where types with a more informal habit are needed. They are difficult to find since the names were changed, but fortunately the former *Chrysanthemum rubellum* 'Clara Curtis', now called *Dendranthema* 'Clara Curtis' (Rubellum group), has kept its cultivar name. This plant has daisy-like flowers and grows up to 70cm (28in). 'Mei-Kyo' (syn. 'Anja's Bouquet')

produces lavender-pink flowers lavishly until frost sets in. 'Flora' is yellow; 'Bronze Elegance' is bronze-brown; 'Duchess of Edinburgh' (Rubellum-group) reddish-brown;

Delphinium 'Astolat'

Dendranthema 'Clara Curtis'

Dendranthema 'Flora'

Deschampsia cespitosa

'Julia' pale pink and 'Mary Stoker' (Rubellum group) apricot-yellow. The chrysanthemums from cuttings, available from nurseries, are best planted in the vegetable garden for cutting purposes, as their unbending habit is a little too stiff for the border.

Deschampsia

Deschampsia cespitosa, or Tufted hair grass has several valuable cultivars. 'Bronzeschleier' has bronze-coloured blades; 'Goldschleier', 1.2m (4ft), golden-yellow; 'Goldtau' is lower 70cm (28in); 'Schotland' is lower still 40cm (16in) with dark-green foliage.

Grasses are infinitely versatile, combining well with small shrubs and perennials. They are fully hardy, although they sometimes disappear for no reason. They will grow in sunny and shady positions.

Deutzia

STEPHANOTIS

The best-known *Deutzia* is certainly *Deutzia x kalmiiflora*, renamed *Deutzia purpurascens* 'Kalmiiflora'.

This decorative shrub, 1.5m (5ft)-high, flowers early, in May with spreading posies of pink flowers, deep pink in the bud, almost white on the inside. But there are many more richly-flowering species of *Deutzia* and cultivars, with white or pale-pink flowers such as *Deutzia x magnifica*; all of them love full sun and fertile soil. Regular pruning is essential to

stimulate free flowering. *Deutzia gracilis* grows up to 75cm (2^1/2ft) and has pure white flowers. *Deutzia x hybrida* 'Mont Rose' has large, plume-shaped clusters of pink flowers.

Deschampsia cespitosa 'Goldtau'

111

Deutzia × magnifica

Dianthus carthusianorum

Dianthus

PINK CARNATION

🛈 ❀ ☀

Many of the low pinks are gems for the rock garden. Here we will introduce you to the taller ones which can be grown in the border. *Dianthus carthusianorum* is a short-lived perennial which lengthens its life by seeding itself. This Carthusian pink bears deep rose-pink flowers on 60cm (2ft)-long stems, a plant for the informal cottage border. Dianthus deltoides, the Maiden pink, is lower, 40cm (16in) also suitable for a cottage border. *Dianthus superbus*, is a magnificent pink, also a short-lived perennial with lavender-pink , fringed flowers on 40cm (16in)-long stems. 'Red Feather' and 'White Feather' are both cultivars. *Dianthus superbus* var. *longicaly-cinus* has slightly longer sepals than the type and a pinkish-purple colour. The taller pinks of the Plumarius group can be planted in the very front of the border. 'Mrs. Sinkins' is noted for her fragrance and 'Musgrave Pink', white with a green eye, is also sweet-scented, but there are so many more. *Dianthus barbatus* is the familiar sweet william, often forgotten as a border plant. These biennial plants are often available in mixed colours, plants or seeds, but also in a single colour. A beautiful, old-fashioned cultivar is 'Nigrescens', with black-red flowers and dark foliage. Sweet williams of the Standard series flower from July until October and are available in white, red and deep, dark red. They form a splendid combination together with foxgloves.

Diascia

As these perennials are only half-hardy they are grown as annuals. Diascias were known in Gertrude Jekyll's day, but they have only been rediscovered in recent years. These are plants which flower profusely from June until well

Dianthus deltoides

Dianthus barbatus in the border

Diascia 'Ruby Field'

Diascia 'Lilac Belle'

into October. There are so many new cultivars that it is impossible to keep up with them. But the species of this South African plant are also used. Diascia anastrepta, with pink flowers is fairly hardy, but only suitable for edging as it is 20cm (8in) high. *Diascia fetcaniensis* grows to 50cm (20in), with pink flowers and is lovely in combination with the grey foliage of lamb's tongue (*stachys*). *Diascia integerrima* has small, pale-pink flowers, close together. This species has a completely different habit with stiff, vertical stalks covered with leaves. *Diascia vigilis* grows up to 50cm (20in) with glossy pale green foliage and pale pink flowers. Well-known hybrid-cultivars are: 'Blackthorn Apricot', the richly-flowering 'Ruby Field', the lavender-pink 'Lilac Belle' and the deep pink 'Rupert Lambert'. The 60cm (2ft)-tall 'Jack Elliot' is a cultivar of Diascia vigilis. These free-flowering plants do very well in tubs, as also in the border.

Dicentra spectabilis

Dicentra exima

Dicentra spectabilis 'Alba'

outer petals are curled. 'Alba' is its white cultivar, 'Stuart Boothman' is pale pink. These dicentras are 25cm (10in)-high.

Dicentra formosa has several slightly taller cultivars.
'Adrian Bloom' has narrow, blue-grey foliage and deep pink flowers; 'Bacchanal' has blood-red flowers; 'Langtrees' is a lovely cultivar with blue foliage and white flowers; 'Luxuriant' has deep-pink flowers; 'Margery Fish' has coarser foliage and pinky-white flowers.

Bleeding-heart is a beautiful plant which blooms early on and both its foliage and flowers play their part. They prefer moist soil rich in humus and a shady spot. The one disadvantage of these pleasing plants is that they withdraw after flowering, leaving large gaps in the border. This can be taken into account beforehand by planning neighbouring plants, willing to fill the gaps.

Dicentra

BLEEDING-HEART

Dicentra spectabilis is the true bleeding-heart, its elegant, arching stems bearing red-and-white, pendent, heart-shaped flowers. The plant has fine, fern-like foliage and flowers in May and June.

They are usually 60 cm (2ft)-high, but in a favourable spot they can grow up to 1m (3ft). The white cultivar 'Alba' is the most popular. *Dicentra eximia* has more finely divided leaves and slender, pink flowers of which the

Dictamnus

In the garden of their country house in Hammerby, Sweden, a daughter of Linnaeus (1707-1778) is said to have shown her father's students that she could set fire to a dictamnus without its burning. This can still be done today, but it has to be a warm and windless summer evening. The flowers exude so much volatile oil that sparks fly if a flame is held to them.

Dictamnus prefers chalky, fairly dry soil and full sun. It may take several years for the plant to flower freely, but by that time it will be a sturdy and reliable plant.

Dictamnus albus, the Burning bush, applies to its white roots, the flowers are pale-pink clusters on upright spikes.

This type grows 80cm (32in)-tall. The cultivar 'Albiflorus' really has white flowers and 'Purpureus' are pinkish purple. The plants flower in June and July.

Dierama

ANGEL'S FISHING ROD   WANDFLOWER
◊ ☼

Dierama pulcherrimum is an unusual bulbous plant from South Africa, unfortunately not at all hardy in our European climate. The tubers must be planted at some depth in well-drained, fertile soil, moist while the plant is growing.

This self-willed plant sometimes chooses its own spot by moving, perhaps from the border to the terrace. The fine, grassy foliage stays green all winter if the frost is not too severe. It can be protected with a covering of dry mulch, but the best method is to lift the tubers and store them in a dry place. The very elegant 1m (3ft)-long arched stems bear bell-shaped pink flowers in late summer.

Dictamnus albus 'Purpureus'

Dictamnus albus 'Albiflorus'

Dierama pulcherrimum

Digitalis purpurea

It is no wonder that they are also known as "Angel's fishing rod" because they are often grown at the edge of a pond.

The plant is often grown in Ireland because it is hardier there and selections have been developed from it. It is well worth trying in your local climate as it is unrivalled among the ornamental grasses.

Digitalis

FOXGLOVE
🌱 ❀ ○ ☀

Digitalis purpurea, the common foxglove, is the best-known of the twenty-odd species of annual and perennial plants. It grows in the wild, but there are also many cultivars of this species, in assorted colours or in one colour.'Lelieblank' is a great favourite among the cultivars; it has white flowers without spots on the inner side of the 'gloves'. 'Alba' is white and spotted. 'Gloxiniiflora' (syn. 'The Shirley') has large flowers in various shades of pink. 'Gelbe Lanze' is a hybrid-cultivar with pale-yellow flowers, no spots. 'Giant Spotted' (syn. 'Glittering Prizes') is a blend of mixed colours; its flowers have a dark-yellow spot on the inside. 'Apricot Beauty' lives up to its name.

These foxgloves grow to about 1.5m (5ft)-tall. Most foxgloves seed themselves. *Digitalis purpurea* subsp. *heywoodii* grows up to 80cm (32in) and has silvery-green foliage and creamy-pink flowers.

Digitalis ferruginea

Digitalis lutea

Goldfinches love the seeds. Once you have teazles in the garden they are there to stay, seeding themselves everywhere. This can be avoided by removing the teazle-heads immediately after flowering. Few people can bear to do this as the heads stay on the plant all winter, even looking lovely when snowcapped. The great teazle *Dipsacus fullonum* (*D. sylvestris*) is the one most often grown. *Digitalis inermis*, a perennial type, looks exactly like C*ephalaria dipsacoides*. They need sun and good garden soil.

Dipsacus fullonum

Digitalis ferruginea is a biennial or perennial, self-seeding, magnificent foxglove; its golden-brown flowers has rust-red veins on the inside. The cultivar 'Gigantea' has larger flowers than the species and both grow up to 1.5m.(5ft) *Digitalis grandiflora* grows to 80cm (32in) and has large, light-yellow flowers. Digitalis lutea grows up to 1m with pale-yellow flowers, suitable for the more informal border and half-hardy. *Digitalis x mertonensis* (Digitalis 'Mertonensis') has glossy dark-green foliage and strawberry-coloured flowers, 80cm (32in)-tall. *Digitalis lanata x grandiflora* 'John Innes Tetra' has all the colours of a sunset and beautiful grey-green foliage besides, 50cm (20in)-tall. These are just a few of the many foxgloves and there is a fitting one for every border.

Dipsacus

TEAZLE

Teazles are suitable for the wilder border where these tall, biennial plants can show off their blooms. The small pale-purple coloured flowers appear first in a circle in the centre of the teazle-head, after which they continue flowering upwards and downwards.

Dipsacus fullonum

Dodecatheon alpinum

Dodecatheon

SHOOTING STARS

❀ ☀ ○

This plant flowers early, in May and June. It needs a successor as most species disappear completely after flowering. The plants are sometimes combined with primulas, to which they are related. But the flowers are more like the cyclamen. From five to twenty flowers are clustered on top of long stems. *Dodecatheon jeffreyi* is variable, between 30 and 60cm (1-2ft)-high. It flowers in April with dark-red to deep-purple flowers.

Dodecatheon meadia is the best-known, with lilac-pink flowers, 30cm (12in)-high. 'Album' is a white cultivar, 40cm (16in)-high and 'Queen Victoria' is lilac pink and grows to 50cm (20in). *Dodecatheon alpinum* is lower. They need medium soil, not too dry, in light shade.

The plants are very good in combination with large-leaved hostas; these will disguise the gaps left when dodecatheon quietly withdraws after flowering.

Dodecatheon meadia

Doronicum

LEOPARD'S BANE

 ☼ ○

When other plants are only just beginning to show their noses above the ground in early spring, doronicum is already there with its cheerful, bright-yellow flowers. *Doronicum orientale* and a few hybrid-cultivars, including 'Miss Mason' are among the early birds. The result of this early flowering is that it is all over by the end of May. *Doronicum pardalianches* with heart-shaped leaves is a very rare old plant. The cultivar *Doronicum pardalianches* 'Goldstrauss' flowers late for a *doronicum*, in June and July. *Doronicum plantagineum* 'Excelsum' flowers in May and June and is downier than the above. D. orientale has smooth foliage. The plants are adaptable but they like moist soil; the types with downy leaves need a place in half-shade.

Dracocephalum

DRAGON'S HEAD

 ☼

The annual and perennial dracocephalum are related to cat-mint and this has led to the occasional exchanging of names between the two genuses. *Dracocephalum sibiricum* is now called Nepeta sibirica.

The annual *Dracocephalum moldavica* is stunning. 'Snow Dragon' flowers freely in white, 'Blue Dragon' in blue (grows in the wild). Both grow up to 60cm (2ft) and are favourites with the bees. D. grandiflora is a fairly low perennial, 20cm (8in) with grey foliage and indigo-blue flowers. *D. isabellae* is taller with bright-blue flowers. *D. ruyschiana*, 40cm (16in) has violet-blue flowers and grey foliage. These plants need well-drained soil. They are not always sold by the correct name.

Dryopteris

 ○ ●

The best-nown *Dryopteris* is the male fern *Dryopteris filix-mas*, still found in moist, light, deciduous woods.

'Grandiceps' has lovely mid-green foliage with more branched fronds, unfurling in spring from brown-scaled rootstocks. 'Linearis Polydactylon' 70cm (28in) is a light and airy fern tipped with forked fronds. *Dryopteris dilatata* 'Crispa Whiteside', 50cm (20in) has

Doronicum orientale 'Miss Mason'

fresh, pale green curled foliage. *Dryopteris erythrosora*, 40cm (16in) has bronze-coloured foliage in spring, returning again in the autumn. *Dryopteris wallichiana* is a 70cm (28in) tall fern with splendid golden-green foliage in spring.

Dryopteris filix-mas

Echinacea purpurea

Echinacea

CONEFLOWER

❀ ☼

This perennial plant will flower in the same year as it is sown, if this is done early enough. The large, crimson flowers of the species are worth growing, but cultivars of *Echinacea purpurea* are the plants most often grown as they are exceptionally strong and tolerant of drought. 'Alba', white, is 1m (3ft) tall; 'AugustkÜnigin' has purple flowers with an orange centre. 'Green Edge' is white tinged with green; 'Magnus' (only variably stable seed) has pinkish-purple flowers with an orange-brown heart and its petals are not pendent but erect. The crimson 'Rubinstern' is not easy to grow, but lovely. 'The King', 80cm (32in) high, is a beautiful shade of deep crimson. 'White Swan' , 50cm (20in) high, (plants sown from seed), and 'White Lustre' (propagated by division) grows up to1m (3ft). The plants flower late, from July into September. The flowers are grown and processed to make a homeopathic remedy.

Echinacea purpurea 'Alba'

Echinops

GLOBE THISTLE

❀ ☼

Most growers agree that *Echinops ritro* 'Veitch's Blue' is the loveliest. The 80cm (32in) tall plants with their thistle-like leaves and global flowers are fantastic in the border. They are distinctive long before the flowering

Echinacea purpurea 'White Swan'

globes appear. They thrive in most garden soils and love the sun, but will also grow in half-shade. *Echinops bannaticus* 'Blue Globe' is suitable for a large border with its height of 1.2m(4ft). *E. bannaticus* 'Taplow Blue' also grows to 1m.(3ft) These plants are easy to grow, but they sometimes need to be tied up. The global flower heads can be dried very well. *Echinops pungens*, 1.5m (5ft) tall, with mouse-grey globes fits well in natural borders.

Echinops ritro in border

Echinops ritro 'Veitch's Blue'

Echium

☝ 🌱 🌸 ☀

Echium vulgare or Viper's bugloss, grows wild in sand dunes. The annual, *Echium plantagineum* is available as a mixture ('Bedding Mixed') of pink and white, all shades of blue ('Light Blue Bedder'), but also in one colour. These pleasant, freely-flowering plants grow up to 40cm (16in), much loved by the bees. *Echium vulgare* 'Drake's Form' is a biennial, deep-blue selection. Viper's bugloss likes the sun and flowers throughout the summer and well into autumn.

Echium

Echium plantagineum 'Light Blue Bedder'

Echium plantagineum 'Bedding Mixed'

Elaeagnus

Elaeagnus angustifolia is a beautiful, grey-leaved shrub with modest cream-coloured flowers, followed by oval, yellow fruits resembling olives. This type does well on dry, poor soil and also tolerates coastal wind. The shrub eventually grows up to 6m (2ft) but it can be checked by pruning. *Elaeagnus angustifolia* sheds its foliage, but *Elaeagnus x ebbingei* is evergreen. The cultivar 'Coastal Gold' has grey-green foliage with a yellow speck in the centre; 'Gilt Edge' lives up to its

name, and the foliage of 'Limelight' has lime-coloured specks. The young stalks of *Elaeagnus umbellata* are silver-coloured and the slender leaves have silvery-grey under-sides. These types can also be kept in check by pruning.

Epilobium- see - Chamerion

Epimedium

These plants flower early, in April and May and as they have splendid foliage for the rest of the year they are well worth growing. Some of them, such as the yellow-flowering *Epimedium x perralchicum* have evergreen foliage tinged with bronze in winter, like the sprouting leaves; they deserve a place in the front of the border. The bright-yellow flower-ing cultivar 'Frohnleiten' has a more compact habit and its yellow flowers emerge from the foliage. The foliage of many evergreen epime-diums should be cut away in February so that the flowers can be seen. The new cultivars are selected to produce flowers which grow clear of the foliage. The flowers of epimedium are fine and decorative, their leaves are leathery. The plants belong to the same family as *Mahonia* and *Berberis*. *Epimedium grandiflorum* is one of the plants to be given an AGM-classification, the Award of Garden Merit, so this is an exceptionally good garden

Elaeagnus umbellata

Epimedium grandiflorum 'Nanum'

123

Epimedium × versicolor 'Sulphureum'

Epimedium × youngianum 'Niveum'

plant. Its fairly large white flowers rise up from the foliage. The cultivars 'Nanum' (white with smaller leaves), 'White Queen', and 'Rose Queen' also have an AGM. The cultivar 'Lilafee' makes good ground cover, with big purple-violet flowers emerging from purple foliage. Epimediums are not always named correctly and a pale-pink Epimedium may sometimes be sold for a 'Rose Queen'.

Epimedium x rubrum has carmine-red flowers and foliage sprouting a lovely red in spring. Epimedium x versicolor 'Sulphureum' dates from 1849 and is still a valuable cultivar. The sulphur-yellow flowers appear simultaneously with the fresh, bronze-green foliage. This is evergreen foliage, also tinged with bronze in winter.

The foliage of evergreen epimediums may die off in winter due to severe frost, but this is only temporary as it always sprouts again. 'Orangekönigin', a light orange plant flowering profusely is a cultivar of Epimedium x warleyense. This species with copper and yellow-coloured flowers is called after Warley Place, the home of Ellen Willmott and it is often sold by its cultivar name 'Ellen Willmott'. Epimedium x youngianum is an uncomplicated, smaller Epimedium with a

snow-white cultivar 'Niveum' and the lavender-pink 'Roseum'. Most epimediums are 25 - 30cm (10-12in) high, excellent ground coverers. New types and cultivars continue to join their numbers.

The Japanese botanist, Mikinori Ogisi has discovered and cultivated more species over the last fifteen years. Wild Epimediums grow in deciduous woods, so they also prefer light shade in the garden. They are strong plants, but most of them need moist loam and all need well-drained soil. They will tolerate sun if the soil is moist enough. Young shoots may be scorched by the midday sun.

Eremurus

FOXTAIL LILY   KING'S SPEAR
❀ ◌ ☀

This is an impressive, perennial plant with tuberous-roots, not normally found at the nursery for perennial plants but available from the bulb grower. It will depend on the type of soil and the position, whether this imposing presence can be welcomed in the border. Planting is important to begin with; the tubers may not be planted too deeply and a few centimetres (1in) of earth over their noses is sufficient.

The foxtail lily needs a sunny position in well-drained, fertile, sandy soil. The plants are

Eremurus robustus with fruit

Eremurus in de border

Erigeron karvinskianus 'Profusion'

grown commercially for their magnificent candles of flowers, for the florist trade and there are many cultivars of *Eremurus x isabellinus*. These cultivars vary in height from 80 - 100cm (32 - 40in). De Ruiters-hybrids, also available in a mixture of different colours, can grow up to 2m (6ft) with 1m (3ft)-long 'foxtails'. *Eremurus* needs protection in the garden in winter, or it may be frozen. *Eremurus himalaicus* is pure white, growing up to 1.2m (4ft). The sensational flowers clustered on tall spikes appear at the end of May or beginning of June. *Eremurus robustus* is a giant at 2.5m (8ft), with pale-pink flowers. One bloom is at least 1m (3ft) long, containing over 800 small flowers. *Eremurus stenophyllus*, formerly called *E. bungei*, is a stately plant with yellow flowers.

Erigeron

FLEABANE
 ☼

Erigeron karvinskianus 'Profusion' must be the most familiar of these flowers resembling

asters, with white to pink flowers. The plant is not fully hardy and should be brought in for the winter, or sown every year.

Like all erigerons, it will seed itself anyway. They love the sun and well-drained soil and they also need sufficient moisture during the growing season. These temporary, free-flowering inhabitants of the border or tubs remain fairly low, flowering throughout the summer. The hybrid-cultivars which are hardy, are generally taller, 50-60cm (20in - 2ft) and good for cutting. They will flower a second time if the deadheads are removed. The colours vary from white - 'Sommer-neuschnee', via shades of pink - 'Dignity', 'Four Winds', 'Foersters Liebling', 'Lilac Jewel', 'Quakeress', 'Rosa Jewel' and 'Rosa Triumph' to shades of blue - 'Dunkelste Aller', 'Schwarzes Meer', 'Strahlenmeer', 'Wuppertal', to deep red - 'Rotes Meer'. Most of these flower in June, July and August, combining well in a summer border.

Erigeron 'Dignity'

Erigeron 'Rosa Jewel'

Erodium resembles *Geranium,* but has five fertile stamens instead of ten

Erodium

STORKSBILL

 ☀

These rewarding plants are related to the popular *Geranium* - not the *Pelargonium* of the tubs, but the garden geranium. To find the difference between an *Erodium* and a *Geranium* all you do is to count the stamens. *Erodium* has five fertile stamens and *Geranium* has ten. Not all erodiums are fully hardy. They do not like wet feet, especially in winter. They prefer sandy or stony, chalky ground, and they need protection in winter. A

piece of glass over the plant will be enough to prevent the roots from becoming too wet. *Erodium manescavii* is one of the stronger types, flowering from June into September, with lavender-pink flowers, 40cm (16in) high. 'Merthsham Pink' is a good pink cultivar. *Erodium x variabile,* a cross between *E. corsicum* and *E. reichardii,* has some beautiful cultivars: 'Album', white; 'Flore Pleno', double pink; 'Roseum', pink, red-veined. *Erodium chrysanthemum* - not fully hardy - has pale-yellow flowers. *Erodium hymenodes* (true name *E. trifolium*) has white-with-pink flowers, growing up to 40cm (16in). Lower types and cultivars will not be dealt with here as they are low-growing rock plants.

Eryngium

SEA HOLLY

♌ ❀ ☀

Bees love the flowers of the lovely, often impressive eryngium which can be dried. They need fairly dry soil and full sun.

Eryngium maritimum or sea holly grows on sandy shores and is becoming so rare that it is an endangered species in some countries. This

Erodium variabile 'Roseum'

Erodium manescavii

Eryngium agavifolium

Eryngium planum 'Flüela'

to 60cm (2ft) and is more like *E. planum* than *E. alpinum*. *Eryngium planum* has light-blue flower heads, 1m (3ft) tall. The cultivar 'Blauer Zwerg', 60cm (2ft) is deep blue, 'Blaukappe', 80cm (32in) is greyish-blue and 'Füela', 80cm, is violet-coloured.

There is also a splendid biennial eryngo, *Eryngium giganteum*, only 80cm (32in) spite of the name. The plant has silver-grey foliage and flowers and seeds itself, creating the illusion that it is perennial. The plant is also known as 'Miss Willmott's Ghost' because Ellen Willmott (not a pleasant personality) used to sow seeds of this plant secretly, while visiting gardens which needed something to wake them up, in her view. Over a year later 'Miss Willmott's Ghost' would appear.

Erysimum

WALLFLOWER

beautiful, all-blue plant and other eryngium will need quantities of sand worked into clay soil if they are to thrive. *Eryngium bourgatii* is the same height, 50cm (20in) with metallic-blue flowers and deeply dissected, white-veined foliage. *Eringium alpinum* is almost twice as tall, with big flower heads surrounded by bracts, like a lace collar. The cultivar 'Blue Star' is deep blue and the most often-grown of these plants. *Eryngium agavifolium* is a very unusual plant, with leaf rosettes exactly like those of the *Agave*, although they are not succulent. The flower heads are greenish-white and the plant is a focal point with its height of 1.5m (5ft). The soil must not be too dry during the growing season. *Eryngium x tripartitum* has smaller dark-blue flower heads, it grows up

Wallflowers are sub-shrubs which will survive the winter with some protective covering. The true wallflower, formerly *Cheiranthus cheiri* and now *Erysimum cheiri* only grows wild on old walls in the southern part of the country. The species has single, yellow flowers; the cultivar 'Harpur Crewe' has double flowers in the same colour; 'Bloody Warrior' has double, dark-red flowers. The plants are usually grown

Erysimum cheiri – mixed

Erysimum 'Constant Cheer'

Erysimum pulchellum 'Aurantiacum'

as biennials, but on dry, limy, well-drained soil these fragrant flowers are hardy. One wallflower which can flower from March until October is the hybrid-cultivar 'Bowles Mauve', 60cm (2ft) with grey-green foliage and mauve flowers. 'Constant Cheer' has brown flowers turning to purple. The hardiest wallflower is the 25cm (10in) high 'John Codrington', with pale-yellow and brown flowers with purple markings. The colour combination of 'Wenlock Beauty', 30cm (1ft) is even stranger; the flowers go from purple to yellow and brown with pink. *Erysimum pulchellum* 'Aurantiacum' is an orange wallflower, 25cm (10in) high.

Escallonia

Escallonia is a beautiful, flowering shrub growing up to 2m (6ft) or higher and it is often evergreen. After the first flowering in June and July the plant will usually go on flowering until October. Escallonias are sometimes planted for hedging because they can be trimmed easily, and they are especially suitable for seaside gardens as they are tolerant to coastal wind. There are many

Escallonia 'Donard Seedling'

lovely hybrid-cultivars but not all are hardy. *Escallonia virgata* is hardy and this elegant, deciduous shrub flowers freely with small white flowers.

The best-known hybrid-cultivar suitable for most climates is the evergreen 'Donard Seedling', with white flowers tinged with red; 'Dart's Rosyred' has spreading growth with arching branches; 'Edinensis' is another of the hardier escallonias, with little pink flowers. 'Pink Elf' and 'Red Elf' have a compacter habit. 'Apple Blossom' is a lovely hybrid-cultivar. Escallonias combine well in a border as they are modest shrubs, with small leaves and pretty clusters of flowers, easy to trim if they grow too large.

Eschscholzia

The California poppy, *Eschscholzia californica* is orange, and the cultivar 'Orange King' is an old-fashioned border plant which conjures up neatly folded orange flowers from under its green cap, when the sun shines. There are cultivars available in other colours. 'Dairy Maid' is white and flowers for a long period; 'Apricot Chiffon' is creamy-yellow, edged with bright orange; 'Dalli' is scarlet with a yellow centre; 'Purple Gleam' is lilac pink and 'Rose Chiffon' is pink with blue-green foliage. There are also mixtures, including 'Thai Silk', with double, pleated petals in all the garish colours and 'Mission Bells', with flowers like small roses.

Eschscholzia caespitosa 'Sundew' has yellow flowers. California poppies are such cheerful flowers and they should be sown outside, on the spot where you want them. They are back in favour now that brighter colours are used in the border.

Eschscholzia californica

Eschscholzia – mixed

Euonymus fortunei 'Dart's Cardinal'

Eschscholzia californica 'Dalli'

Euonymus – fruits

Euonymus

 ☼ ○

Euonymus is often too coarse to combine with perennials, but *Euonymus nanus* var. *turkestanicus* is an exception. This small shrub, 1m (3ft) fits into the border, providing lovely red fruits with orange seeds. *Euonymus alatus*, the Winged spindle, is a fairly compact shrub, about 2m (6ft) high with striking brownish-grey margins of cork along its branches.

The leaves take on a glorious red in the autumn. *Euonymus alatus* 'Compactus' grows up to 1m (3ft) with a spread of 3m (9ft). This cultivar has hardly any cork edging, but its dark-red autumn colouring is splendid. *Euonymus fortunei* includes many evergreen shrubs which will also fit into the border with a little discretion and the necessary pruning. 'Dart's Cardinal' grows up to 1m (3ft) in height and spread, with fresh, green foliage and many fruits. The silver-variegated 'Emerald Gaiety' grows up to 1.2m (4ft) in height and spread; 'Emerald 'n Gold' and 'Canadale Gold' are gold-variegated.

Eupatorium

BONESET
❁ ☼ ○

Eupatorium is a tall, imposing plant with clusters of flowers for butterflies and bees in search of nectar to land on. *Eupatorium cannabinum* can still be found growing wild by the waterside. *Eupatorium cannabinum* 'Plenum' has double, old-rose coloured flowers in big clusters, growing up to 1.5m (5ft).

The plant flowers in August and September. *Eupatorium purpureum*, a native of the USA, grows up to 2m (6ft). Several beautiful cultivars of *Eupatorium maculatum* are available: 'Album' , with white clusters, growing well over our heads to 2.5m (6_ft). 'Atropurpureum', the same height with wine-red clusters on red stems.

Eupatorium maculatum 'Atropurpureum'

Eupatorium purpureum

Eupatorium cannabium 'Plenum'

A magnificent plant, covered with umbels of flowers on a fine day. 'Glutball' is lower, with brighter-red clusters. 'Purple Bush' grows to a 'mere' 1.4m, (5ft) suitable for the smaller garden. 'Riesenschirm', 2m (6ft)tall, lives up to its name with enormous, wine-red flower heads. Eupatoriums flower in August, September and October. They require good, moisture-retentive soil in the sun or partial shade.

Euphorbia

MILKWEED SPURGE

Euphorbias are popular and it is really no wonder. They owe this to their combination of flowers, foliage and overall habit. They are not fully hardy in colder regions so it is best to choose them with care and to plant them in a sheltered, sunny place. The euphorbias which we grow in the garden are nearly all perennial plants. There are a few annual euphorbias such as *Euphorbia marginata* 'Early Snow', 'White Top' and 'Late Snow', with grey-green and white leaves, often used in bouquets. But these cannot compare with their perennial relatives. *Euphorbia amygdaloides* var. robbiae (*Euphorbia robbiae*) is an evergreen ground-cover plant, 40cm (16in) high, with lovely lime-green clusters of flowers. The plant puts out runners and may grow rampant. E. amygdaloides 'Purpurea', 40cm (16in), 'perennial of the year 1995' has lime-coloured flower heads and dark, grey-green foliage with a purple blush in winter.

Euphorbia griffithii 'Fireglow'

Euphorbia characias 'Lambrook Gold'

Euphorbia palustris 'Walenburg's Glorie'

The plant is susceptible to mildew in spite of this qualification. *E. characias* subsp. *wulfenii*, 1.2m (4ft) has lime-coloured clusters with a dark centre and is less hardy. *E. characias* 'Lambrook Gold', 1.2m (4ft) is one of the loveliest flowering euphorbias. *Euphorbia coralloides*, 60cm (2ft) deserves more recognition, according to Brian kabbes. Its lime-green flowers appear in May and the plant flowers into the autumn. When it sheds its leaves in winter, the stems take on a flaming coral colour. *Euphorbia dulcis* 'Chameleon', 30cm (1ft) has finely coloured foliage, sprouting grey-purple, turning deep purple later. The plant needs a sunny position to retain the lovely colouring of its foliage. This *Euphorbia* will do well in place of the susceptible *Euphorbia amygdaloides* 'Purpurea'. *E. griffithii* 'Dixter',80cm (32in) purple-red foliage and orange umbels of flowers, like E. griffithii 'Fireglow', except that this has green foliage and combines well in a red border. *E. palustris*, the native spurge of the marshes, has fresh green foliage and lime-green flower heads. One of its lovely cultivars is 'Walenburg's Glorie', 1m. (3ft) *E. polychroma* or *E. epithymoides*, 50cm (20in) is

well-known, but none the less beautiful with its yellow umbels, later turning green. *E. polychroma* 'Candy', 40cm (16in) has yellow flowers and purple foliage. However many more lovely ones there are, the last to be named here is *Euphorbia wallichii*, 60cm (2ft) with very large pale-yellow bracts and purple foliage with a broad white midrib. All types of milkweed contain poisonous milky sap.

Exochorda

🌿 ☼

Exochorda x macrantha 'The Bride' is a really beautiful, freely flowering and compact shrub, 2m (6ft) tall. In late spring/early summer this Exochorda is one huge bridal bouquet of white flowers against a background of dark-green foliage. *Exochorda giraldii* var. *wilsonii* also flowers white, but grows taller. *Exochorda* thrives in sun or half shade and is tolerant of any soil.

Exochorda giraldii var. *wilsonii* in flower

Exochorda giraldii var. *wilsonii* – fruit

Fargesia murielae 'Simba'

Fargesia

⚬⚬ ☼ ○

Fargesia murielae is the new name for *Arundinaria* and if this does not sound familiar, it applies to bamboo. It is a very lovely bamboo from China which does not grow runners, growing up to 2.5 - 3.5m (8-9ft). This exotic-looking plant is frost hardy and also evergreen. It exchanges most of its leaves in the autumn for fresh green foliage a few weeks later. The species is at a point in its growth cycle where the plant is weakened and will eventually die, so that one of its cultivars is a better choice. 'Simba', a seedling of this type, grows less vigorously to a height of 1.5m (5ft). Unfortunately these bamboos are frequently sold when in flower. Do not buy plants of this kind as the pleasure will be short-lived. Cultivars are 'Eisenbach' or 'Nymphenburg'. *Fargesia nitida* grows as high but with brown stems and narrow foliage.

Felicia

♀ ✿ ⚘ ☼

In a South African book on plants, *Felicia amelloides the Blue marguerite*, is described as a sky-blue daisy with a bright-yellow centre, 1m (3ft) high, that flowers from spring onwards throughout the year. In our climate this sub-shrub is found with the annuals. The plant loves the sun but does not thrive in wet

Festuca glauca 'Azurit'

Fargesia nitida 'Nymphenburg'

conditions. It is a rewarding plant, flowers for a long period in pots or in the border with bright-blue flowers and a yellow centre. The species can grow to 50cm (20in) while the cultivars 'Read's Blue' and 'Read's White' are lower. There is also a cultivar with variegated

Felicia amelloides

Felicia in border

Festuca glauca

foliage. These felicias are propagated by cuttings. *Felicia amoena* has dark-blue flowers and downy foliage and has to be classed with the annuals. This type also has cultivars with variegated foliage. *Felicia bergeriana* is not grown so often, not because its flowers are less pretty, but because they only flower in the morning, and then only if the sun shines.

Festuca

Festuca can be grown in dry soil and especially those types and cultivars of which the foliage is blue-tufted, is useful in the border.

The best-known is *Festuca glauca*, or Blue fescue, with blue clumps and creamy-white plumes. The cultivar 'Blauglut', 30cm (12in) is one of the loveliest, with pale blue-grey foliage and dark brown spikelets of flowers. 'Azurit' is fairly tall, 'Blaufuchs' has bluish-green foliage and 'Harz'is olive-green. *Festuca glauca* 'Elijah Blue' is taller, 50cm (20in) also tufted with blue. This plant needs a spot in the full sun.

Filipendula

MEADOWSWEET

❀ ☼ ○

Filipendula ulmaria, can be seen growing wild in boggy meadows and by the side of a ditch. This plant feels at home in a natural garden beside the pond. If you have no pond there is no need to do without the beautiful plumes of flowers because there are more species and cultivars too, which do not grow rampant and which will grow on dry land. *Filipendula palmata* for instance, slightly taller (90cm) than *Filipendula ulmaria*, 80cm (32in) with pale pink plumes. The cultivar 'Nana' is a miniature, 20cm (8in) high, with deep-pink plumes, lovely for the edge of the border. *Filipendula ulmaria* 'Aurea', 80cm (32in) has golden-yellow foliage, later cream-coloured with yellow-white plumes. This plant may not be placed in the sun. *Filipendula camtschatica* comes from Japan and forms large clumps, 2m (6ft) high with pale pink, almost white flower plumes. *Filipendula purpurea* has carmine plumes, 70cm high. 'Elegans' is pale pink and 'Alba' is creamy-white. 'Nephele', 1.2m (4ft), looks very good in a natural garden, flowering from pink to

Festuca glauca in flower

Filipendula ulmaria

Filipendula rubra 'Venusta Magnifica'

white; 'Pink Dreamland' has branched, red stems and pink plumes of flowers while 'White Dreamland, 70cm (28in) is also loved for its sweet scent. *Filipendula rubra* 'Venusta' is an exceptionally beautiful, 1.5m or higher plant with fluffy pink plumes, still lovely after flowering. The cultivar 'Venusta Magnifica' is often taken for a synonym of 'Venusta', but this is incorrect. 'Venusta Magnifica' has wider, dark carmine-pink heads of flowers.

Filipendula vulgaris,- Dropwort, -is the only filipendula which can grow in dry soil. 'Plena' is a double, white cultivar. All the other filipendulas need moisture-retentive soil,

Filipendula vulgaris 'Plena'

especially when sprouting. If it is not moist enough, the best method is to cover the soil around the plant with compost or rotted manure in April. The plants can grow in the sun or in light shade, excepting *F. ulmaria* 'Aurea' which does not tolerate sun.

Foeniculum

FENNEL

❀ ☼

Foeniculum vulgare or fennel, is more familiar as a culinary herb than as a border plant. Tea made from fennel is known as a remedy against babies' colic pains and the seed and leaves can be used in many recipes. The finely divided leaves of fennel can also decorate the border with a haze of green. Or this haze could be bronze-coloured.

There are cultivars with purple-brown foliage 1.5m (5ft) high, known as bronze fennel, which look wonderful in the border. That is - if they will grow, because this is not at all certain. They need fertile soil, in a sunny position and there is no guarantee that this perennial plant will return year after year. It is well worth trying one of the bronze cultivars as the colour is beautiful and the yellow umbels of flowers go so well with them. 'Purpureum', 'Smokey' and 'Giant Bronze' are similar, growing to 1.8m (5¹/₂ft) tall and perhaps of the same variety.

Foeniculum vulgare 'Purpureum'

Forsythia - hedge

Forsythia

 ☼ ○

Few people are not familiar with this widely known flowering shrub. The yellow, bell-shaped flowers appear brazenly early in April, on bare, leafless branches. *Forsythia x intermedia* has many cultivars, of which 'Spectabilis' is the best known. 'Beatrix Farrand' and 'Lynwood' can be clipped to make good hedges. The attractive feature of a forsythia hedge is that the yellow flowers will

Forsythia – trimmed for the border

adorn the bare branches in spring in spite of being trimmed. This opens up a new possibility for the border. Those who find *Forsythia* too untidy for the mixed border can trim it into a globe or any other shape. Those who dislike trimming can plant *Forsythia ovata* 'Tetragold', a low, bushy shrub, 1m high flowering early with large flowers. Forsythias will grow in any well-drained soil. Do not prune until after they have flowered or you will cut away the flowering branches. Some of these branches of *Forsythia* can be brought on indoors to flower much earlier. If you leave them where they are after they have stopped flowering, they will grow roots.

Fothergilla major in flower

Fothergilla major – autumn colours

Fothergilla

 ☼ ○

Both species of *Fothergilla* are worthwhile plants for the garden. *Fothergilla gardenii* or Witch alder, is a low shrub, 60 - 80 cm (24-32in) with grey-green foliage and 2-3cm (1-1_in)-long clusters of cream-white flowers in April and May. *Fothergilla major* , 2m (6ft) has fragrant cream-white flowers in spring with bristling stamens, like a bottlebrush. These shrubs need moist, fairly acid soil. They take on splendid colours in the autumn.

137

Fragaria

STRAWBERRY

The pink-flowering *Fragaria* 'Pink Panda', introduced to the market a few years ago, is now called Fragaria 'Frel', still the same pink. Like all strawberries this forms ground cover, spreading by root-forming rosettes on trailing runners.

The foliage is typical of the strawberry and the pink flowers give no inkling that edible strawberries might ensue. But this strawberry is pretty rather than edible. 'Lipstick' is the same, with carmine-red flowers. *Fragaria chiloensis* 'Variegata' has white flowers and decorative greenish-white streaked foliage. The wild strawberry, *Fragaria vesca* with its delicious, fragrant little fruits, is at home in a wild garden, but it is less suitable for a tidy border because of its spreading habit. *Fragaria vesca* 'Alexandria' does not put out runners but its strawberries are bigger.

The border is no place for strawberry plants - they belong in the kitchen garden, valued for their delicious fruits and not for their coloured flowers or striped leaves.

Fragaria 'Frel' ('Pink Panda')

Fuchsia

Most fuschias are still grown in pots and and brought in before the frost. But frost-hardy fuchsias are on the increase and gradually making their mark. No fuschia is fully hardy and there are always conditions. The flowering season also has an effect; if a fuschia flowers before 15th July, it will be fully hardy, if before 15th August, frost hardy, after 15th August half hardy. Hardy fuschias require

Fragaria 'Lipstick'

Fragaria vesca 'Alexandria'

safe side before the frost really sets in. *Fuchsia magellanica* var. *gracilis* has small, red flowers with violet. This fuchsia can be seen in the Irish landscape forming long hedges. *Fuchsia magellanica* var. *molinae* is white, *F. m.* 'Aurea' has yellow foliage. *Fuchsia magellanica* 'Ricartonii' is most often used as the garden-hedge fuchsia. *F. magellanica* var. *molinae* is white, *F. m.* 'Aurea' has yellow foliage. Many more fuchsia cultivars are now available which may be termed hardy, under certain conditions.

Fuchsia magellanica var. *molinae*

good soil, rich in humus and well-drained. Fuchsias will not tolerate wet feet, especially in winter.

They will grow in almost any situation, except in deep shade. They can tolerate more sun in summer when planted in the open ground, than in a pot. When the temperature begins to drop a few degrees below zero at the end of the growing season, it is time to protect them with a mound of earth and a layer of leaves and above all, do not cut the branches back yet. You can take a few cuttings to be on the

Fuchsia magellanica 'Aurea'

Gaillardia 'Kobold'

Gaillardia

BLANKET FLOWER

We do not often see these flowers now and they are no longer mentioned in many of the growers' catalogues. It may be that they do not combine in a modern border with their gaudy colours. They can be pushy too, with their very large flowers. Be that as it may, there are annual and perennial blanket flowers which look good in the border. The annual *Gaillardia pulchella* has cultivars with single or double flowers, in one or two colours. 'Blood Red' is a single red one, 70cm (28in) high; 'Lollipop Bicolor', 35cm (14in) has double flowers in red and yellow. 'Crimson Giant' (90cm) is a mixture of single flowers in different shades of red with yellow markings. 'Lorenziana Mixed Colours', 60cm (2ft) is a mixture of double flowers in many colours. 'Lorenzia Lollipop' is a lower mixture of double flowers. 'New Pastels' 60cm (2ft) is a mixture in quieter colours, with white and many shades of pink and yellow. *Gaillardia aristata*, the perennial species, flowers so profusely that it exhausts itself and must be considered as a short-lived perennial or an annual. We usually see the hybrid-cultivars and not the species. 'Aurea Pura' is pure yellow, 60cm (2ft) high; 'Bremen' is yellow with a red circle, 50cm (20in)high; 'Burgunder' is a beautiful wine-red, also 50cm (20in) high; 'Kobold' has cheerful red flowers with a yellow edge. It is best to sow the annuals at intervals if you want them to flower from July until October. The perennials do this of their own accord. As the perennials are not

Left: *Gentiana lutea*

Galega 'Duchess of Bedford'

fully hardy, they should be given a winter blanket of branches and leaves. They love sun and dry soil.

Galega

GOAT'S RUE

Galegas are huge plants with spikes of pea-like flowers in June, July and August, excellent for a large border. *Galega officinalis* grows up to 1.2m (4ft) with lilac-pink flowers. The cultivars of the Hartlandii group are most often grown, formerly taken to be a cross between *Galega bicolor* and *Galega offici-*

141

nalis, now listed in catalogues as *Galega x hartlandii.* This is another of those cases where a difference of opinion only causes confusion. The truth is that *Galega bicolor is* a synonym for *Galega officinalis* and a cross between the two is impossible. For the sake of clarity we will name cultivars only here. 'Alba' has long spikes of beautiful white flowers and light-green foliage, growing up to 1.3m (4¹/₂ft). 'Candida' is very similar with the same height (the same cultivar?); 'Her Majesty' has pale-purple and white flowers; 'Duchess of Bedford' has lavender-blue flowers and 'Lady Wilson' has lilac-pink flowers (these last two cultivars are often confused with each other). Galegas need staking if they thrive and it is best to place sticks early on so that the plants can grow through them for support.

Galega orientalis, 1.2m (4ft) tall, grows so vigorously that it does not need staking. Its bright -blue flowers rise above the foliage. This plant has a tendency to grow rampantly and it will cover several square metres on sandy soil. As long as *Galega* is in the sun it can tolerate both dry and moist soil.

Galium

LADY'S BEDSTRAW

Sweet woodruff, formerly *Asperula odorata* is now called *Galium odoratum,* an excellent, fully hardy ground cover. Whorls of leaves bear posies of little white flowers.

Galium odoratum

Galega 'Her Majesty'

Galtonia

Galtonia candicans

Sweet woodruff only grows to 20cm (8in), suitable for the edge of a shadow border and as ground cover in a shrub border. The plant may tend to overgrow its low neighbours, but it is easily checked. *Galium verum* 40cm (16in), is lady's bedstraw with yellow flowers, suitable for a wild garden. Sweet woodruff flowers early, in May and June; lady's bedstraw flowers from June into September.

Galtonia

A bulbous plant from South Africa, not fully hardy. The bulbs have to be lifted before winter and stored frost free. In South Africa the bulbs are left in the ground all the year round and the advice given in gardening publications there is to leave them severely alone to achieve the best results. We shall have to make do. *Galtonia candicans* grows from 80 - 110cm (2^1/2ft - 3^1/2ft) high and combines well in the border with its spikes of white, pendent hyacinth-like flowers. Planted in the garden at the beginning of April, they will flower from July into September. They require fertile soil. *Galtonia viridiflora* grows as high, with light-green flowers and bluish-green foliage. It may be worth taking a risk by covering the bulbs before the winter with a 10cm-(4in) thick blanket of mulch. If the

winter is mild and the ground not too wet, they may survive. Nothing ventured, nothing lost, but you may prefer to lift them.

Gaultheria

An evergreen shrub, grown for its foliage and fruits rather than the flowers, although the clusters of pink flowers of *Gaultheria shallon* are decorative. The broad, oval, leathery foliage of this 80cm-(32in)high shrub is often used in bouquets and sold by its generic name. The berries of this Gaultheria are black, in contrast with the much lower *Gaultheria procumbens*, 15cm (6in) which are bright red.

Gaultheria procumbens

Gaultheria shallon

This sub-shrub is sold in pots at Christmas time, because its berries make a lovely contrast with the purple-brown winter foliage. But after months of the dry climate indoors it does not take kindly to the cold garden outdoors. It is better to buy the plants from a grower and to plant them outdoors directly for that purpose. Both of these gaultherias make excellent ground cover.

The crushed berries have a strong aroma of the oil which is obtained from the berries of *Gaultheria procumbens.* The ointment used in sport massage has the same, distinctive aroma.

Gaura

Gaura lindheimeri is a splendid border plant, 1 m (3ft) high, flowering with pinkish-white flowers from July into October. Cultivars are

Gaura lindheimeri

'Corrie's Gold', with gold-variegated foliage and 'Whirling Butterflies' which is most often grown. 'Whirling Butterflies' has white, butterfly-like flowers on long, sturdy stems. The only disadvantage of gauras is that they are short-lived. They lose their vigour after two or three years and have to be replaced. The plants like fertile, well-drained soil.

Gazania

In their native land South Africa, these plants are perennial. They are usually grown as annuals in Western Europe.
But if the plants are kept in a conservatory

Gazania rigens 'Freddie'

Gaura lindheimeri 'Corrie's Gold'

Gazania rigens 'Ministar Mixed'

Gazania rigens 'Golden Delight'

they will flower every year. Most gazanias are available in a mixture, 'Ministar Mixed', but there are also self-coloured selections such as 'Freddie', yellow with a dark ring; 'Golden Delight', yellow; 'Ministar White'; 'Magenta Green', purple; 'Silver Beauty', with silver foliage and pale yellow flowers; 'Tangerine', a subdued orange with yellow-margined foliage and 'Vimmer's Variegated'. Most of them are 20 to 30cm (4-12in) high, suitable for the edge of the border. Many gazanias have a dark ring around the centre. They are cheerful flowers for a colourful border.

Genista

BROOM
☙ ☼

Genista is a beautiful shrub for a garden on dry, sandy soil. It flowers so freely that it is more like a perennial than a shrub. *Genista hispanica* 60cm (2ft) is one mass of yellow flowers in May and June. *Genista Lydia* needs protective covering in severe frost. *Genista pilosa* has some lovely cultivars for ground cover: 'Goldilocks' and 'Vancouver Gold'. *Genista sagittalis*, is another good ground coverer, 30cm (1ft) high.

Gentiana

GENTIAN
❀ ☼ ○

The name 'gentian' is usually enough to call up a vision of the low alpine gentian with its big, blue bells. There are higher gentians more suitable for the border.

Gentiana asclepiadea, 50cm (20in) high with dark-blue flowers on arched stems. 'Alba' is the white cultivar. Both prefer a cool, moist and shady spot, flowering from July into September. *Gentiana lutea* makes a change with yellow flowers instead of the gentian-blue. This slow-growing plant with elegant leaf rosettes eventually grows to 1.5m (5ft) and prefers light, chalky soil. The plant flowers in June and July, but only after taking years to establish itself in its position, and then not reliably. *Gentiana tibetica* 60cm (2ft)has

Genista sagittalis

Gentiana acaulis

cream-white flowers and *Gentiana triflora* 'Royal Blue' 1m (3ft)has blue flowers and prefers soil without chalk. All gentians need well-drained, cool soil and moisture while growing.

Gentiana lutea – fruit

Geranium

CRANESBILL
❀ ☼ ○

Geraniums are like stamps: if you have one, you want more and in no time you have a collection. Growers have at least forty different types and cultivars, so what is the attraction? They have almost everything: if you are looking for something between 5cm (2in) and 1.5m (5ft) high that flowers in many colours, that will grow in deep shade or in the heat of full sun, on boggy ground or on almost pure sand, there is a *Geranium* for every situation. *Geranium sanguineum* 'Ankum's Pride', 20cm (16in) high, is a long-flowering plant with bright-pink flowers and dark veins. *Geranium pratense* 'White Lady' is a sturdy plant, 60cm (2ft)high with pure white flowers. *Geranium maculatum* 'Shameface' is beautiful as also *Geranium phaeum*. *Geranium maculatum* 'Chatto', 40cm (16in) with shell-pink flowers is one of the loveliest early-flowering geraniums.

A good cultivar of *Geranium phaeum* is 'Album'. The hybrid-*cultivar Geranium* 'Philippe Vapelle' has lovely blue flowers, 35cm (14in) and Geranium psilostemon 'Iwan' is 70cm (28in) high, lighter in colour than the species. This 'Iwan' should really be 'Ivan', after Ivan Louette and it is a hybrid-cultivar, not a cultivar of *G. psilostemon*. *Geraniums* deserve a book to themselves, but we will mention a few of the numerous geraniums which are suitable for the border.

'Ann Folkard' is a cross between *G. procurrens* and *G. psilostemon*, visible in the 1.5m (5ft)-tall plant with maroon flowers and a dark centre. It will need protection from frost during its first winter. 'Anne Thomson' is 40cm (16in) high and more suitable for a neat border, with the same colour but without the trailing stems of the former. 'Brookside' is a beautiful new one with blue flowers which blooms for three whole months. It has a promising, sturdier seedling, 'Orion', which flowers even longer. *Geranium x cantabrigiense* is a carpeting plant, 30cm (12in) high, with rose-pink flowers which will grow in the shade. The cultivar 'Biokovo' has white to pink flowers, 'Lohfelden' white and 'Cambridge' lilac-pink. *Geranium clarkei* has several lovely 35 to 40cm-(14 -16in) high cultivars, including 'Kashmir Pink', 'Kashmir Purple' and 'Kashmir White' which has white flowers with lilac veins. The flowers of this last, very popular plant are larger than of the other cultivars. *Geranium endressii* 'Wargrave Pink' has deep pink flowers and grows to 35cm (14in). 'Dilys' is an unusual plant with long, non-rooting tendrils bearing

Geranium 'Ann Folkard'

pinkish-purple flowers, only 20cm (8in) high. *Geranium macrorrhizum* is a strong, creeping ground cover, 40cm (16in) high with aromatic foliage and magenta to pink and white flowers. The cultivar 'Album' has white flowers and 'De Bilt' is pink. 'Ingwersen's Variety', with a compacter habit is pale pink and 'Spessart' is white. 'Nimbus' is a new hybrid-cultivar with deeply cut foliage and bluish-purple flowers with a white centre. This plant grows up to 60cm (2ft) with a spread of 1m (3ft). *Geranium x oxonianum* 'Claridge Druce' is for those who want a strong plant with vigorous growth, 70cm (28in) high with pink flowers. Not for the tidy border, but

Geranium psilostemon 'Ivan'

pleasant under tall shrubs. 'Thurstonianum' is lower, 40cm (16in), with very narrow petals, flowering a splendid reddish-purple. This colour (slightly less glowing), and the large leaves were inherited from *G. psilostemon*, the long period of flowering from *G. x oxonianum*. The hybrid-cultivar 'Patricia', 1m (3ft) is another good plant which has inherited the best features from both parents. *Geranium psilostemon* is a magnificent plant with large foliage and flowers with the brightest colour of all geraniums. Some call it magenta, others carmine or cyclamen red. The flowers have a black centre and if you buy this plant, be very careful where you put it. The combination with grey-leaved plants and *Nepeta x faassenii* 'Six Hills Giant' is stunning. Other shades of pink and red should be kept out of their way, as *G. psilostemon* always wins. 'Spinners' is a beautiful, tall cultivar with large, intense blue flowers. There are enough geraniums to choose from.

Geum

AVENS

❀ ☼ ○

Pleasant, free-flowering plants for good moisture-retentive soil. The following are lovely hybrid-cultivars: 'Beech House Apricot'; 'Bulgaricum', orange-yellow; 'Karlskaer', bright yellow; 'Feuermeer', orange-red; 'Georgenberg', orange-yellow; 'Lady Stratheden', double, yellow; 'Prinses Juliana', orange-yellow; 'Red Wings', semi-double, scarlet and 'Rijnstroom', copper-orange.

Geum rivale, the water avens, is fast disappearing in the wild, but there are some splendid cultivars of this species: 'Album', 40cm (16in), with greenish-white flowers; 'Leonard's Variety', 40cm (16in) with arching, copper-coloured flowers; 'Lionel Cox', 30cm (12in) with pale-yellow flowers; 'Salmon Bells', with salmon-coloured flowers. Also worth planting are *Geum x heldreichii* 'Mammoet', 30cm (12in) orange-red and *Geum pallidum* 'Elpenbeen', 40cm (16in), ivory-coloured. One very familiar *Geum* is *Geum chiloense* 'Mrs. Bradshaw', with scarlet, semi-double flowers. There will always be room for a Geum in the border.

Geranium 'Brookside'

Geranium clarkei 'Kashmir White'

Geranium macrorrhizum 'De Bilt'

Geranium × oxonianum 'Claridge Druce'

Geum rivale 'Album' with white aquilegia

Geum chiloense 'Mrs Bradshaw'

Geum rivale 'Leonard's Variety'

dies off in winter. Small white flowers with red calyces and stems emerge from plumes of red buds in June and July. Brown seed capsules appear later which combine splendidly with the autumn colours of the foliage. *Gillenia* does well in the border and for cutting purposes as the flowers keep well in water. It is quite a demanding plant: the soil must be fertile and moisture-retentive, well-drained and not too dry, cool and not chalky. It takes several years to establish itself and slugs and snails devour the young shoots in spring. But it remains a fantastic plant for the border and the worst possible scenario described above may never happen.

Gilia

 ☼

The annual *Gilia tricolor* bears the lovely name of 'Birds Eyes' .The single blooms have three or four bands of colour, starting with a yellow centre, purple in the middle and edged with pale blue. They flower in late spring to early summer, 20 to 30cm (8-12in) high. 'Snow Queen' is a white cultivar. *Gilia capitata* grows from 30 to 60cm (1-2ft) high with small, rounded blue flowers, close together. As gilia is a native of desert-like areas, it prefers light, well-drained soil and full sun. Most suitable for a cottage garden.

Gillenia

❀ ☼ ○

Gillenia trifoliata is an exceptional plant growing from 80 cm to 1.2m, (2^1/$_2$-4ft) depending on its position. The plant resembles a shrub as it is very sturdy with a shrub-like habit, but this member of the Rosaceae family

Gillenia trifoliata

Gladiolus callianthus 'Murilae'

Gladiolus callianthus 'Murilae'

Gladiolus

◊ ☼ ○

The common 'gladdy' is best planted in the kitchen garden for cutting, but the Abyssinian gladiolus, formerly called *Acidanthera murilae* and now *Gladiolus callianthus* 'Murilae', is suitable for the border.

A group of these corms does well there with sweet-scented, elegant white flowers with deep-purple centres. They love the sun, but will also grow in half shade. As they are not fully hardy the corms should be lifted before winter and stored frost-free.

The botanic species *Gladiolus papilio* has bell-shaped flowers in distinctive shades of grey-green.

Godetia

 ☼

This annual plant resembles the clarkia so strongly that all godetias are now classified as clarkias. But we will mention them individually here because most seed catalogues still do the same.

There are single and double godetias, available in multi-coloured mixtures or self-coloured. To name a few, 'Double White', 'Double Nain Cherie Sweetheart' and 'T&M Tall Double Mixed'. Among the single godetias are 'Aurora', salmon pink; 'Furora', deep red; 'Lilac Lady', pale purple and 'Pink Joy'. In order to enjoy godetias throughout the

Godetia bottiae 'Pink Joy'

Godetia

Gypsophylla paniculata 'Fairy Perfect'

Gypsophylla repens 'Rosa Schönheit'

summer it will be necessary to sow several times. They can also be sown in the autumn. They need light, moisture- retentive soil.

Gomphrena

GLOBE AMARANTH
ⓘ ☼

Gomphrena globosa, the globe amaranth is mainly grown for its clover-like flower heads for drying, but it is also useful in the border. It is a modest plant; of which there are pink, red and purple cultivars. *Gomphrena haageana* has orange-coloured cultivars. They like full sun and fertile, well-drained soil. Gomphrena globosa has tall cultivars suitable for the border and lower ones for tubs. 'Professor Plum' is plum-coloured, 'White Innocence' and 'Blushing Bride' are true to their names. They grow up to 60cm (2ft) *Gomphrena haageana* is pale orange and 80cm (2¹/2ft) high. If you can part with them in the border, pick them for drying.

Gypsophila

ⓘ ✿ ☼

There are annual and perennial gypsophilas. "Snow Fountain', 'White Monarch' and 'Snowflake' are white flowering cultivars of the annual *Gypsophila elegans;* 'Rosea' has pale-pink flowers; 'Carminia' is carmine-pink and 'Kermesina' crimson. These are all attractive flowers for a mixed bouquet, but *Gypsophila elegans* 'Covent Garden' is most suitable for this purpose. These plants grow from 60 to 70cm (24-28in) tall, interweaving with other border plants. The perennial

Gypsophila paniculata 'Bristol Fairy' is a familiar plant, 1.2m (4ft) tall and always highly valued in the border. The plant is enveloped in a haze of small, double white flowers. 'Fairy Perfect' has slightly larger double flowers; 'Flamingo' has pale-pink, double flowers and 'Schneeflocke' is a lower, white one, 70cm.(28in)

The hybrid-cultivar 'Rosenschleier' is the loveliest in its pink cloud, 40cm (16in) high. *Gypsophila repens* is only 20 to 30cm (8-12in) high and is useful as an edging plant. 'Rosa Schönheit' is pure pink and 'Rosea' is pink and flowers earlier. Most gypsophilas flower in July and August, preferably in well-drained soil and full sun. They dislike wet soil in winter and thrive on chalky soil. They are decorative in a border and useful for filling the empty places after bulbs and early-flowering plants have had their day.

Gypsophylla repens 'Rosea'

Hamamelis mollis in the winter

Hamamelis and maple in the autumn

Hamamelis

WITCH HAZEL

Witch hazel conjures up unusual, fragrant flowers in the depth of winter and early spring, sometimes snowcapped. These are shrubs which grow up to 4m (12ft) eventually, but they grow slowly and adapt well in the shrub border or mixed border. *Hamamelis x intermedia* 'Arnold Promise' flowers freely in March, with pale-yellow flowers. 'Diane' bears large, bronze-red flowers in February. 'Jelena', (called after Jelena de Belder of the "Arboretum Kalmthout" in Belgium), flowers in December and January with coppery, orange flowers. *Hamamelis mollis*, the familiar Chinese witch hazel, flowers in January and February (sometimes even in December), with large golden-yellow, sweet-scented flowers. The cultivar 'Pallida' has numerous, big, sulphur-yellow flowers. The foliage of many witch hazels has yellow or red autumn colouring.

Hedera

IVY

The familiar climbing ivy has many species and cultivars which are excellent ground coverers

Helenium 'Wyndley'

Hedera helix 'Arborescens' in the winter

and there is also ivy which is particularly suitable for the shrub border. *Hedera colchica* 'Arborescens' 1.2m (4ft)high with the same spread, has large, oval foliage. The lovely rounded, yellow-greenish flowers appear from September until November, followed by black fruits.

Hedera helix 'Arborescens' (1.8m) (5½ft) has smaller foliage and greenish-yellow flowers in October and November and fairly small, black berries. *Hedera helix* has several bushy cultivars: 'Arbori Compact' is lower and denser; 'Arbori Purple' has purple foliage in winter; 'Erecta' has upright twigs growing up to 50cm, (20in); 'Goldheart' has dark-green foliage with a golden-yellow centre.

Hedera helix subsp. *poetarum* grows up to 1.5m (5ft) and has unusual, orange-yellow

Hedera helix 'Goldheart' edging the border

Helenium autumnale 'Pumilum Magnificum'

fruits. Plant them in fertile, moist soil. The flowers are a good source of nectar for bees.

Helenium

SNEEZEWEED

The helenium is a very strong border plant, always recognizable by its flowers with global hearts and the colourful skirt of petals around them. The flowers are yellow, orange or red-brown coloured, very good for cutting. The plants vary in height from 60cm to 1.2m (2-4ft) and may need staking. *Helenium Autumnale* 'Pumilum Magnificum' has pale-yellow flowers and is 90cm tall.(3ft) Good hybrid - cultivars are: 'Baudirektor Linne', brown-red; 'Bruno', ochre; 'Crimson Beauty', brown-red; 'Dunkle Pracht', brown-red with a green centre; 'Kupfersprudel', coppery-brown; 'Kupferzwerg', red-brown; 'Moerheim Beauty', brown-red and 'Wyndley', bronze-yellow. Two more beauties are 'Meranti', red-brown and 'Oudgoud', golden-yellow. *Helenium* does well in fertile soil, enriched with manure and it must not be dry. It flowers late, usually from July into September; 'Rotgold' does not flower until September and October. This hybrid - cultivar comes from a strain which can include

Helenium 'Bruno'

inferior plants so it is best to get them from a reputable grower.

Helianthemum

ROCK ROSE

The name 'Rock rose' suggests that it belongs in the rock garden rather than the border, but you could plant a few of these at the edge of

Helianthemum 'Mrs. C.W. Earle'

Helianthemum 'Sulphureum Plenum'

Helianthemum 'Wisley Pink'

green foliage and single white flowers, 40cm (16in) high. A few of the many cultivars are: 'Jubilee', with pale-yellow double flowers; 'Lawrenson's Pink', pink with an orange centre; 'Mrs. C.W. Earle' ('Fireball'), bright red; 'Sulphureum Plenum', bright yellow, double; 'The Bride', one of the best single cream-white rock roses, with grey-green foliage. 'Wisley Pink', the same foliage and deep-pink flowers and finally 'Wisley White'. Rock roses are frost tender and need a protective covering of mulch in winter.

Helianthus

SUNFLOWER

☿ ✿ ☼

That one, particular sunflower does not exist because there are over seventy species of these annual and perennial plants growing in the wild in North and South America. They are versatile, striking plants with excellent cutting flowers, a source of nectar for the bees and their large seeds are also widely appreciated. The big cultivars of the annual sunflower, *Helianthus annuus* have particularly large seeds which attract finches and other seed-eating birds. Sunflowers are also grown especially for their seeds, used in the manufacture of sunflower oil and cattle food.

There is another sunflower, a useful perennial *Helianthus tuberosus*, the Jerusalem artichoke. It is grown for its edible tubers which make a delicious vegetable or salad, also used as fodder. This sunflower can also be grown as a windscreen. It is not a decorative plant as it may only produce a few small flowers in a very good summer and it is also invasive, not welcome in the border. The cultivar 'Bianca' flowers every year. There are other sunflowers worthy of a place in an autumn border,

Helianthus debilis subsp. *cucumerifolius* 'Italian White'

the border. They love the sun and well-drained, chalky soil. They should be cut back lightly directly after flowering to keep them in shape. They flower from May to September. Many hybrid-cultivars are between 20 and 30cm (8-12in) high. *Helianthemum apenninum* is the exception, a small shrub with grey-

Helianthus 'Lemon Queen'

Helianthus salicifolius

including *Helianthus atrorubens* 'Gullick's Variety', 1.8m (5^1/2ft) tall with small golden-yellow flowers. Or *Helianthus decapetalus* 'Capenoch Star', with pale-yellow flowers, or cultivar 'Triomphe de Gand', with yellow flowers. The first of these flowers early, in July and grows to 1.5m (5ft) and the second flowers in August growing up to 1.8m.(5^1/2ft) *Helianthus microcephalus* is a very strong border plant with small, sulphur-yellow flowers wich can grow to a height of 2m.(6ft) The strangest of the perennial sunflowers is *Helianthus salicifolius*, the Willow-leaved sunflower, which is grown for its foliage. It only produces small yellow flowers in a beautiful summer. The remarkable thing about the plant is that its long, erect stems are covered with narrow, willow-like, elegantly-drooping leaves, hence the generic name. The hybrid-cultivar 'Lemon Queen' grows to a height and spread of at least 2m,(6ft) flowering as from August with lovely yellow flowers. This gigantic plant needs no support. These perennial sunflowers are not suitable for a border with delicate plants, but for those who like to think tall in the border, they will do very well.

The annual sunflower *Helianthus annuus* has very many, beautiful cultivars with flowers varying in colour from yellow to brown, in size from small to big and in the height of the plants from 30cm to 3m (1-9ft) or higher. The stems of some varieties are branched, others are not. The tall sunflower is a rewarding plant in the childrens' garden because it grows so fast that it leads to exciting competitions as to who has the highest sunflower. 'Russian Giant' and 'Uniflorus Giganteus' are competition-sunflowers of this kind. Lower ones are better for the border, such as 'Velvet Queen', a dark-red one, 1.6m; (5^1/2ft) 'Tayo', golden-yellow with a black centre; *Helianthus debilis* 'Vanilla Ice', 1.5m (5ft) with creamy-yellow flowers and a black centre on a strongly branched plant or one of the sunflowers with cucumber-like foliage: *H. debilis* subsp. *cucu-*

Helichrysum cassianum 'Gabriel Pink'

merifolius 'Italian White', the loveliest, almost white sunflower, 1.4m (4½ft) high. The last two are especially suitable for the border because they are branched, like shrubs. Sunflowers will grow on any well-drained soil and they appreciate a dressing of old, rotted manure.

Helichrysum

STRAWFLOWER
⚲ ✿ ☼

The annual strawflower, *Helichrysum bracteatum*, is more familiar as a strawflower than a garden flower. All the same, these flowers can decorate the border because they are now available self-coloured as well as in a mixture. The 'King Size Formula Mixture', 1m (3ft) high, or the lower 'Bright Bikini' mixture of white, yellow, pink, red and orange papery flowers that rustle, are still there for those who

Helichrysum bracteatum 'Bright Bikini'

Helichrysum subulifolium 'Yellow Star'

prefer this. For those who prefer their colours separate, there are the sulphur-yellow 'Frosted Sulphur', the bronze-orange 'New Orange', the crimson 'New Red' and the pale pink 'Silvery Rose', all the same height. *Helichrysum subulifolium* 'Yellow Star' is smaller 50cm (20in) and has yellow flowers of which the centre is visible. *Helichrysum cassianum* has very fine little pink strawflowers grouped in clusters. 'Gabriel Pink', 'Lichtrosa' and 'Select' are cultivars 50cm (20in) high. There is a perennial *Helichrysum*, formerly *Anaphalis triplinervis* 'Schwefellicht', now called *Helichrysum* 'Schwefellicht'. The plant resembles the *Anaphalis* strongly but it has yellow flowers, instead of white, and grey foliage. *Helichrysum italicum* is an evergreen plant with grey foliage, 50cm (20in) high and twice as wide with insignificant yellow flowers which can be cut. The foliage smells of curry. All helichrysums need very well-drained soil and a sunny position.

Heliopsis

✿ ☼

It is a pity that this sturdy borderplant is out of favour as there is nothing wrong with it. It is strong, fully hardy and the flowers are good for cutting. Perhaps the colour is to blame or it may be too common, or it is just out of fashion. Fortunately it is still available, if sparingly. *Heliopsis helianthoides* 'Benzinggold' has big, yellow-orange flowers and needs no support although it grows up to 2m (6ft) high. 'Goldgefieder' has double, golden-yellow flowers and is 1.3m (4½ft) high; 'Light of Loddon' has single yellow flowers; 'Goldgrünhertz' is double and bright yellow with a greenish-

Heliopsis helianthoides 'Light of Loddon'

Heliopsis helianthoides 'Karat'

Heliotropium in the border

yellow centre 1.2m (4ft);'Hohlspiegel' is orange-yellow, semi-double with large flower heads 1.3m (4¹/₂ft); 'Karat' is yellow, single and the best type for cutting; 'Spitzentänzerin is yellow and 1.2-1.4m (4-4¹/₂ft) tall; 'Summer Sun' has bright-yellow flowers and grows up to 1.5m (5ft) ; 'Venus' has large, yellow-ochre flowers, 1.3m (4¹/₂ft) high and excellent for cutting. Mien Ruys combined them long ago with blue delphiniums, grey *Artemisia and Helenium* 'Moerheim Beauty'. These plants will tolerate poor, dry soil, but they thrive on fertile, moisture-retentive soil.

Heliotropium arborescens

Heliotropium

🌿 ☼

Heliotropium peruvianum is now called *Heliotropium arborescens*; its flowers are usually blue and very fragrant with an illusive scent that is difficult to define, but its name, 'Cherry Pie' describes it well enough. This rather stiff sub-shrub is really a pot plant as it is not hardy, but it can still play a part at the edge of the border when it is used as an annual. There are various cultivars in every shade of blue, from pale violet to dark blue, and there is even a white one. These are usually sold as bedding plants without the cultivar-name label. You can also sow them, but they do not germinate with any regularity and they need to be kept very moist. Give them fertile soil and a spot in full sun.

Helipterum

IMMORTELLE
ⁱ ☼

This is an 'immortelle' or everlasting flower - a lovely name for plants which keep their colour when dried.
Helipterum roseum (syn. *Acrolinium roseum*), 50cm (20in), is white or pink, an ideal, papery flower for drying, with a yellow centre. It has a looser, less formal habit than the strawflower *Helichrysum bracteatum*. 'Red Bonny' is pink and 'Blanche' is white. They flower more freely on poor soil and produce more foliage on good soil. *Helipterum manglesii* (syn. *Rhodanthe manglesii*) 40cm (16in) is a very decorative immortelle with small pink and white flowers. The plants are slightly more branched.

Helipterum roseum

Helipterum roseum 'Red Bonny'

Helipterum manglesii

Helipterum humboldtianum (syn. *Pteropogon humboldtianum*) 40cm (16in) is quite different with clusters of small yellow flowers. All these annuals love a warm and sunny summer. As everyone still knows them as *Helipterum* and as they are still listed as such in the seed catalogues, they can also be found by that name in this book. What's in a name? They are very useful in the border, combining well with other plants.

Helleborus

CHRISTMAS ROSE   LENTEN ROSE
❁ ○ ◑

If you have once seen christmas roses in flower, you have to grow them. They start flowering in winter and continue well into spring. The white christmas rose, *Helleborus niger,* often flowers at Christmas.

It is tempting to buy one in a pot and enjoy it indoors over Christmas and then to plant it outdoors. Unfortunately this is usually a disappointment; the buds often fail to open and the plants never thrive.
It is best to buy *Helleborus niger* for the garden from a good grower and to plant it outside at once. These plants are the seedlings, specially selected, of large-flowered christmas roses. But Helleborus orientalis-hybrids are much stronger, hardier and less susceptible to disease.

Helleborus 'Primrose'

Helleborus – flowers in a bowl

Helleborus argutifolius

Helleborus foetidus

These fantastic plants flower from February into April, not at Christmas. Some nurseries organize special 'Christmas rose' days in early spring. The plants available are usually self-coloured seedlings, but there is so much variation in the flowers that they are all different. The flowers may be white, green, pink, red or almost black, sometimes spotted. Most growers sell selected seedlings sown from the seed of their own mother plants, but some sell divided plants.

The Helleborus orientalis group of plants has been much improved by English growers and new cultivars appear frequently. We will not name them all here, but it is always best to buy these plants for your garden in a satisfactory colour from a good grower.
Helleborus argutifolius is the most often grown of the other species. It has evergreen,

Hemerocallis 'Corky'

shrubby foliage and flowers from February into April with big clusters of pale green flowers.
Helleborus foetidus, the Stinking hellebore has lovely, deeply divided evergreen foliage which smells of elderberry; it flowers in December with pale green flowers with a brownish-red margin. The christmas rose prefers semi-shade or a shady position in fertile soil enriched with well-rotted manure.

Hemerocallis

DAYLILY

This is an immoderate genus of plants so easy to cross that more than 40,000(!) hybrid-cultivars have been registered and these are joined by 1000 new ones every year. The demand can hardly justify such quantities and a few new hybrid-cultivars of good quality every year would be much better all round. Fortunately there are wise growers who provide a selection of plants suitable for the climate from the complex supply.

Hemerocallis is a plant which needs full sun to thrive and there are modern hybrid-cultivars which hardly bloom at all if the summer is not perfect.

Large-flowered daylilies sometimes look the worse for wear after a shower and many red-flowering cultivars do not come into full flower in bad weather. There are enough daylilies left with beautiful flowers and foliage. The narrow, grassy leaves are very decorative and slugs also find them tasty. The lightly-fried buds of *Hemerocallis* also taste delicious. The

Hemerocallis 'Princess Blue Eyes'

Hemerocallis 'Stella de Oro'

lime-green throat; 'Siloam Red Toy', 50cm (20in), red with green throat; 'Siloam Uri Winniford', probably the loveliest with its small, creamy flowers and purple eye, but it is in short supply; 'Stella de Oro', 40cm (16in), yellow with green throat; 'Suzie Wong', 60cm (2ft), lemon-yellow. These erect plants will grow in most soils, even when dry, but they need fertile soil to flower freely.

Hesperis

DAME'S VIOLET
🌱 ✿ ☼ ○

The Dame's violet, *Hesperis matronalis*, is sometimes confused with honesty, *Lunaria*, but of these two crucifers the dame's violet is the most fragrant. There is no trace of this by day, but at dusk the scent is strong. This perennial plant is easy to sow and usually behaves as a biennial.

Hesperis with ferns and *Digitalis*

Hesperis matronalis 'Alba'

faded flowers can be used if you cannot bring yourself to eat the buds. The following are just a few of the tens of thousands of hybrid-cultivars: 'Corky', 80cm (32in) with small, pale yellow flowers and reddish-brown buds; 'Duke of Durham', 60cm (2ft). orange-brown, lovely in a red border; 'Gentle Shepherd', 70cm (28in), white with lime-green throat; 'Green Flutter', 90cm (3ft), greenish-yellow flowers; 'Helle Berlinerin', 1.2m (4ft), cream with orange; 'Lullaby Baby', 80cm (32in), apricot-coloured; 'Nugget', 80cm (32in), orange-yellow, bell-shaped flowers do not open wide; 'Princess Blue Eyes', maroon with

Heuchera 'Chocolate Ruffles'

Heuchera × brizoides 'Taff's Joy'

Heuchera americana

The rosette appears in the first year, the flower in the second year and the plant fails to return in the third year. But the single-flowered plant sows itself so freely that there will always be one somewhere else. It is over a metre (3ft) high and combines well in a border. Hesperis matronalis is very like Phlox paniculata in lilac-pink. The best-known cultivar, 'Alba', is white and not only fragrant in the dark, but luminous too. 'Alba Plena' has double, white flowers and 'Lilacina Flore Plena' has double, pale purple flowers. Hesperis violacea (syn. Hesperis steveniana according to "T& M") is lower, 40cm (16in), with dark-purple flowers.

Heuchera

ALUM ROOT

Alum root is known for its large, sturdy clumps of evergreen foliage. The long flower stems with white, sometimes pink plumes emerge from the clumps. in May and June. They like light shade, but cultivars with red foliage need more sun. *Heuchera x brizoides* has several lovely cultivars, including 'Taff's Joy'. *Heuchera americana* grows up to 50cm (20in), has green and white foliage and white flowers. Many new cultivars with red foliage are grown in America. The best known is certainly *Heuchera micrantha* 'Palace Purple', with deep purple foliage and small white plumes of flowers. 'Molly Bush' is a selection ùf these with larger and darker leaves. 'Purple Ace' is another cultivar resembling 'Palace Purple'. 'Pewter Moon', a cross between 'Greenfinch' and 'Palace Purple', has leaves with deep purple undersides and silvery markings on top. 'Chocolate Ruffles', true to its name, is chocolate-coloured with ruffled leaves and it flowers profusely. *Heuchera* is very suitable for the border and it is also beautiful in a large pot.

Heucherella (X)

× *Heucherella* is a cross between *Heuchera* and *Tiarella* and it has inherited the best features from both parents. The plants grow lower than the *Heuchera*, 30-40cm (12-16in); they make good ground cover with beautiful autumn colouring. The young foliage is green with brown spots and the older leaves are dark green. They flower more freely than the *Heuchera*.
× *Heucherella alba* 'Bridget Bloom' flowers with bright pink plumes of flowers and ×

X *Heucherella tiarelloides*

X *Heucherella alba* 'Bridget Bloom'

Hibiscus – fruit in winter

Heucherella alba 'Rosalie' is slightly lower with pink plumes. × *Heucherella* tiarelloides has pink flowers and sends out runners, in contrast with × *Heucherella alba*. × *Heucherella* tiarelloides is an excellent ground coverer which flowers well and needs good, moisture-retentive soil.

Hibiscus

ALTHEASTRUIK
🌿 ☼

Hibiscus syriacus is known to have about 125 cultivars which bloom with big single or

Hibiscus syriacus 'Woodbridge'

double flowers from the end of August into October. The flowers are large for shrubs with a diameter of 6-12cm (2-5in). These fairly stiff shrubs, 1-2m (3-6ft) high love a sunny position. There are several good cultivars: 'Coelestis', blue with a dark centre; 'Hamaba', pale pink, tinged with dark red; 'Lady Stanley', white, tinged with pink and red in the centre and does not grow vigorously; 'Oiseau Bleu'/ 'Blue Bird', blue with a dark

Hippophae rhamnoides

Hippophae salicifolia

centre; 'Red Heart', pure white, centre tinged with bright red; 'Speciosus', double flowers, pure white with a red centre; 'William R. Smith', pure white; 'Woodbridge', deep red. All are single-flowered except for 'Speciosus'. The types with double flowers are not as hardy. These upright shrubs can provide some beautiful colours in the autumn border and their fruits are decorative in the winter border.

Hippophae

✿ ☼

Hippophae is an ideal shrub for dry, sandy soil and grows well in coastal gardens. *Hippophae rhamnoides* or Sea buckthorn, is covered with spines and has long narrow leaves and orange berries. 'Leikora' is a beautiful cultivar, growing up to 3m (9ft);this shrub bears many big, orange berries, especially if the 'Pollmix' pollinator is nearby. Buckthorns are dioecious so that the female shrubs only bear berries if they are planted near a male one. *Hippophae salicifolia* is a small tree with arching branches, grey-green foliage and orange fruits.

Holodiscus

✿ ☼ ○

Holodiscus discolor, 2m (6ft), is almost unknown as a shrub, with large, arching sprays of cream-coloured flowers in July and

August. It prefers humus-rich, moist soil and sun. Its light and airy habit combines well with other shrubs in a shrub border.

Hosta

FUNKIA

❀ ☼ ○ ◗

Most people cannot resist hostas. They are grown for their foliage but some also have splendid flowers. Over a thousand cultivars have already been registered and there are still more new ones to come. Hostas reach their permanent height after six years and the plants are at their best and thrive if left to themselves in good garden soil enriched with rotted manure. Do not water in the evening as this

Hosta undulata 'Mediovariegata'

attracts slugs and snails which are very partial to hostas, especially those with thin leaves. It helps to discourage them by putting some ashes around the plants in spring and removing the snails by hand. Almost all hostas can be grown in pots, as long as they have enough water and nutrients. A little vaseline around the edge of the pot will form an insurmountable obstacle to the slugs. Hostas are excellent border plants, varying in height from low, 30-40cm (12-16in) to 70cm (28in) and higher. They prefer light shade and will tolerate some sun if the soil is sufficiently moist. Variegated and yellow-leaved hostas such as *Hosta undulata* 'Mediovariegata', are better out of the sun. Blue hostas should not

Hosta × fortunei 'Gold Standard'

Hosta sieboldiana 'Elegans'

Hosta lancifolia

Hosta sieboldiana 'Frances Williams'

Hosta × fortunei 'Moerheim'

be planted under dripping trees as this will damage the wax layerof their foliage. The familiar and beautiful *Hosta sieboldiana* 'Frances Williams' is called after the American garden designer who collected hostas from 1930.onwards; it grows up to 60cm (2ft) with gilt-edged bluish-green foliage. The hybrid-cultivar 'Reversed' (40cm/16in) does not grow as vigorously as 'Frances Williams' and reverses the colouring, with yellow foliage edged with bluish-green.

Hosta sieboldiana 'Elegans' is a familiar blue hosta, 80cm (32in) high. 'Sum and Substance' is a spectacular hosta with very thick, golden-green leaves not favoured by slugs or snails. 'Big Daddy' and'Big Mama' resemble H. sieboldiana 'Elegens', but grow taller and 'Big Mama' has longer, slender leaves. *Hosta x fortunei* has some very good cultivars: 'Albopicta', which originated in the botanical gardens of Leiden in the 1860s, has yellow leaves with a dull green edge; 'Francee' has lavender-blue flowers and dark green foliage with a white edge; 'Hyacinthina' is a lovely,

Houttuynia cordata 'Chameleon'

Houttuynia cordata

Houttuynia cordata 'Chameleon'

old -fashioned hosta with grey-green foliage and lilac flowers; the foliage of 'Gold Standard' is pale green at first with a dark green edge, later turning golden-yellow in the middle, given enough sunlight;

The leaves of 'Moerheim' have broad, yellow edges turning white later. *Hosta x tardiana* 'Halcyon' is a bluish-grey hosta with small leaves, 40cm (16in) high. Hosta lancifolia has small, narrow, dark-green leaves.

Houttuynia

Care is needed when planting houttuynia in the border,as it will not fit in everywhere. This is due to its highly variegated foliage, especially of the cultivar 'Chameleon'. The leaves are flecked with green, yellow and red in a set pattern, usually green in the centre, yellow and red at the edge.

Houttuynia cordata has dull, dark-green foliage. Both have insignificant, white flowers. 'Plena' is a cultivar with double flowers. These plants need extremely moist soil and prefer to grow beside a pond.
They grow 30 to 40cm (12-16in) high and become invasive with spreading rhizomes. They need protective covering in winter.

Hydrangea

ℒℯ ○

The cultivars of *Hydrangea macrophylla* are the best known. There are two groups, the Lacecap hydrangea with wide, flat flower heads and the Hortensia or mophead with domed flower heads.

Macrophylla cultivars may react to the iron content of the soil and grow a beautiful blue instead of pink. Growers add a chemical to the soil to create blue hydrangeas. The blue hydrangea which you plant in your garden this year may well bear pink flowers next year. 'Otaksa', 1m (3ft), is the only one which remains a pinky-blue without help. 'Bouquet Rose' grows up to 2m (6ft), with pink flowers; 'Adria' is blue depending on the amount of iron and acid in the soil; 'Masja' is dark red and retains this colour for a long period; 'Leuchtfeuer' is also red; 'Hobella' has three colours, but not all at once: the flowers are pink at first, then brown, turning red. These cultivars of *H. macrophylla* flower from August into October and look superb in a mixed autumn border. They usually grow up to 1m (3ft).

Hydrangea paniculata 'Limelight'

Hydrangea arborescens 'Annabelle' is much loved and often planted. It grows to 1.2m

Hydrangea in the border

Hydrangea serrata 'Blue Bird'

(4ft) high, like 'Grandiflora' and 'Hills of Snow', with slightly larger, white, domed flower heads. *Hydrangea aspera* 'Macrophylla' is a splendid shrub, 1.75m (5^1/2ft) high, with broad, lilac to white flower heads. Not all macrophyllas have rounded flower heads; some cultivars such as the Lacecap 'Mariesii Perfecta' (syn H.m. 'Blue Wave') 1.5m (5ft) high, bears flat bluish-pink flower heads.

Hydrangea paniculata, 2m (6ft) high, can show off at the back of a mixed border with its conical flower heads. These are almost all white, including 'Unique', 'Kyushu' and 'Silver Dollar'. Other colours include 'Pink Diamond', a creamy 'Dolly' and the green-white 'Greenspire'. *Hydrangea paniculata* 'Limelight' is a brand new, beautiful debutante. The clusters of this cultivar are white to green and slightly shorter.*Hydrangea quercifolia* grows up to 2m (6ft) high with lovely foliage like that of the American oak, (Quercus rubra) and plume-shaped flower heads. *Hydrangea serrata* 'Bluebird' 1m (3ft), has blue ray flowers and 'Intermedia', 1.75m (5^1/2ft) has pink ray flowers. Hydrangeas need plenty of water and grow in the sun or in light shade. The domed flower heads can be dried very well if they are picked as soon as the flowers feel crackly.

Hypericum

✣ ⚜ ☀ ○

Hypericum is grown in the garden for its flowers and it is used in bouquets for its fruits. These sub-shrubs are not very tall and quietly

Hypericum androsaemum 'Orange Flair'

Hypericum androsaemum

Hyssopus officinalis 'Ruber' ('Purpurascens')

Hypericum calycinum

combine with perennials and other shrubs in the border. *Hypericum androsaemum* is the best known, a broad sub-shrub, 80cm (32in) high with big, golden-yellow flowers from June into September. The fruit capsules are brown-red at first, later black. This species has some lovely cultivars: 'Autumn Blaze', 1m (3ft), with small golden-yellow flowers and brown berries, familiar from bouquets; 'Dart's Golden Penny', with large leaves and big, black berries; 'Gladys Brabazon', 50cm (20in), half hardy, with unusual green, pink and white variegated foliage and berries red at first, later black; 'Orange Flair', grown for its beautiful orange berries.

Hypericum calycinum or Rose of Sharon, is an ideal ground coverer with large golden-yellow flowers, it needs plenty of room. *Hypericum beanii*, 70cm (28in), half hardy, flowers freely and long with clusters of yellow flowers. The new Danish cultivar 'Elda', 1m (3ft), has arching branches and big, deep yellow flowers. *Hypericum hyssopifolium*, a perennial from Southern Europe has narrow leaves and unbranched stems bearing large, yellow flowers. *Hypericum x inodorum*, 1m (3ft) is a familiar, frost tender Hypericum often grown, with golden-yellow flowers and brown-red berries turning brown-black later. The cultivar 'Elstead', 75cm (2½ft) has striking red fruits. These shrubs need humus-rich, moist soil.

Hyssopus

HYSSOP

Hyssop belongs in a herb garden, but there is no reason why this aromatic herb should not be planted in the border.

There are some very suitable cultivars: *Hyssopus officinalis* 'Albus' has spikes of small white flowers; 'Ruber' ('Purpurescens') is purple and 'Roseus' is pale pink, so are 'Pink Delight' and 'Stella's Pink'. The plants grow up to 50cm (20in), they love full sun, dry feet and some chalk in the soil. The plant may be damaged by severe frost, but it will return.

Iberis amara 'Impuded White Spiral'

Iberis umbellata 'Fantasia'

Iberis 'Candituft Dwarf Mixed'

Iberis

CANDYTUFT

☽ ⊛ ⊶ ☼

Iberis amara, *Iberis umbellata* and their cultivars are most often grown of the varieties of the annual candytuft. The first has white or purple and white flowers; the cultivar 'Mount Hood', 40cm (16in) has white flowers in little clusters followed by pretty seed capsules. 'White Pinnacle', 50cm (20in) is as white as 'Iceberg', 30cm (12in). Their clusters of flowers are sometimes compared with hyacinths; this certainly applies to 'Impuded White Spiral' and although the the flowers are quite different, the clusters are as big as those of hyacinths. *Iberis umbellata* is larger with a flatter flower head. The colour of this species is variable, but usually purple. There are several mixtures of this type: 'Flash', 'Fantasia' and the lower 'Candituft Dwarf Mixed', with many shades of pink, white, carmine and lilac,

matching each other perfectly. Mixed colours are more difficult to combine in a border than a uniform white, but they can certainly be recommended for edging and cutting. The perennial *Iberis sempervirens* is a familiar, low sub-shrub (20cm- 8in) which is evergreen in a mild winter. Like the annual candytuft, this plant loves full sun and fairly dry, chalky soil. It flowers early in March and April. There are various cultivars, some of which flower longer, or later, with larger or whiter flowers than the species. 'Autumn Beauty' flowers in spring and autumn; 'Findel' has big, white flowers; 'Snowflake' forms clumps and 'Weisser Zwerg' is only 15cm (5in) high.

Iris 'Ola Kala'

Ilex

HOLLY

Holly can be evergreen or deciduous; the best known is evergreen holly with splendid red berries which is used for Christmas decoration in many homes and gardens. These berries can also be yellow, orange or black according to the species and the cultivar, but they only appear on the female plants. and then only if both sexes are present as holly is unisexual. Cultivar names do not help matters when it appears that *Ilex aquifolium* 'Golden Queen' is male and *Ilex x altaclarensis* 'Golden King' is female.

Many species of holly will grow too big for a shrub border, but this need not be a problem as they are easy to clip. There are so many green and variegated cultivars of the species *Ilex x altaclarensis* and *Ilex aquifolium* (For instance, *Ilex aquifolium* 'Argentea Marginata'), that we will mention some less familiar, unusual cultivars of *Ilex x aquipernyi* (*Ilex aquifolium x Ilex pernyi*), *Ilex crenata, Ilex x meserveae* (*Ilex aquifolium x Ilex rugosa*) and *Ilex glabra. Ilex verticilata* is also worth planting.   First the cultivars of *Ilex x aquipernyi*; 'Dragon Lady', a slender shrub with dark green foliage and big red berries; 'China Boy', a broad bush with green foliage

Ilex aquifolium 'Argentea Marginata'

and without berries; 'China Girl', a broad bush with bright red berries. Next the cultivars of *Ilex crenata,* the Japanese holly with tiny Box-like leaves and black berries; 'Convexa', a female plant with glossy green, very convex foliage; 'Fastigiata', conical with dark green leaves; 'Golden Gem', with greenish-yellow foliage, very effective in winter and spring, with few berries and a compact habit; 'Green Lustre', a low, dense bush with glossy dark green foliage.

The cultivars of *Ilex x meserveae* come from the USA and are known as the blue hollies there because the young shoots and some of the leaves are bluish-green.

'Blue Angel' has glossy, bluish-green foliage and large, red berries; 'Blue Boy' has no berries; 'Meseal' ('Blue Bunny') has dark green foliage and red fruits; 'Blue Princess' has purplish-blue young shoots, bluish-green foliage and glistening red berries; 'Mesan' ('Blue Stallion') has no berries and is suitable for hedging, as is 'Golden Girl', with fresh green foliage and yellow berries. *Ilex glabra,* the Inkberry, grows up to 2.5m (8ft); it has several dense, low-growing cultivars including 'Compacta' and 'Nana'.
Holly is tolerant of most soils and prefers light shade,

Incarvillea delavayi

Incarvillea delavayi 'Alba'

Incarvillea

✿ ☼

Bulb growers sometimes sell these plants as dried rhizomes in a packet with a pretty picture on it. In fact they are perennial plants and hardy if treated with care. Given some protective covering they will survive the winter, if it is not too wet. They need well-drained soil and their roots do not tolerate wet soil. The best-known is *Incarvillea delavayi,* a plant with a rosette of green, feathered leaves which flowers from May into July with deep pink, trumpet-shaped flowers on stems between 40 and 50 cm (16-20in) high. 'Alba' has white flowers with yellow ochre throat, often available under the incorrect name of 'Snow Top'. It will be easier to combine in the border than the brighter coloured *I. delavayi.* *Incarvillea arguta* is one of the loveliest species, a kind of sub-shrub which does not die off completely in winter so that it needs to be well-covered. The plant flowers throughout the summer with small, dark pink or white flowers.

All these plants love full sun and well-drained soil. They are very suitable for growing in tubs, where they will need plenty of water during the growing season and hardly any while resting. They should be stored frost-free in winter.

Indigofera

❀ ☼ ○

This shrub flowers throughout the summer and well into autumn because the clusters of flowers grow from the leaf axils of young shoots It is deciduous with decorative compound leaves. It will grow in any soil, even when dry, but it needs sun. Even when damaged by frost in severe winters it will usually return. *Indigofera amblyantha* grows up to 1.5-2m (5-6ft) with very elegant little rose-red flower clusters. *Indigofera decora* f. *alba* is only 50cm (20in) high and flowers all white. *Indigofera heterantha* grows to 1m (3ft) and has dense spikes of bright pink flowers. *Indigofera kirilowii* is 1m (3ft) high with deep pink flowers in long spikes. *Indigofera pseudotinctoria* grows up to 1m (3ft) with short clusters of small, bright pink flowers. A valuable addition to the border with its beautiful foliage and flowers.

Inula

ALANT
✿ ☼ ○

Inulas can be giants or dwarves, but high or low they all have cheerful, yellow, daisy-like flowers. The sunny flowers indicate that they love full sun and well-drained soil. Inula

Inula hookeri

Inula orientalis 'Grandiflora'

ensifolia, which flowers from June into August is low, bushy and strongly branched. The term 'Senior' indicates that the plant was propagated vegetatively and that it is not a cultivar. *Inula helenium* is a very tall Greek plant which can grow up to 2m (6ft). This plant can be found in herb gardens as it has medicinal properties and it is suitable for woodland conditions. It tolerates light shade, in contrast to other inulas. *Inula hookeri* is between these two in height at 60cm (2ft), with oval, hairy foliage, flowering freely in summer with daisy-like flowers. Inula orientalis, 60cm (2ft), has orange-yellow flowers, very good for cutting. The flowers of *Inula orientalis* 'Grandiflora' are larger. *Inula rhizocephala* grows over 1m (3ft) high, branched, with big yellow flowers. In general inulas are really too coarse for a neat and tidy border; they feel more at home in a wild border.

Iris

✿ ☀

The most familiar iris must be the Yellow flag which inhabits watersides with splendid clumps of yellow flowers and orange berries later on. But there are many more; this particular *Iris pseudacorus* also has a double-flowered version - 'Flore Pleno'- and even one

Left: Indigofera kirilowii

with variegated foliage - 'Variegata'. It also has some very tall cultivars and some that are almost white The exquisite flowers of the iris make this a most unusual plant. The flowers consist of six petals, of which the inner 'standards' are erect and the outer 'falls' curl downwards. Bearded irises also have coloured hairs growing along the middle of each fall. There are over 300 species of the iris divided into subspecies and sections. Hundreds more hybrid-cultivars were developed in the past century.

Iris innominata, brown to yellow, with a natural habit, 30cm (1ft) high; Iris unguicularis, a lilac-blue version, 60cm (2ft) high. *Iris chrysographes* is 50cm (20in) high with black to purple, velvety flowers, and as a complete contrast there is the free-flowering white *Iris sibirica* 'Little White', 1m (3ft).

Iris pseudacorus – flower

Iris siberica 'South Coombe White'

Two splendid cultivars are 'Black Knight' of *Iris chrysographes* and 'Perry's Blue' of *Iris siberica*. There are two favourites in the Germanica group: 'Ambassador', a flesh-colour combined with purple and the bright pink 'One Desire'. Finally, *Iris germanica*

Iris pseudacorus – fruit

'Florentina', with grey-blue flowers. This iris from Florence is grown in italy for the perfume industry. The dried rhizomes which smell of violets are used for this, not the flowers. The best-known irises are those of the Germanica group with large flowers on stiff, branched stems and tuberous roots growing on the soil rather than in it. They come in shades of blue, violet, white, brown, green and yellow ('Ola Kala'). The following are beautiful irises: 'Bianca', white; 'Ginger', 'Glacier', white to blue, 'Harbor Blue', bright blue; 'Sable', deep purple and 'Susan Bliss', lilac-pink. These impressive irises flower in May and June, preferably in well-drained soil and full sun. The Siberian irises, such as the lilac-pink cultivar 'Sparkling Rose', are more at home in a natural border. The cultivars of *Iris sibirica* need good, moisture -retentive soil, especially in April, May and June and they love full sun. Some lovely ones are: 'Berlin Bluebird', 90cm (3ft); 'King of Kings', white, (over 1m -3ft); 'Polly Dodge', maroon; 'Silver Edge', blue with a white edge. The Stinking iris, *Iris foetidissima*, has insignificant lilac-green flowers, followed by striking orange seeds. Two irises with variegated leaves are *Iris foetidissima* 'Variegata', green foliage with a white edge and *Iris pallida* 'Variegata', combining pied foliage with lavender-blue flowers. Two irises go by the same name of 'Variegata', one with golden stripes, the other silver, now known as 'Aurea Variegata' and 'Argentea Variegata' respectively. The following irises are for those who prefer simple shapes and natural colours: *Iris x chrysofor*, with mustard-coloured, drooping petals; *Iris orientalis*, deep- purple flowers; *Iris setosa*, lance-shaped leaves and purple-violet flowers; Iris versicolor, the Blue flag iris with purple-blue flowers. There are more than enough irises to choose from.

Itea

🌿 ☼ ○

This shrub is not well-known, sometimes confused with *Clethra*. It needs well-drained soil, but not dry. Itea ilicifolia, which resembles holly, is not fully hardy in all regions.

This is an evergreen shrub, 3m (6ft) tall with long, green, fragrant catkins in late summer. *Itea japonica* 'Beppu' is a new cultivar from Japan.

A small shrub, not high, but spreading in width, with scented flowers in July and August and foliage turning red in the autumn. *Itea*

Iris with peony

Iris sibirica 'Sparkling Rose'

virginica is a deciduous shrub with upright, creamy spikes of flowers in summer, turning a lovely red in autumn, lower than the former. 'Henry's Garnet', 1.2m (4ft) high is a beautiful cultivar with red foliage in the autumn and white flower spikes in summer.

Jasione laevis

Jasione

The common *Jasione montana* grows in the wild in regions where the soil is poor, dry and sandy, lacking in chalk. It forms pleasant little clumps with sky-blue flowers. It has a more fashionable relative for the garden, *Jasione laevis*, or Sheep's bit, with an even better cultivar, 'Blaulicht'. *Jasione laevis* 'Blaulicht' has flowers of a brighter blue than the species, grows up to 30cm (1ft) high and prefers the same open, poor dry soil as its wild relatives. The flowers are like those of *Scabiosa* but it is no relation. Jasione will flower from June into August at the edge of a sandy border.

Kalmia

The flowers of this shrub are more effective than its foliage. *Kalmia latifolia* or Calico bush is an evergreen with a habit resembling a *Rhododendron*. The shrub is 2-4m (6-12ft) tall and flowers in late spring with clusters of flowers at the end of its stems. This type has deep pink buds becoming pale-pink when they open. There are several cultivars of this species, usually from America, including *Kalmia latifolia* 'Pink Frost'.

Kalmia is the 'national' flower of the state of New York. 'Myrtifolia' is a low shrub with white flowers, 'Olympic Fire' has bright red flowers and 'Ostbro Red' has large red flower buds opening to reveal a pink flower with a white centre. The flowers of *Kalmia angus-*

Kalmia latifolia 'Pink Frost'

tifolia or Sheep laurel, 1.5m (5ft) high, are smaller and the foliage is narrower. Its cultivar 'Rubra', with deep pink flowers is most often grown. This species and the cultivar are both poisonous so take care with children and pets. Kalmias thrive in the same conditions as rhododendrons and they need acid soil.

Kniphofia 'Alcazar'

Kalmia latifolia 'Myrtifolia'

Kalmia angustifolia

Kerria

JEW'S MALLOW

Kerria japonica or Jew's mallow grows up to 1.8m (5¹/₂ft) with graceful, arching branches. These are a glossy green, making a focal point in winter when its leaves have fallen. The species has single, yellow flowers, but there are also cultivars with double flowers. They like moist, well-drained soil which must not dry out in summer. Their large flowers need protection from the bright midday-sun to prevent fading. Yellow cultivars with single flowers are 'Golden Guinea', with large flowers and 'Variegata', combining yellow flowers and green foliage with an irregular, broad white margin. 'Pleniflora' or 'bachelor's

Kerria japonica

Kerria

buttons' has double, yellow flowers. 'Albiflora' has creamy-white flowers which combine very well in the border.

Kirengeshoma

Kirengeshoma palmata is a splendid plant for a shdow border, if the ground is sufficiently moist; if not, its buds will hang their heads. The plant has lovely, firm foliage and in late summer clusters of bobbing yellow flowers, with petals fanning outwards, appear above the leaves. The flowers of *K. palmata* are only half open. The plant grows up to 1m (3ft). The experts are in doubt as to whether there is another species, but the *Kirengeshoma*

Kirengeshoma palmata

Knautia macedonica in the border

koreana is mentioned in most publications; it is taller and its stems are more upright with flowers opening wider.

Knautia

 ☼

Knautia arvensis or *Scabious*, with lilac flowers is becoming increasingly rare in the wild. *Knautia arvensis* 'Albion' flowers from June into September, pure white, 1.3m (4¹/₂ft)

high. *Knautia dipsacifolia* was recently found growing wild; it differs from the scabious in that its leaves are undivided. The blue flowers attract bees and butterflies.

The *Knautia* which we grow in the garden is usually *Knautia macedonica*, 60cm (2ft) high, producing dark, burgundy-flowers throughout the summer and well into autumn. The plant will be more robust if it is grown in fairly poor soil. Stake it early on with sticks, or put it where it can weave itself among other plants.

Kirengeshoma palmata

Knautia arvensis

Kniphofia 'Shining Sceptre'

Kniphofia 'Little Maid'

Knautia looks very good in combination with grey-leaved plants such as artemisias. Give it a place in the sun.

Kniphofia

RED-HOT POKER   TORCH LILY

✥ ☼

The name 'Red-hot poker' immediately conjures up the fiery orange spikes of flowers produced by these striking plants.

There are over sixty species and just as many hybrid-cultivars, with 'pokers' varying in colour from white, yellow, orange, red and apricot-coloured, to green, mustard and salmon-pink. There is no point in going to a nursery to buy some cultivars straight away because it is not so easy. So many cultivars are not hardy, in fact there is not one red-hot poker which will survive the winter without protective covering.

The best method is to tie up the foliage before the onset of winter and to pile a thick layer of dry leaves around the base of the plant. Even then the plant may not return after a severe winter. 'Shining Sceptre', with lovely creamy-white pokers is a good choice for a colourful border. 'Ice Queen' has impressive, greenish-white pokers, 1.5m (5ft); 'Alcazar', bright orange and 'Toffee Nosed', creamy-white with

the tips turning brown and orange. Even people who do not like the red-hot poker will appreciate 'Little Maid' which was selected in Beth Chatto's garden.

This is a small plant, 60cm (2ft) high with

Kochia scoparia, in the border

Kolkwitzia amabilis

narrow leaves and modest, creamy-white pokers. It needs full sun and fertile, well-drained soil.

Kochia

♀ ☼

Kochia is now known as *Bassia,* an annual foliage plant. It is no wonder that it is taken for a conifer because it is pillar-shaped, 60cm (2ft) high with narrow, light green leaves. Planted with care, its rather stiff habit can form a focal point of rest in the border between all the different colours. *Kochia scoparia f. trichophylla*, the Burning bush, or Summer cypress, takes on beautiful brown to red colours in the autumn. So does the cultivar 'Autumn Red'.

'Childsii' and 'Evergreen' do not change colour. There is also a variegated cultivar, 'Acapulco Silver'.

Kolkwitzia

⚜ ☼ ○

Kolkwitzia amabilis, the Beauty bush, is a familiar, exuberant shrub, 2-3m (6-9ft) high, covered with bell-shaped, yellow throated, pale pink flowers in May and June. It grows in any garden soil, preferably in the sun. 'Pink Cloud' has bright pink flowers and is lower.

Kochia in the border

Lamiastrum galeobdolon 'Herman's Pride'

Lamiastrum galeobdolon 'Silberteppich'

Lagurus

HARE'S-TAIL GRASS

Hare's-tail grass is an annual plant which has its soft, white spikes of flowers to thank for its name. It grows up to 50cm (20in) on sandy, well-drained soil and - like quaking grass - it combines well with other border plants. The plants can be sown from seed in autumn, brought indoors for the winter and planted in the border in spring. The tails are excellent for drying.

Lamiastrum

Lamiastrum galeobdolon was formerly *Lamium galeobdolon* and many experts still call it so. It grows rampantly and is only suitable for a shrub border.

It will grow in any soil and even tolerates shade. The species has green foliage and yellow flowers. The cultivars have variegated leaves and yellow flowers. 'Florentino' has leaves variegated with silver. 'Herman's Pride', (discovered by Herman Dijkhuizen in Dalmatia in 1972) is not rampant and has wonderful silvery-variegated leaves.

Leucanthemum vulgare 'Maikönigin'

The leaves of 'Silberteppich' are almost entirely silver-coloured. The plants, which flower in May and June, are grown for their foliage.

Lamium

DEADNETTLE

Lamium album, the white deadnettle, is so common that we do not plant it in the border, where it would also spread alarmingly. It feels at home in natural surroundings, for instance with forget-me-nots and primulas. It is good for cutting. Some of the other deadnettles are easier to live with. Cultivars of *Lamium*

Lamium maculatum 'Shell Pink'

Lamium orvala 'Album'

maculatum give the border a natural look without encroaching too much. 'Beacon Silver' has green-margined, silvery foliage with mauve flowers; 'James Boyd Parselle' flowers in pink with silvery-white leaves; 'Shell Pink' has pale pink flowers and white and green variegated foliage; 'White Nancy' combines white flowers with silvery-white foliage. All these deadnettles are good for cutting, especially effective when the various shades are combined in a bouquet. *Lamium orvala*, 60cm (2ft) looks quite different, the first shoots of foliage growing dark red at first, turning green later. The large flowers are a deep pink. The cultivar 'Album', 40cm (16in) is just as pretty with white flowers. Neither of these is rampant and both like well-drained soil in light shade or shade.

Lantana

❀ ⚜ ☼

Lantana is better known as a tub plant than a border plant, but this shrub verbena can also be grown in a sunny border. *Lantana camara* is a shrub which is not fully hardy, with many cultivars, often bicoloured. They can be sown from seed. 'Camara Mixed' is a mixture of red with yellow, pink with yellow, lilac and white

Lamium maculatum 'Beacon Silver'

Lantana camara-hybrids

Lathyrus vernus

Lantana, yellow

Lathyrus 'Brian Clough'

flowers. Gardeners can make their own selection of favourite colours from this. The plants are sold self-coloured which makes it easier to fit them into the planting layout. Parent plants can be stored frost-free in winter and cuttings are easily made. Butterflies love the flowers.

Lathyrus

PRONKERWT

Climbing plants may not seem suitable for the border, but with support they can add some height where necessary. *Lathyrus odoratus*, the fragrant annual Sweet pea, has low cultivars such as 'Bijou' and 'Knee-Hi', which need no support, weaving themselves in among other plants and flowering from June into September. Climbing cultivars can make a splash of colour against their support. There are several perennial, non-climbing sweet peas suitable for the border. A few sticks will

Lathyrus aureus

Lavandula angustifolia 'Rosea'

Lavandula stoechas subsp. *pedunculata*

Lavandula angustifolia 'Hidcote Blue'

provide the necessary support. *Lathyrus aureus*, 60cm (2ft) high, with unusual brownish-orange coloured flowers. *Lathyrus davidii* has creamy-yellow flowers turning to ochre later, 80cm (32in). *Lathyrus vernus*, the spring sweet pea, has maroon, later bluish-green flowers, 50cm (20in). The cultivar 'Albiflorus' has creamy-white flowers and 'Alboroseus', pale pink. The nice part about these species of lathyrus is that they also have lovely foliage. The perennial *Lathyrus latifolius* is a climber; the various cultivars 'Pink Pearl', 'Red Pearl', 'Rose Queen' and 'White pearl' all need support 1.5m (5ft) high to enable them to climb properly. They flower in July and August, not as long as the annual climbing lathyrus. In order to give their all, flowering so long and freely, they will need plenty of care in the autumn, when the soil must be loosened and dressed with manure.

Lavandula

LAVENDER

Lavender does not grow in every garden and a severe winter can be fatal. Some people no longer plant it as a hedge for this reason. *Lavendula stoechas*, or French lavender is an excellent tub plant, not fully hardy; it is always recognizable by the large, purple bracts at the tips of its flowers. *Lavandula stoechas* var. leucantha has white flowers. *L. stoechas* subsp. *pedunculata* has larger spikes of flowers and bracts. The plant can survive a mild winter and a few degrees of frost if it is in well-drained soil. The cultivars of *Lavandula angustifolia* are stronger, but they should be tip-pruned after flowering; if they continue to

flower for a long period it is best to remove the flowers during the second half of August. In this way the plant is forced to grow shoots. The situation is very important with lavender as it needs full sun and chalky soil. 'Bowles Early' flowers early, in June. 'Hidcote Blue' is a very dark blue lavender; 'Hidcote Pink' has lilac-pink flowers and those of 'Loddon Pink' are a pallid pink, like 'Rosea', 'Alba' has greyish-white flowers. 'Twickel Purple' is lavender-blue, its foliage often has a purple blush in winter. We need hardly add that lavender flowers can be dried.

Lavatera

TREE MALLOW

The annual *Lavatera trimestris*, with a stiff habit and large mallow flowers combine very well in a border for perennial plants. The plant

Lavatera 'Ice Cool'

Lavatera 'Rosea' in the border

is 60cm (2ft) high, with flowers in colours ranging from white in the varieties 'Mont Blanc', 'White Regis' and the lower 'White Cherub', 25cm (6in), to pink - 'Silver Cup' and deep pink - 'Ruby Regis'. The best known tree mallow is surely the hybrid-cultivar 'Barnsley', which can grow up to 2.5m (8ft) in the right spot. It has whitish-pink flowers with a pinkish-red centre. 'Rosea', 1.8m (5¹/2ft) high is another familiar favourite in the border. It flowers abundantly from July into October with pink flowers. If 'Rosea' is too high there

Lavatera trimestris

is also 'Shorty', 1m (3ft) high. 'Pretty Flamingo' resembles 'Rosea', but is less vigorous; 'Burgundy Wine' has wine-red flowers, 1.3m (4¹/2ft) high; 'Ice Cool' has small white flowers with a green centre, 1.2m (4ft) high; 'Candy Floss', 1.5m (5ft) high has pale pink flowers. The species *Lavatera cachemiriana*, 1.5m (5ft) high, is a short-lived perennial plant with pale pink flowers. All the perennial lavateras need a sheltered position in full sun. The plants may be frozen in a severe winter and fail to return. It is best to be on the safe side and store a few cuttings frost-free.

Leonurus

Leonurus cardiaca has almost disappeared in the wild. We can make up for it by planting this robust shrub, 1.2m (4ft) high, in the wild border. *Leonurus cardiaca* 'Grobbebol' has crenated leaves and is lower than the species (1m -3ft), but with the same flowers. It attracts bees.

Lespedeza

This is a late-flowering shrub which becomes a colourful and casual bouquet at the end of summer, very useful in a mixed or shrub border. It is easy to grow and tolerates any soil. One disadvantage is that it grows shoots early in spring when it may be damaged by frost. *Lespedeza bicolor* or 'Ezo-Yama-Hagi' in Japanese, has some lovely cultivars. 'Summer Beauty' grows up to 1.5m (5ft) high,

189

Leonurus cardiaca

Leucanthemum vulgare

Leucanthemum 'Wirral Supreme'

with clusters of maroon flowers in the leaf axils. 'Yakushima' is only 30cm (12in) high, with small, purple clusters. *Lespedeza thunbergii* has arching stalks and grows up to 2m (6ft). The large, purple-pink plumes flower from July into September. These plants need a sunny position and sandy soil.

Leucanthemum

MARGUERITE
✿ ☼

It is a very festive sight when *Leucanthemum vulgare*, the wild marguerite, flowers in the fields and verges at the end of May. They prefer moisture-retentive, poor soil.

The flowers keep well in water - a bunch of wild flowers used to consist of marguerites, poppies and cornflowers. If you prefer larger flowers than the species, there are cultivars, including 'MaikÜnigin', or the double flowered 'Plenum'.
As this species and its cultivars tend to grow rampant in the border, we recommend planting the cultivars of the Superbum group: 'Christine Hagemann' with double flowers is 70cm (28in) high; 'Dwarf Snow Lady' is only 25 cm (10in) high; 'Wirral Supreme' has pure white, semi-double flowers and grows up to 90cm (3ft).

Leucothöe

🌿 ○ ●

Leucothöe walteri (L. fontanesiana) is a small, evergreen shrub, 1m (3ft) high with arching shoots flowering in May and June with small, white, flower clusters. The cultivar 'Rainbow' has strongly variegated foliage with pink, yellow, orange and green markings. This shrub was found as a seedling at Hilliers' well-known nurseries in England, but, according to

Leucothoe 'Zeblid'

G. Krüssmann, an authority on the subject, it came from Ohio in the USA. The hybrid-cultivar, 'Zeblid' ('Scarletta'), 60cm (2ft), has unusual foliage: glossy green when young, turning a darker green when mature and crimson in autumn and winter.

The plant does not take on such colours when in the shade. It is used for cutting and thrives in well-drained soil, rich in humus and without lime.

Leycesteria

❀ ☼ ○

Leycesteria formosa, the Himalayan honey-suckle, 1.6m (5¹/₂ft) is a striking shrub, with very attractive, hanging clusters of white flowers with purplish-red bracts from July into September, followed by large, shining, reddish-purple berries. This shrub grows in any soil and tolerates lime, coastal wind and pollution, but it needs a sheltered position as it is not fully hardy. Those that die off down to the ground in winter always return, right as rain again in spring.

Leycesteria formosa

Liatris

GAY FEATHERS

❀ ☼

This plant was despised for a long time - and perhaps it still is, probably due to its use in bouquets. The stiff, ramrod -like spikes of flowers used to be bunched together and stayed fresh far too long in their unbending arrangement. But if we look at the habit of this plant as a whole, especially the white cultivars

Liatris spicata

Liatris spicata 'Alba'

like *Liatris spicata* 'Alba' and 'Floristan Weiss' (supposed to be one and the same cultivar), then this 80cm (32in)-high plant turns out to be of value for those same stiff spikes of flowers, softened by the narrow, grassy leaves. Even the notorious mauve species and its lower, mauve cultivar 'Kobold', 40 cm (16in), seem to combine well in some colour schemes. These plants are as strong as iron, their spikes flower from July into Sep-

Liatris spicata

tember from the tips downwards. They need good, well-drained soil and full sun.

Libertia

Libertias are not fully hardy and need a protective covering of mulch in winter and not in a damp site. They form large clumps with narrow, grassy foliage and spikes of white flowers followed by decorative seed pods. *Libertia grandiflora*, the New Zealand satin flower, grows to 80cm (32in) and flowers in

July and August; *Libertia formosa*, which comes from Chile, flowers a little earlier with ivory flowers; it can withstand short periods of -15°C (5°F). Libertia resembles *Sisyrinchium striatum*, but the flowers are not so well - distributed over the stems. This plant prefers well-drained, slightly acid soil.

Ligularia

These splendid plants need moist soil as the large-leaved types will otherwise soon wilt. A

Libertia grandiflora

Ligularia dentata

Ligularia przewalskii

Ligularia wilsoniana

windy day will have the same effect. The plants are at their best in a shadow border, or by the waterside. Apart from its large and decorative leaves, *Ligularia* also has beautiful flowers in shades of yellow and orange. The leaves and stems of some cultivars are dark in colour. Ligularias are impressive plants in themselves, but they are also very effective planted in groups, or a whole row of them along the waterside instead of the odd specimen. They would also look good in a moist, shady border. *Ligularia veitchiana* and *Ligularia wilsoniana* have large, coarse foliage,that of *Ligularia przewalskii* is finer. Some have dark leaves, including *Ligularia dentata* 'Desdemona' and 'Othello'. The height of these plants varies from 80cm (32in)

in *Ligularia dentata* - to 1.8m (5¹/2ft) in *Ligularia stenocephala* 'The Rocket'. The stems of this plant are dark in colour and the long, upright flower heads are yellow. *Ligularia x palmatiloba* has palmate, dissected leaves and large, showy flowers appearing a month earlier than the others, in July and August or August and September. These are strong, fully hardy plants.

Ligustrum

PRIVET

⚘ ☼ ○

The privet hedge is familiar to everyone, but it is not so well known that some species and

Ligustrum quihoui – flower

Ligustrum quihoui – berry

cultivars form lovely shrubs if they are allowed to grow freely. Florists often use the black berries in flower arrangements. 'Lydia' is one of the berried varieties used in public gardens. *Ligustrum obtusifolium* has the lovely, lower cultivars 'Dart's Dressing' and 'Dart's Spreader'. The common semi-evergreen *Ligustrum ovalifolium* has a silver variegated cultivar 'Argenteum' and the golden privet 'Aureum'. 'Dart's Golddust' has yellow and green leaves with a bronze-yellow sheen. *Ligustrum quihoui* is a specially beautiful semi-evergreen privet. The fresh, green leaves are joined by long, cream-white plumes of flowers in August and September, followed by black berries. Privet will grow anywhere, but it needs fertile soil to flower nicely.

Lilium

LELY

◇ ☼ ○

Lilies are to be found at a bulb grower's, not at a nursery for perennial plants. The flowers are usually available from florists, but they are still not a regular feature in most gardens. All the same, there are some lilies which combine well in a mixed border, between low shrubs, or in a border for perennial plants. The lilies with very large flowers could be used, such as the

Lilium 'Black Dragon'

Golden-rayed lily of Japan *Lilium auratum*, the Regal lily *Lilium regale* and hybrid-cultivars including 'Black Dragon', with trumpet-shaped white flowers, purplish-red on the outside, or the bright yellow 'Connecticut King',- but lilies with smaller flowers would be more suitable. *Lilium cernuum* is a beautiful,

Lilium 'Connecticut King'

Lilium martagon

low lily, 50cm (20in) with fragrant lilac pink flowers. Lilium henryi is a sturdy, tall lily, 1.5m (5ft) with yellow-orange flowers. *Lilium martagon*, also 1.5m (5ft) with bowed, purple flower heads of which the petals curve backwards, turkscap-style. *Lilium pumilum* is 50cm (20in) high with red flowers and recurving petals.The plants are fully hardy. The bulbs only last for a few years, but the plants seed themselves. There are many more suitable 'border' lilies, but the last one to be mentioned here is *Lilium speciosum*. This lily

Limonium sinuatum 'Market Grower's Light Blue'

is almost hardy and grows to 1.5m (5ft) with pink flowers and recurved petals with pink or red-spots. Lilies should be planted quite deeply, 8-10 cm (3-4in), preferably immediately after buying them as they are very vulnerable. The soil all round the lilies must also be well-loosened before planting as the one thing they do not tolerate is wet feet. The orange lily beetles and their voracious larvae can cause great damage by nipping flowers in the bud.

Limonium

SEA LAVENDER

The only true sea lavender must be the wild *Limonium vulgare*, of the salt marshes and sea embankments. This plant also has cultivated annual and perennial relatives. *Limonium sinuatum (Statice sinuata)* is a stiff plant in comparison with perennial sea lavenders. The straight, winged stalks bear

Limonium altaïcum 'Pioneer'

Limonium sinuatum

crests of tiny white, yellow, pink and purple papery flowers, good for drying. The less brightly-coloured, annual varieties of sea lavender, such as 'Apricot Beauty' and 'Market Grower's Light Blue' look good in the border. On the whole, the perennial *Limonium latifolium* is much prettier, the flower heads looser and just as easy to dry. The large leaves of this species form a rosette from which the stems emerge in July and August, 50 cm (20in) high, bearing large clusters of small, lilac-blue flowers. This species has several lovely cultivars including the blue 'Blauer Diamant', and 'Violetta', with violet-blue flowers. *Limonium altaïcum* 'Pioneer', a new *Limonium* from Japan, has silvery-blue flowers, eminently suitable for both the cut-flower trade and the garden. Sea lavender grows anywhere, by the sea and inland, as long as it has well-drained soil in a sunny spot.

Linaria

TOADFLAX

☀ ☼

Linaria vulgaris is the toadflax which grows in the wild on sandy soil, railway embankments and dry meadows. It used to have a blue

Linaria maroccana 'Fairy Bouquet'

Linaria maroccana 'Antique Silver'

Linaria purpurea

sister, *Linaria arvensis* which grew in the fields, but this has not been seen since1936. *Linaria maroccana*, the Moroccan toadflax, is much more striking and usually available in mixtures. 'Fairy Bouquet' and 'Northern Lights' are colourful mixtures of this kind. 'Antique Silver' is a silvery-white cultivar. The perennial toadflaxes, especially *Linaria purpurea* and its cultivars are favourite border plants. They often grow over 1m (3ft) high, with narrow, grey-green foliage and the species has long spires of purple-violet flowers from July into September. 'Canon J. Went' with pale pink flowers and 'Springside White' are good cultivars The plants seed themselves fairly satisfactorily.

Lower toadflaxes for the border are *Linaria x dominii* 'Carnforth', 60cm (2ft) high, with lilac-pink flowers, and 'Yuppie Surprise', 70cm (28in), with lilac flowers. The cultivar 'Kir Royal', 50 cm (20in), has large, lilac-pink flowers which do not set seed. These toad-flaxes are short-lived plants which propagate themselves. The soil should not be too rich and they prefer a sunny spot.

Lindheimera

STAR DAISY
☿ ☼

An annual plant from Texas, *Lindheimera* is not an uninteresting plant, but the genus consists of only one species, so there is little to tell. This species, *Lindheimera texana* has only one cultivar - 'Sunny Boy'- that we could find, but there may be more. It is an easy plant to grow and can be sown indoors in early spring, or outdoors later, on the spot. The large, star-shaped, yellow flowers appear throughout the summer and well into autumn, 70cm (28in) high. *Lindheimera* will grow in any well-drained soil, in full sun.

Linum

FLAX
☿ ✿ ☼

Linum usitatissimum, the true flax, 90cm (3ft) high, is grown for the manufacture of linen. It has tiny, pale blue flowers which turn into seed capsules. The cultivar 'Sutton's Blue' has slightly bigger, sky-blue flowers and the 'Common Flax' is azure; they are lower than the species. *Linum grandiflorum* has much larger flowers and the colourful cultivars are nothing like the humble blue flax. 'Bright Eyes' has large, white flowers with a red centre and 'Rubrum' has incredibly large red flowers. Blue is back in perennial flax, *Linum perenne*, short-lived but self-seeding. This type grows up to 60cm (2ft), the same height as the white cultivar 'Album'.

Liriope muscari

'Diamond' is white, only 25cm (6in) high, like the blue 'Saphir'. There are species which do not resemble common flax , including the yellow *Linum flavum*, 40cm (16in) and *L. dolomiticum*, 30cm (12in). To end with blue, there is *Linum narbonense*, 40cm (16in) high, a perennial plant producing large, sky-blue flowers over a long period. Flax likes sandy soil and sun.

Liriope

LILYTURF
✿ ○ ●

These peculiar plants resemble grasses until

Linum perenne

Linum grandiflorum

Lobelia × *gerardii* 'Rosenkavalier'

Lobelia × *speciosa* 'Fan Scarlet'

Lobelia siphilitica

suddenly, in August, fat little spikes of violet flowers emerge from its narrow, arching, glossy leaves. *Liriope muscari* is the most-grown species and it has several cultivars with various foliage or flower colours. 'Majestic' has lilac flowers, 'Variegata' has yellow-edged leaves. These are evergreen perennials sometimes used as edging plants. They can survive a temperature of -15°C (5°F) but it is best to cover them with a mulch in winter. They tolerate dry conditions but not wet feet and need well-drained soil.

Lobelia

Annual lobelias are usually better-known than the perennials. They are the familiar blue (or white) bedding plants which also grow well in pots and hanging baskets. Perennial lobelias look quite different, but a good look at the flowers reveals the similarity. They are not fully hardy and especially those with dark foliage should be protected with a thick layer of mulch in winter. *Lobelia fulgens* 'Queen Victoria' has red-brown foliage and bright red flowers, growing over 1m (3ft) high. *Lobelia x gerardii* 'Blue Knight' flowers from July into September; 'Rosenkavalier' has pink flowers and 'Vedrariensis' has purplish-violet flowers; all three are 1m (3ft) high. *Lobelia x speciosa* also has some lovely cultivars;they like very rich soil and need fortnightly dressings of manure if the soil is poor. 'Complexion' has apricot-pink flowers; 'Dark Crusader' has blood-red flowers in beautiful contrast with the dark red foliage; 'Pink Flamingo' has deep pink flowers, 'Fan Scarlet' bright red and 'Russian Princess' deep pink. 'Tania' is a hybrid-cultivar, 70 cm (28in) high with brown stems and dark red spikes. The foliage is orange-red when it begins to sprout, turning green later. *Lobelia siphilitica*, 70cm (28in), flowers in August and September with sapphire-blue flowers, fully hardy.

Lonicera

HONEYSUCKLE

We usually think of Lonicera as a climbing plant, but there are some non-climbing loniceras which do well in the border. The cultivars of *Lonicera nitida* are the most suitable, such as 'Baggesen's Gold', an evergreen shrub, 50cm (20in) with golden-yellow foliage in summer, bronze in winter. This small bush can light up a dark corner of a yellow border like a ray of sunshine. 'Maigrün' has a compact habit and glossy, green foliage; 'Red Tips' is a new cultivar with shining crimson leaves. *Lonicera korolkowii*, 2m (6ft) has blue-green foliage and pale pink flowers. *Lonicera fragrantissima* bears fragrant creamy -white flowers on leafless stems from January to March, followed by dark red

Lonicera pileata

Lunaria annua

Lunaria annua 'Variegata'

berries. *Lonicera pileata* is a small, evergreen shrub with beautiful cultivars including 'Moss Green' and 'Stockholm'.

Lunaria

HONESTY

The biennial honesty, *Lunaria annua* resembles a perennial, but it disproves this by contiually changing places. Fortunately honesty seeds itself freely, but if you want to be sure of having one in its place at all times, plant a perennial *Lunaria rediviva* in the border. Like its biennial relative, this plant will flower with pale lilac plumes, also followed by long, silver seed pods instead of the round ones of *Lunaria annua*. It seems that the perennial species was difficult to improve on - it has no cultivars. *Lunaria annua* has several, including 'Alba' with white flowers; 'Alba Variegata' has white flowers combined with white-variegated leaves; 'Variegata' with the same foliage and purple flowers; 'Munstead Purple' has purplish-violet flowers. Honesty does not like dry soil and prefers a spot in light shade or partial shade. The flowers of perennial honesty are fragrant, those of the biennial are not.

Lupinus

LUPIN
🕯 🕸 ⚘ ☼ ○

There are all kinds of lupins: annuals, peren-

Lupinus nanus 'Pixie Delight'

Lupinus 'Chandelier'

Lupinus in the border

nials and shrubs. The annual lupins begin to flower when the perennials have finished. *Lupinus luteus* is one of the annual species; its blooms are yellow and it grows in the wild in Italy. Sow the seed mixture 'Pixie Delight', a cultivar of *L. nanus*, and you will have low lupins, 30cm (12in) in shades of pink, white and blue. The familiar perennial garden lupin, *Lupinus polyphyllus*, has hybrid-cultivars in many colours: 'Chandelier' is golden-yellow; 'My Castle', aptly, brick-red; 'Noblemaiden', creamy-white; 'The Governor', blue with a white flag; 'The Pages', carmine; the well-known Russell-hybrids, in mixed colours. The Gallery series has lovely self-coloured, compact plants. This perennial lupin flowers fairly early, sometimes in May, usually in June and July. *Lupinus arboreus*, the Tree lupin, is a semi-evergreen shrub with beautiful, light green foliage and fragrant, yellow flowers. 'Snow Queen'; 'Golden Spire', and 'Mauve Queen are true to their colourful names. The plants need some protection in winter.

Luzula

WOODRUSH
🕸 ○ ◖

Luzula is an evergreen rush which likes the shade. The species itself, *Luzula nivea* 40cm (16in), or Snowy woodrush is beautiful and it has two even lovelier cultivars which wave their grassy wands and plumes in May and

Luzula nivea

Luzula luzuloides

'Tauernpass' forms large clumps of broad blades which are sensitive to the sun in winter; 'Wäldler' has narrower foliage and blooms early in April. These plants ensure that the border will go on looking attractive in the autumn and winter.

Lychnis

CUCKOOFLOWER

❀ ☼

There is hardly a genus with more common names, such as ragged robin and cuckooflower for *Lychnis flos-cuculi*, Jerusalem cross or Maltese cross for *Lychnis chalcdedonica*; and there are many more without common names, including *Lychnis x arkwrightii* 'Vesuvius', 30cm (12in) high, with striking brownish-red foliage and beautiful, matching orange-red flowers from July into August. The cultivars of *Lychnis chalcedonica*, the Jerusalem or Maltese cross, 80cm (32in), are not all as fiercely vermilion as the species. 'Alba' is almost white, and 'Carnea' has pale pink flowers. 'Plena' flowers longer than the type with bright red, double flowers. The true cuckooflower, *Lychnis flos-cuculi*, has fringed, pink flowers. 'Alba', 40cm (16in), is white and 'Nana', 10cm (4in), is pink. *Lychnis coronaria* has crimson flowers contrasting strongly with the hairy, grey foliage; 'Alba' is a pure white variety. Lychnis viscaria has pink

Lychnis viscaria 'Splendens'

June. 'Schattenkind', 50cm (20in) forms wide clumps with narrow blades and 'Schneehäschen', 70cm (28in) has white-haired foliage and white flower spikes. *Luzula luzuloides*, the White woodrush is becoming rare in the wild, it is sometimes seen on old estates. *Luzula sylvatica*, the Greater woodrush is also rare, except in some southern areas. It is an endangered species almost everywhere, but it has several lovely cultivars: 'Ausleze' 35cm (14in), with broad leaves and brown flower spikes in May and June; 'Hohe Tatra' 50cm (20in) also has broad blades and loose clusters of flower spikes; 'Marginata' has yellow-edged leaves at first, later white-edged;

Lychnis coronaria 'Alba'

Lychnis chalcedonica

and white cultivars, including 'Plena' with double, magenta flowers, 'Schnee' is white and 'Splendens' has large, bright red flowers. All these plants are useful in a sunny spot in

Lysimachia clethroides

the border, in fertile soil.

Lysimachia

LOOSESTRIFE

Lysimachias are plants for moist soil and natural borders The familiar Garden loosestrife, *Lysimachia punctata*, 70cm (28in), can become a nuisance in a neat border by growing

Lysimachia fortunei

Lysimachia ciliata

Lythrum salicaria 'Morden Pink'

rampant, if the conditions are to its liking. Lysimachia ciliata is more modest, though also inclined to spread. This plant is 70cm (28in) high, with light brown foliage in spring, blooming with pale yellow flowers. Its lovely cultivars are: 'Firecracker', with really chocolate-coloured leaves and lemon-yellow flowers and 'Purpurea', with deep purple foliage and pale yellow flowers. *Lysimachia fortunei* 70cm (28in) flowers from July into September with white, upright spikes of flowers. *Lysimachia clethroides*, 80cm (32in) seems only to exist in bouquets, but it also does well in the garden - sometimes too well. We should not grumble if such a beautiful plant grows a little rampant. The elegant white, completely horizontal spikes of flowers have nothing in common with the loud yellow flowers of the country bumpkin, *Lysimachia*

punctata. Lysimachia ephemerum, 90cm (3ft) has grey-green foliage and long, upright spikes of white flowers. This plant needs protection in winter as it is not fully hardy. It is one of the loveliest loosestrifes and does not grow rampant. Lysimachias are generally easy to grow.

Lythrum

PURPLE LOOSESTRIFE

Lythrum salicaria is a native of the water-sides, peat bogs, marshes and reed-lands. Its cultivars are at home by a pond and in the border too, because they also grow well in dry soil. The characteristic lilac-pink shade of Purple loosestrife returns in almost all the cultivars, except in 'Blush', which is pale pink; 'Feuerkerze' ('Firecandle') has deep pink spikes of flowers; 'Happy' is red; 'Lady Sackville' purplish-pink; 'Morden Pink' a clear pink; 'Zigeunerblut' dark red, is also the tallest, 1.2m (4ft). The rest are 80cm (32in) high, except for 'Happy', which is 60cm (2ft) high. The seedlings of these cultivars are not stable. *Lythrum virgatum*, 1.2m (4ft) is more elegant and finer than *Lythrum salicaria* and the lilac-pink flowers are on arching stems. The cultivar 'Dropmore Purple', 1m (3ft) high is crimson. Purple loosestrife flowers for months on end with beautiful autumn colours as a bonus.

Lythrum salicaria 'Feuerkerze'

Macleaya cordata

Macleaya

PLUME POPPY

This is an imposing plant, 2-3m (6-9ft) tall, suitable for a high border. It tends to spread alarmingly, forewarned is forearmed. *Macleaya cordata* is less guilty of this than *Macleaya microcarpa*. Plume poppies are attractive because of their grey-green, deeply lobed leaves and their plumes of flowers. Macleaya cordata has pale pink plumes, its cultivar 'Flamingo' has pink plumes and those of *Macleaya microcarpa* 'Kelway's Coral Plume' are coral pink. They need fertile, well-drained soil. A group of macleayas in a lawn can be splendid, and the spreading growth can be kept within bounds by mowing away the surplus.

A clump of this plant in the border can be curbed in spring by removing the shoots. They can be planted to form a row in a strip between the house and a path, where the wall and the path will prevent its spreading.

Macleaya with *Crocosmia*

Mahonia

The *Mahonia* is usually seen as a prickly bush planted in public gardens to discourage dogs and children. This is very effective, as *Mahonia aquifolium*, the Oregon grape and its many cultivars form excellent ground cover. A particularly lovely one is the cultivar 'Green Ripple', 1m (3ft) high with glossy green foliage turning dark brown in winter with yellow flowers in April. The foliage of this cultivar is often used for cutting. *Mahonia bealei* is a decorative shrub, 1.5m (5ft) high with compound leaves, 40cm (16in) long, above which the upright, pale yellow plumes of flowers, (15cm-6in) can be seen in December and January. The fruits are blue-green. The shrub is more elegant than its unbending, leathery foliage suggests.

Mahonia bealei 'Hivernant'

Mahonia × wagneri 'Fireflame'

The leaves of *Mahonia bealei* 'Hivernant' (Mahonia japonica 'Hiemalis') can grow to a length of 50cm (20in). *Mahonia x media* 'Charity', 2m (6ft) has even longer foliage, up to 60cm (2ft) with upright spikes of flowers 40cm (16in) long, flowering in December and January. This *Mahonia* may not survive during severe frost as it is not fully hardy. 'Buckland' and 'Winter Sun' are also splendid, but not reliably hardy. *Mahonia wagneri* 'Fireflame' is a wide shrub with blue-green foliage, taking on a bronze hue in winter. The cultivars of *Mahonia aquifolium* need hard pruning after flowering to promote fresh young growth in the shrub. The other mahonias do not need this treatment. They will grow in any soil, in sun or shade.

Maianthemum bifolium

Maianthemum

MAY LILY
❀ ○ ◑

This magnificent ground-covering plant grows in deciduous woods and on wooded banks. The sprays of white, star-shaped flowers of this may lily, *Maianthemum bifolium*, are followed by red berries. Plants situated in acid soil will produce many berries, while there will be hardly any on those in limy soil. The plant is also known as the 'false lily of the valley', which it resembles in its habit. *Maianthemum canadense* has large, glossy leaves, slightly narrower and with shorter stems than *Maianthemum bifolium*, but with the same sprays of white flowers and red berries. The may lily forms good ground covering in a wood, natural garden or shrub border. The plants may spread if the conditions suit them; they prefer light, acid soil, rich in humus and they dislike wet feet.

Malope

⚲ ☼

Malope trifida is an annual plant, a little like *Lavatera*, but less stiff and it is stronger. It forms nicely branched shrubs, 1-1.5m (3-5ft) high. The petals of Malope grow narrower at the base so that the green of the calyx shines through them. The seed is available in mixtures of white, pink and red, but also self-coloured as in 'White Queen', 'Pink Queen' and 'Red Queen' They combine well in the perennial border.

Malva

MALLOW
⚲ ❀ ☼

Malva includes annuals and perennials, most of them perennials. These behave like annuals in that they flower during the same year that they are sown. *Malva alcea*, the quinate mallow, with pink flowers has become rarer in the wild, but its population is stable at present.

The plant is suitable for a wild border, but it seeds itself everywhere. 'Fastigiata' has deep pink flowers on upright spikes, 1m (3ft) high. *Malva moschata*, the musk mallow is quite widespread in the wild and has naturalized in some areas. This decorative plant with large, bright pink flowers has a white cultivar, 'Alba', with more deeply-divided leaves, 60cm

Malva moschata

Malva sylvestris 'Primley Blue'

Malva moschata 'Alba'

(2ft) high, like the species. *Malva sylvestris* also grows in the wild on banks, verges and dikes. A familiar, mauve-blue cultivar is 'Primley Blue' 50cm (20in), which needs protective covering in winter as it is not fully hardy.

Marrubium

HOREHOUND
✿ ☼

The true horehound, *Marrubium vulgare* has become very rare in the wild and may soon disappear altogether. Fortunately it has relatives which are sold as garden plants by nurseries where they are valued for their grey foliage. This plant is very acceptable as an alternative for *Ballota acetabulosa*. *Marrubium cylleneum*, 30cm (12in), a pot plant, not hardy, comes from Greece and Albania, *Marrubium incanum* from Italy and the Balkans, *Marrubium supinum* from Spain and *Marrubium velutinum* from northern and central Greece. The latter is a little higher, 50cm (20in) and is most often grown. The small flowers are insignificant.

Marrubiums need full sun and well-drained soil which must never be sodden in winter. In spite of all the care and attention given to them, they are often frozen.

Matteuccia

OSTRICH FERN
✿ ○ ◐

Matteuccia struthiopteris, originally from Central Europe, is often seen in gardens and has also become naturalized as though it were a native - a sure sign that the climate suits it.

The plant, 1m (3ft) high, has sterile, fresh green fronds which die off in winter, but the dark brown, fertile fronds appearing in the centre can survive the winter.
The fronds of this fern form a beaker and its creeping rhizomes can spread far and wide. *Matteuccia pensylvanica* does not spread so quickly. This species from North America is

Matthiola in the border

smaller, 60cm (2ft). Both these ferns are easy to grow, at home in the shade and in moisture-retentive soil.

Matthiola

STOCK
î îî ☼

Stocks are familiar mainly as very fragrant cut flowers.
They are grown for flower shows, and competitions, especially in England. Many biennial stocks are grown as annuals and sold as stiff bedding plants in mixed colours.

Matthiola incana 'Bavaria White' has pure white flowers, 80cm (32in) high; 'Cinderella Lavender', with lavender-blue flowers is small, 20cm (8in).

Self-coloured stocks will combine better in the border than mixed colours. If you only want to enjoy the scent, then sow *Matthiola longi-petala (Matthiola bicornis)* in the border, an annual with inconspicuous flowers.

This is the night-scented stock, so delicious in the evenings.

Matthiola in a flower bed

Meconopsis cambrica

Meconopsis

BLUE POPPY

Meconopsis betonicifolia is the blue poppy most likely to succeed if you feel you have to try one in your garden, whatever everyone says. This one has the best chance of taking and returning, with luck. Once you have seen this unusual, sky-blue poppy you will want it in your own garden. The striking blue colour makes it difficult to combine in the border. It can grow up to 1m (3ft) in the right conditions

Meconopsis betonicifolia

Meconopsis grandis

- sandy soil, rich in humus, moisture-retentive, but not wet in winter. It needs a cool and shady spot, with some protection in winter, not of mulch or branches, but preferably under glass or a cloche.

Melittis melissophyllum

Mertensia echioides

Mertensia virginica

Meconopsis grandis, can grow over 1m (3ft) high, an imposing figure with the same, characteristic blue colour. For those with the right conditions who welcome the challenge of growing difficult plants, there are many more species, in yellow, orange, red and white. *Meconopsis cambrica* 'Welsh Poppy', 50cm (20in), is easy to grow, seeding itself freely. This cheerful 'poppy' combines well in a natural border and will spill over onto the terrace without a by-your-leave, but once you have it in your garden it is there to stay. 'Frances Perry' is a red cultivar.

Melittis

BASTARD BALM

This labiate relation of the *Lamium* grows wild in central and southern Europe. It is a sturdy plant, 50cm (20in) high with white flowers and a purple lower lip. The colour of the flowers is variable in the wild, some species have all-purple, pink or white flowers; for this reason a number of subspecies have been defined. *Melittis melissophyllum* flowers in May or June; it prefers a spot in light shade and limy soil rich in humus.

Mertensia

Mertensia virginica, 50cm (20in) is the most often-grown species of *Mertensia*. The flowers in the bud are pink, when open they are a shining blue which means that they are related to the *Pulmonaria*. The leaves are blue-green and the plant flowers very early, in April or

May. After flowering the whole plant dies off above ground. The vacancy in the border then needs filling with other plants. Many people assume that the plant is dead when it dies off, but it turns up again happily the following spring. Not all mertensias do this; *Mertensia echoides*, 50cm (20in) flowers later, from May into July with sky-blue flowers and blue-grey leaves. *Mertensia pterocarpa*, 35cm (14in), flowers in May and June with gentian-blue flowers. It is really a low form of the very variable species in the wild, *Mertensia sibirica*, 50cm (20in), which also flowers in May and June, with sky-blue flowers.
Finally, *Mertensia simplicissima* (*M. asiatica*, 20cm -8in), with blue foliage and azure

Mimulus in the border

Mimulus 'Orange Glow'

flowers which loves a sunny spot, in contrast with other mertensias. Most mertensias prefer a cool position in partial shade and soil rich in humus.

Meum

Meum athamanticum or Baldmoney, or Spignel is the only species of this genus. It is a fragrant plant with fine, light green, fern-like foliage, flowering in May and June with heads of tiny white flowers. It is a good plant for a natural border and will grow in any good garden soil in the sun.

Milium

Milium effusum 'Aureum' is the cultivar of the wild Wood millet (Milium effusum); it has greenish-yellow foliage, stems and flower heads. Milium suffers from scorching in bright sunlight. The flower head is a large plume which brings the height of this grass up to 80cm (32in).

Mimulus

MONKEY MUSK

The flowers of monkey-faced Mimulus often look so garish that they are difficult to combine in the border. But there are various hybrid-cultivars with such lovely colours that they deserve a place in the border. For instance, 'Andean Nymph', 25cm (10in) high,

Mimulus aurantiacus

with pink and cream-white flowers which will bloom a second time if you cut them back after their first flowering. The plants will cover the ground in a moist, sunny to partially -shaded situation. 'Wisley Red' has dark carmine flowers; 'Bees Major', yellow spotted with brown-red; 'Orange Glow', pure orange; 'Bees Scarlet', a dark orange-red; 'Shep', yellow spotted with brown. All the cultivars mentioned are hardy, with reservations. Mimulus aurantiacus is a sub-shrub, 60cm (2ft) high with orange flowers, sometimes

planted in a hanging basket. Mimulus is not always fully hardy and it is often grown as an annual for that reason.

Mirabilis

FOUR O'CLOCK FLOWER
MARVEL OF PERU

ⓘ ⊗ ☼

Mirabilis jalapa is a perennial plant, but it is always grown as an annual. If the temperature does not fall below -5°C (23°F), the tuberous roots will survive. These tubers resemble

Mirabilis jalapa, red and yellow

dahlias and can also be brought indoors for the winter, but they are usually sown every year. The flowers of the Four o'clock flower open around tea-time, very fragrantly, to attract moths. The flowers can be pink, red, yellow and white; The strange thing is that these different colours can all appear on one plant. "It is a miracle", sighed Linnaeus, and that was how the plant came by its botanical name. This old-fashioned plant is in fashion again.

Miscanthus

⊗ ☼

The cultivars of *Miscanthus sinensis* decorate the summer with their foliage and plumes of flowers, followed by their ornamental frosted outlines in winter. 'Ferner Osten' (2m - 6ft , September/November) has narrow blades, loose spikelets of flowers and wonderful autumn colours; 'Flamingo' (1.8m - 5½ft, August/ October) has pink, arching spikelets of flowers; 'Flammenmeer' (1.8m, August/ October) is known for its autumn colouring; 'Goliath' (3m - 9ft, September/ November) is true to its name with impressive plumes of flowers, suitable for a hedge; 'Gracillimus' (1.2m - 4ft) is a *Miscanthus* which does not flower, with narrow leaves; 'Graziella' (1.5m - 5ft) has narrow leaves and silvery-pink spikelets of flowers. The following will grow in heavy soil: 'Grosse Fontäne' (2.5m - 8ft, July/Oct), a robust plant with a wide spread and red-bron spikes of flowers; 'Kaskade' (2m - 6ft, September/November), with arching stems and pink plumes turning white; 'Kleine Fontäne' (1.8m - $5^1/2$ft, July/October); 'Kleine Silberspinne' (1.6m - $5^1/2$ft, August/October); 'Malepartus' (2m - 6ft, August/October), with golden-brown plumes of flowers, turning silver; 'Morning Light' (1.6m), with variegated leaves; 'Pünktchen' (2m - 6ft, September/October), with golden-yellow striped foliage and red-brown spikes of flowers; 'Roland' (2.5m - 8ft, September/October), with arching plumes of flowers; 'Rotfuchs' (2.2m - $6^1/2$ft, September/October), with red-brown plumes of flowers; 'Samurai' (2m - 6ft, September/October), with brown-red plumes and yellow colouring in the autumn; 'Silberpfeil' (1.5m - 5ft, September/October), with white variegated leaves; 'Silberspinne' (2m - 6ft, September/November), with brown plumes of flowers; 'Silberturm' (2.5m - 8ft, August/October), a genuine 'silver tower' in winter; 'Sirene' (2.5m), with brown-red plumes; 'Undine' (2.2m - $6^1/2$ft), with silvery plumes of flowers; 'Zebrinus', with horizontal white or yellow stripes on the leaves. Nearly all of these

Miscanthus sinensis 'Rotfuchs'

Miscanthus sinensis 'Gracillimus'

Miscanthus sinensis 'Zebrinus'

Molinia caerulea 'Moorhexe'

Molinia caerulea 'Variegata'

Molucella laevis

cultivars make excellent specimens and the lower ones are very good border plants. They all love the sun.

Molinia

Molinia caerulea is one of those native grasses that we take for granted, but we can use it, or one of the cultivars in the border. The species grows up to 60cm (2ft) high, flowers from July into October and seeds itself freely. It has stunning autumn colouring which all its cultivars have inherited. 'Dauerstrahl' (90cm - 3ft, July/October) is a sturdy plant with upright, dark spikes of flowers; 'Heidebraut' (1.2m - 4ft, July/October) with loose spikelets; 'Moorhexe' (70cm - 28in, July/October) has dark spikes; 'Overdam' (60cm - 2ft, July/October) has fine blades; 'Variegata' has dark green with cream-white striped leaves. *Molinia arundinacea* also has some lovely cultivars: 'Fontäne' (1.8m - 5^1/2ft, July/October) with arching spikes; 'Karl Foerster' (2.2m - 6^1/2ft, July/October) upright; 'Transparent' (2.2m, July/October), most suitable for the border with its loose spikelets;

Molucella laevis

'Windspiel' (1.5m - 5ft, August/October), with arching spikes, turning yellow in the autumn.

Moluccella

BELLS OF IRELAND

⚲ ✾ ☼

This annual plant, 60cm (2ft) high, has three lives: as a border plant, a cut-flower and a dried flower. The inconspicuous little pink flowers are surrounded by striking, bell-shaped green calyxes. *Moluccella Laevis*, the Bells of Ireland or Shell flower, can be sown and brought on under glass or in the border. The plant combines well with perennial plants and prefers a sunny spot.

Monarda

BERGAMOT

⚲ ✾ ☼

Monarda citriodora is an annual bergamot, a native of central and southern USA with the scent of lemons as its name suggests, sometimes called 'lemon mint'. *Monarda didyma* or bee balm, has many cultivars with

Monarda 'Balance'

Monarda 'Fishes'

hooded flowers forming jolly mopheads in their calyxes. These plants used to have a bad reputation for their sensitivity to mildew. There are many new hybrid-cultivars which are less, or not at all sensitive to mildew. The Dutch grower Piet Oudolf has selected and introduced healthy hybrid-cultivars in several colours. Monardas are tall plants, from 80cm (32in) to 1.6m (5$\frac{1}{2}$ft), very useful in the border. They need good soil, moisture-retentive but not too wet and full sun. The pink monardas are: 'Balance', 1.2m (4ft) pink with brownish -pink calyxes; 'Beauty of Cobham' 1.2m, bright pink with red calyxes; 'Blaustrumpf', 1.2m, purplish-pink; 'Cherokee', 1.6m (5$\frac{1}{2}$ft), pink with pinkish-brown calyxes; 'Comanche', 1.8m (5$\frac{1}{2}$ft), pink with red calyxes; 'Fishes', 1m (3ft), pale pink with light green calyxes, one of the loveliest according to Piet Oudolf; 'Ou' or 'Oudolf's Charm', 80cm (32in), pale pink with dark red calyxes; 'Pawnee', 1.7m (5$\frac{1}{2}$ft), pink-lilac with green calyxes; 'Talud' 1.2m (4ft), reddish-pink. The following are red monardas: 'Purple Anne' 1.2m (4ft), crimson flowers and calyxes; 'Squaw' 1.2m, bright red, a good alternative for 'Cambridge Scarlet' which is sensitive to mildew. Violet monardas are as follows: 'Scorpion' 1.4m (4$\frac{1}{2}$ft), violet with dark calyxes; 'Aquarius' 1.3m (4$\frac{1}{2}$ft), violet, in layers.

Lilac-coloured monardas are: 'Chippawa' 90cm (3ft), pale lilac with a light green centre; 'Elsie's Lavender' 1.4m (4$\frac{1}{2}$ft), lavender-blue

Monarda 'Mohawk'

with green calyxes; 'Mohawk', lilac-pink with dark calyxes. There is a purple monarda called the 'Kardinal', 1.2m (4ft) because it resembles a cardinal's hat when in the bud. Finally there are the white monardas: 'Sioux' 1.6m (5^1/2ft) white with a touch of lilac and light green calyxes; 'Snow queen', white with lilac - this plant is unusual for a white monarda in that it is not susceptible to mildew.

Myosotis

FORGET-ME-NOT

Forget-me-nots are usually grown as biennial plants. The true garden forget-me-not, *Myosotis sylvatica* has the cultivars 'Blue Ball, 'Pink Ball' and 'White Ball', all 15cm (6in) high. The higher cultivars 'Blue Giant', 40cm (16in) and 'Blue Basket', 30cm (12in) are also good cutting flowers. *Myosotis sylvatica* of the woods still grows in the wild, or naturalized.

They are grown as biennials because they are short-lived perennial plants. If they are sown

Myosotis sylvatica

in June, they flower early in the following spring. Forget-me-nots and tulips are a lovely combination in the border, so are forget-me-nots and camassias. They grow best in moist soil and they need plants to succeed them after flowering.

Myosortis, pink and blue

Nectaroscordum siculum subsp. *bulgaricum*

Nemesia 'Danish Flag'

Nectaroscordum siculum subsp. *bulgaricum*

Nectaroscordum

○ ⚘ ○

Nectaroscordum siculum subsp. *bulgaricum* is a flowering bulb that was called *Allium* for a long time. The plant smells strongly of onion and its habit is similar. The strong stems are 80cm -1m ($2^1/2$-3ft) tall, bearing twenty to thirty drooping, green flowers flushed with purple and with a cream-white edge, or the flowers may be purple tinged with green. A good colour combination in general for the border. Honeybees and bumblebees love these plants, which are still attractive after flowering in May and June, as they have lovely seed pods, good for drying and flower arrangements. Plant plenty of the bulbs together so that they form a harmonious group. They will grow in any soil, in sun or shade. They need well-drained soil, especially in winter, otherwise the bulbs may rot and the pleasure they give will be short-lived.

Nicotiana sylvestris

219

Nemesia fruticans

Nemophila menziesii

Nemesia 'Carnival Mixed'

between *Nemesia fruticans* and a *Linaria;* research on this is underway. These plants are perennials, but they are grown as annuals because they are not hardy. They flower so brightly in the border and they look lovely if they are self-coloured. A mixture is difficult to combine, except perhaps 'Pastel Shades', a mixture of quiet colours.

Nemophila

⚲ ☼ ○

A very pretty little annual plant. *Nemophila menziesii*, known as Baby blue-eyes, 25cm (10in), flowers long, with sky-blue flowers. *Nemophila menziesii* 'Atomaria' 15cm (6in), has white flowers with black spots, (also available as var. atromaria or 'Snowstorm').

Nemophila menziesii 'Discoidalis' looks wonderful, with near-black flowers edged with white (also available as var. *discoidalis* or 'Penny Black').

Nemophila menziesii 'Atomaria'

Nemesia

⚲ ☼

Nemesia, 'the wild snapdragons' of South Africa, belong in every South African garden in springtime, according to the South African professor Kristo Pienaar. The seed of the original wild *Nemesia versicolor* was brought to England years ago where the plants were improved and new cultivars became available. These found their way back to South Africa, where the people now enjoy their own improved plants from England. Nemesias can be very colourful, red-and-white or blue-and-white, but there are also self-coloured nemesias, or more subdued, matching colours available. There is a perennial *Nemesia*, often confused with *Diascia*, called *Nemesia fruticans*. The cultivar 'Innocence' is white and 'Joan Wilder' is lilac-pink. Joan Wilder herself thinks that this cultivar is a cross

220

Nemophila maculata

Nepeta sibirica

The white petals of *Nemophila maculata* are tipped with purple, hence the name 'Five-spot baby'. These babies grow in the sun or light shade.

Nepeta

CATMINT

There is something about nepetas which causes growers to select and introduce new cultivars. *Nepeta racemosa* 'Grog', 35cm (14in), like all catmint needs full sun, it has lemon-scented foliage and bluish-purple

Nepeta grandiflora 'Dawn to Dusk'

flowers blooming freely in May, with a second flowering in the autumn. *Nepeta grandiflora* 'Dawn to Dusk' has pink flowers, grey-green foliage and is 1m (3ft) high. *Nepeta nuda* 'Anne's Choice' grows up to 1.2m (4ft) with big clusters of pinkish-blue flowers. *Nepeta x faassenii* has several familiar, very beautiful cultivars: 'Superba', 30cm (12in) lovely purplish-blue flowers; 'Snowflake', white tinged with blue; 'Walker's Low' 60cm (2ft), a familiar, good edging plant for the border. These cultivars are sometimes classed with *Nepeta racemosa* in the catalogues and there is some difference of opinion on this. It is best to go by the cultivar names to be sure of the right plants, as most of the new cultivars belong to this species. *Nepeta govaniana* is an unusual catmint with yellow flowers instead of blue, 1m (3ft) or higher. This nepeta differs from the others in preferring moist soil in the shade; it has sweet-scented foliage. *Nepeta subsessilis* grows up to 70cm (28in) with bluish-purple flowers. *Nepeta nervosa*, 30cm (12in) flowers with dense blue spikes. *Nepeta clarkei*, 50cm (20in) has blue flowers with a white lip, flowering for only two months in June and July, in contrast with most nepetas which flower from July into September. They should be pruned in spring and cut back after flowering. *Nepeta sibirica* (*Dracocephalum sibiricum*) is a magnificent and imposing plant, like *Nepeta x faassenii* seen through a magnifying glass. The species takes up more space and is slightly higher than the cultivar 'Souvenir d'André Chaudron' ('Blue Beauty'). The true 'Souvenir d 'André Chaudron' is much lower, 35cm (14in) and hardly spreads at all. Seedlings sold under this name are usually identical to *Nepeta sibirica*. Nepeta is not called catmint in vain; cats love it, especially *Nepeta x faassenii*. They can ruin the plants completely by sitting on them

Nepeta nervosa

or rolling about in them. A plaything filled with catmint is always a huge success with cats.

Nicandra

♀ ☼

A sturdy, branching annual, grows up to 1m (3ft) or more. Bell-shaped, blue flowers appear in late summer or early autumn, only opening for a few hours in the afternoon. Nicandra is usually grown for its fruits, hidden in miniature Chinese lanterns, good for drying. Nicandra is suitable for a natural border where it will seed itself freely. The plant is not

Nicandra physaloides

to be trusted as it is related to the potato; it should be planted in a spot where small children cannot reach it. It does not need staking, in spite of its height. The only species, *Nicandra physaloides*, has a number of cultivars: 'Alba', white petals and 'Violacea', with bluish-white petals. 'Black Pod' is a fictitious cultivar, the species is sold under this name.

Nicotiana

TOBACCO PLANT

♀ ☼ ○

Nicotianas are among the loveliest plants for the border. The modest *Nicotiana langsdorfii* with the lime-green, drooping bells can grow up to 1m (3ft), combining well with everything. *Nicotiana sylvestris*, or Flowering tobacco grows up to 1.5m (5ft), with large clusters of pure white, arching flowers, sweet-scented at night. *Nicotiana glutinosa* has salmon-pink, beige flowers and blue-green, heart-shaped leaves. The white, pendent flowers of *Nicotiana alata* 'Grandiflora' are fragrant at night. *Nicotiana x sanderae* 'Lime Green', is

Nicotiana 'Promenade Lime' and 'Promenade Red'

Nicotiana langsdorfii

lower. There are more hybrid-cultivars in white, red or pink. Flowering tobacco is related to the true tobacco and it follows that all the plants are just as poisonous. It would be more dangerous to smoke the tobacco leaves in their natural state as they are usually treated beforehand.

Nigella

♀ ✿

The loveliest of these is *Nigella damacena*, the common blue Love-in-a-mist. Of course there are some good cultivars: 'Cambridge Blue', light blue, 'Oxford Blue', dark blue and 'Albion', white. 'Mulberry Rose' and 'Red Jewel' are for those who prefer pink.

'Miss Jekyll Hybriden' is a mixture of semi-double white, pink and blue flowers.

Gertrude Jekyll loved these flowers and sowed them freely in her borders. 'Persian Jewels' is a mixture of white, pink, red and purple. *Nigella hispanica* has larger flowers than *N. damascena*, but fewer of them.

The stamens of flowers of this species are striking and there are some cultivars.

Nigella orientalis has yellow flowers and unusual seed capsules which can be bent over when ripe; ('Transformer' is another name for

Nigella damascena 'Albion'

Nigella damascena 'Mulberry Rose'

the species, not a cultivar). All nigellas flower from July into September, followed by lovely seed capsules, excellent for drying.

Nigella damascena

Oenothera fruticosa subsp. *glauca*

Oenothera speciosa

Oenothera

EVENING PRIMROSE

♀ ♊ ✿ ☼

The cultivars of *Oenothera fruticosa* are more suitable for a wild garden. They are 50 -80cm (20 -32in) high, flowering freely from June into August; these are not tidy plants. 'Fyrverkeri' has bright yellow flowers and deep red buds, like 'Hohes Licht', which is slightly higher; 'Glaber' has brown-red foliage, yellow flowers and red buds; 'Yellow River', green buds, red stems and yellow flowers; 'W. Cuthbertson' has red buds and yellow flowers. *Oenothera fruticosa* subsp. *glauca (Oenothera tetragona)* has broader leaves. There is a large, biennial evening primrose, *Oenothera glazioviana (Oenothera erythrosepala)* 1.5m (5ft),

Osmunda regalis

of which the flowers open at night, to attract moths. *Oenothera speciosa* is the odd man out as it does not have yellow flowers. The flowers of the species are white or pink, or they turn pink later. 'Rosea', is lower and has pink flowers, Evening primroses love full sun and well-drained soil, preferably fairly dry.

Omphalodes

♀ ♊ ✿ ☼ ○

The annual *Omphalodes linifolia*, or Venus's navelwort, resembles a white forget-me-not with grey leaves. This plant is 20 - 30 cm (8-12in) high and can be sown directly in the border where it will seed itself. The *perennial Omphalodes* fits in any border, in the role of a

Omphalodes cappadocica

Omphalodes verna

Onopordum in de border

Onopordum nervosum

perennial forget-me-not. *Omphalodes cappa-docica* is a splendid plant with small blue flowers, hardy in mild winters. The cultivar 'Cherry Ingram' ('Ingram's Form') is even more intensely blue and 'Starry Eyes', 30cm (12in) has different, white-edged blue flowers.The modest *Omphalodes verna* does not flower so profusely. 'Grandiflora' has larger flowers, so that it seems to flower more freely. 'Alba' flowers in May and April, like the other cultivars. The perennial *Omphalodes* needs humus-rich soil and light shade; the annual loves the sun.

Onopordum

SCOTCH THISTLE

Perennial plants, reaching 2m (6ft) or more, easily. They form a grey rosette during the first year, from which an imposing, grey-leaved plant grows higher and higher. *Onopordum acanthium*, the Cotton thistle or Scotch

thistle grows in the wild in dry and sunny areas and sand dunes, but it is quite rare. It is grown widely as an ornamental plant, traditionally in the vegetable garden.

Onopordum nervosum (*O. arabicum*), is most often grown, with magenta flowers and larger, spiny foliage. If you would like a few of these plants in your border, it is best to remove the dead flower heads thoroughly as the plants seed themselves with gusto, but leave a few as this biennial plant will die after flowering. The plants like good, slightly chalky soil.

Ophiopogon

These members of the lily family are grown for their foliage, the flowers are inconspicuous. *Ophiopogon jaburan* has dark green, fairly wide, grassy leaves and white clusters of flowers. This species is very strong, although it is often labelled 'not fully hardy'. Cultivars with variegated leaves are most often grown, including 'Vittatus', with light green-striped foliage and a cream-white edge.
This plant is sensitive to frost. *Ophiopogon*

japonicus and *O. planiscapus* are hardier and more often grown. It is also a good waterplant, but will not flower in that case. The common or garden species has dark green foliage and white to pale lilac clusters of flowers.

There are a few very compact cultivars, more suitable for the rock garden than the border. *Ophiopogon planiscapus* 'Nigrescens' ('Niger') 25cm, (10in) with dark purple-black foliage and white clusters of flowers tinged with pink to lilac in May and June, followed by black berries. If the plant seeds itself, the seedlings will not all have this dark foliage.

The plant is often used to edge the border or as ground cover under shrubs. It needs well-drained soil and plenty of moisture during the growing season.

Ophiopogon planiscapus 'Nigrescens'

Ophiopogon planiscapus 'Nigrescens' and *Salvia officinalis* 'Purpurascens'

Origanum laevigatum 'Herrenhausen'

Origanum

DITTANY

❀ ⚲ ☼

Origanum is not only suitable for the herb garden. There are species and cultivars which do very well in the border. *Origanum laevigatum* is one of them, 40cm (16in) high, a branched plant with small, grey-blue foliage and mauve flowers; it has some fine cultivars: 'Herrenhausen', 50cm (20in) has lilac flowers, a stunning combination with its deep purple bracts. 'Hopleys', 70cm (29in), not fully hardy, needs protection in winter. *Origanum* 'Ernetank' (*O. x hybridum*), 50cm (20in) has strongly branched spikes covered with tiny lilac-pink flowers. The hybrid-cultivar 'Rosenkuppel' is a robust plant, 70cm (28in) high with the same colouring. 'Rotkugel' is a smaller version of the same plant, 40cm (16in). *Origanum vulgare*, or Wild marjoram has some yellow-leaved cultivars including 'Aureum' and 'Thumble's Variety'. The first needs light shade as its foliage may otherwise be scorched; The leaves of the second are bigger and will not scorch. *Origanum vulgare* 'Snow Storm', 50cm (20in) was a seedling which appeared unexpectedly in a garden. This marjoram flowers from July until the end of September with silvery-white flowers

Origanum 'Rosenkuppel'

without seeding itself. The nice thing about marjoram is that the flowers attract hundreds of insects, including butterflies and the leaves can be dried. Its hybrid-cultivars are not so aromatic.

Osmanthus

🌿 ☼ ○

Osmanthus x burkwoodii is an evergreen shrub, a little like holly but no relation. It grows up to 2.5m (8ft), with narrow, leathery foliage and white, fragrant flowers in April and May. *Osmanthus decorus* is wider than it is

high (2.5m - 8ft), with less striking flowers than *O. x burkwoodii;* it is planted mainly for its evergreen foliage and dome-shaped habit. *Osmanthus heterophyllus* is a shrub 2m (6ft) high with spiny leaves like holly. Its sweet-scented flowers appear in September. The leaves are opposite, those of holly are scattered. The cultivar 'Aureomarginatus' has yellow-edged leaves; those of 'Goshiki' are white, flecked with grey and bronze when in the sun. These evergreens are tolerant and will grow in any soil.

Osmunda

ROYAL FERN
🌼 ○ ● ☼

Osmunda regalis, the Royal fern is a regal figure. It is not often seen in the wild and is now protected. Orchids and other epiphytes used to be grown on its roots.The smooth light green, divided fronds and the decorative spore-bearing flower spikes can grow up to 2m (6ft) high. When the fronds of this fern sprout in spring they are bronze-brown, turning light green first and yellow and brown in the autumn; they die off in winter. The Royal fern is often planted by the waterside as a specimen where it will even grow in full sun.

Osmunda cinnamomea, the Cinnamon fern is

Origanum vulgare

Osmunda regalis

only 60cm (2ft) high with pale green fronds and cinnamon-coloured fertile plumes. *Osmunda lancea*, 1m (3ft) is a Japanese fern with fertile plumes of the same colour and palm-like fronds. *Osmunda regalis* has some attractive cultivars: 'Crispa', 80cm (32in) with fringed fronds and 'Cristata', 60cm (2ft) with more fringing.

The young fronds of 'Purpurescens', 1.2m (4ft) are a brownish-purple, the fertile plumes are purple throughout the season. These ferns are beautiful in a shadow border with moist soil.

Oxalis

☀ ✿ ○ ●

Oxalis acetosella, or Wood sorrel grows wild in coniferous and deciduous woods and on the shady banks of ditches. It is not so much a border plant as an excellent ground coverer, mainly suitable for the shrub border. The plants are only 10cm (4in) high, with white flowers in spring.

Wood sorrel spreads by means of creeping rhizomes and may cover too much ground in time. *Oxalis magellanica,* from South America and southern Australia does not spread, is half hardy with little clover-like leaves and white flowers in May and June. *Oxalis adenophylla* has pink flowers and grey foliage; it is not fully hardy and needs protection in winter.

Oxalis valdiviensis is an annual wood sorrel which seeds itself well. This plant is also very much at home in a greenhouse, a charming weed, but out of control under the benches. 'Lucky Gold', 30cm (12in) is a cultivar with larger, yellow flowers. The half hardy *Oxalis regnellii* has lovely white flowers. They all need moist soil in a cool situation.

Oxalis regnellii

Pachysandra terminalis

Pachysandra

This familiar ground cover plant is related to box, an evergreen plant very suitable for the shrub border. The leaves are clustered together at the tips of the stems, ensuring good ground covering with the aid of creeping stolons undergound.

The sub-shrub *Pachysandra terminalis* is very useful. The species is only 30cm (12in) high; the cultivars 'Green Carpet'and 'Variegata' remain lower. 'Green Carpet' is smaller and stiffer altogether.'Variegata' has grey-green foliage with a white margin and does not grow so vigorously. These plants are easy to grow, as long as they are not in full sun, or in a windy situation. They prefer partial shade and any fertile soil.

Paeonia lutea

Paeonia

PEONY

A selection from the two best-known groups of peonies: the perennial Lactiflora-hybrids stemming from the Chinese peony *Paeonia lactiflora* - and the tree peonies, cultivars of *Paeonia suffruticosa* - *P. delavayi* and *P. lutea*. To start with the tree peonies, not usually found at the nursery for perennial plants but at a tree nursery, because they are shrubs. Tree peonies are often sold in a single colour which is a pity as there are so many to choose from. Two familiar species are *Paeo-*

Persicaria amplexicaulis

nia delavayi, 1.8m (5¹/₂ft) with single,velvet-red flowers and yellow stamens in May and June - and *Paeonia lutea*, same height with single, yellow flowers. Both types have decorative seed pods. The cultivars of *Paeonia suffruticosa* usually stem from the Far East with exotic names to match and the spelling not always uniform. 'Hakushin' has semi-double white flowers; 'Hanadajin' or 'Hana-daigiu' (magnificent flower), double purple flowers; 'Hanakisoi', pink, semi-double; 'Kaou', (king of flowers) large, double scarlet flowers; 'Renkaku' (flight of cranes) single, white; 'Rimpou', double, dark red; 'Shichifukujin', pink, semi-double; 'Taiyo', bright red, semi-double; 'Yukisasa', white, semi-double. The height of tree peonies ranges

Paeonia 'Lady Alexander Duff'

Paeonia 'Bowl of Beauty'

deeply it will never bloom well, so plant them near the surface. The tuberous root should be covered with only 3cm (1½in) of earth. Peonies will begin to flower well after a few years, not during the first year. After that they will grow more beautiful with more and more flowers, if they are treated well. Here are some of the many hybrid-cultivars: 'Bowl of Beauty', 80cm (32in) high, a fuchsia-pink, anemone-form peony; 'Claire de Lune', with single, pale yellow flowers and orange-yellow stamens; The old 'Duchesse de Nemours' from 1856, with double white flowers and a greenish-yellow centre; 'Jan van Leeuwen', the most beautiful single white flowering plant which can even weather a storm; 'Kelway's Glorious', with double, carmine flowers tinged with pink; 'Lady Alexander Duff', double, pale pink; 'Mrs. Franklin D. Roosevelt', the same; 'Raspberry Sundae', very full, with different shades of pink in one flower; 'Sarah Bernhardt', double and deep pink; 'Shirley Temple', pale pink turning white, very large flowers 20cm (8in); 'White Wings', with large, single white flowers. There are many more, each more beautiful than the one before. The single-flowered peonies combine best in the border in general, but double-flowered varieties are also well-worth planting.

A row of peonies for cutting purposes in the vegetable garden is a possibility, and what about a peony border?

Panicum virgatum 'Rotstrahlbusch'

from 1-1.8m (3-5½ft); the fact that these are expensive shrubs reveals that it costs growers valuable time and trouble to nurse them up to the required standard. They also need care and very well-drained soil in the garden, preferably with some lime. It is advisable to plant them in spring in a sheltered spot and to protect them from frost in winter.

The perennial peony plants are magnificent, robust plants with single, semi-double, double or anemone-form flowers, all very imposing. Fortunately they are increasingly seen as cut-flowers - there is nothing lovelier than a large vase full of peonies, usually the double flowers. If you have enough of them in the garden you can pick them, but wait until the buds are open, otherwise they will not bloom. Peonies are not difficult plants once they start growing, but until then the following points are important to remember.

They need fertile soil. Enrich the soil before planting with quantities of rotted manure or compost and give more manure every year in spring and autumn. If a peony is planted too

Panicum

⚪ ❀ ☀

Panicum miliaceum is the familiar annual, millet and it has a perennial brother from America, *Panicum virgatum*, or panic grass which has the following excellent cultivars for the border: 'Heavy Metal', 1.2m (4ft) with foliage in a metallic colour, not the pollution suggested by the name; The plant flowers with lovely, loose blades. 'Rehbraun', 1.2m (4ft) has foliage which turns reddish-brown in late summer and loose spikes of flowers; 'Rotstrahlbusch' (Hènse Herms), 80cm (32in) colours red in the autumn, contrasting nicely with the flower spikes; 'Squaw', 1.5m (5ft) has lovely autumn colours and arching, brown-red spikes of flowers; 'Strictum', 1.5m has stiff, upright foliage and slender spikes. These grasses flower long, from July into October.

Papaver

POPPY

⚪ ⚫ ❀ ☀

Many of these annual, biennial and perennial plants are very suitable for the border. The annuals first: *Papaver rhoeas*, which used to adorn the cornfields and now grows in the verges, has some attractive cultivars. The best-known of these are the Reverend Wilkes's Shirley Poppies (he used to live in Shirley). These poppies, 80cm (32in) high are often sold in a brilliant mixture of all shades between white and red, with or without contrasting edges. There are also double ones now in more colours than the clergyman could ever have dreamed of. Another annual is *papaver commutatum* of which the lovely 'Lady Bird', 70cm (28in) has bright red petals with a black spot at the base of each. The

Papaver somniferum

Papaver nudicaule

Opium poppy, *Papaver somniferum* of the blue poppy seeds, is also an annual and a very imposing one, with its grey-green foliage, height of 1.2m (4ft) and mauve flowers followed by splendid seed pods. 'Maxi', 90cm (3ft) has the largest seed pods and 'Hen and Chickens' (90cm) the most peculiar; as the large seed pod is surrounded by tiny pods.

The Peony-flowered Series of poppies, 90cm (3ft), are available self-coloured, from deep purple to pink, orange, red, yellow and white. 'Danebrog' has unusual red and white markings which led to the name 'Danish Flag'. *Papaver nudicaule*, the Iceland poppy is a perennial plant but it is best grown as an annual.

They are available self-coloured, but a mixture of pastel shades, or of white, yellow, pink, red and orange is beautiful. Finally we come to the perennial poppies of which the *Papaver orientale*, the Oriental poppy and its cultivars are foremost.

Papaver orientale 'Perry's White'

They were neglected for a while, their large buds and garish colours did not seem to be so welcome in the border. But fortunately they are back in fashion again and we see more of them. Their colours are more subdued. For instance, 'Juliane', 1m (3ft) is a dusty pink; 'Karine', 60cm (2ft) has small pink flowers with red spots at the base of each petal; 'Kleine Tènzerin', 60cm has big, pink flowers with a black spot; 'Lilac Girl' has lilac-pink flowers; 'Mrs. Marrow's Plum' is a typical dark plum colour; 'Perry's White' has a black-purple spot at the base of each white petal.

The bright orange and red-flowering poppies such as *Papaver orientale* 'Allegro' and 'Beauty of Livermere' are still with us and look very good in a red border. Their only disadvantage is that they leave such gaping holes after flowering, which have to be filled with neighbouring plants.

Paulownia

 ☀

This is the story of how a tree became a shrub. No-one could call a 9-12m (27-36ft)-tall tree a border plant. But if you make it into a shrub it will be most effective in the border. *Paulownia tomentosa* can be cut down to the ground every spring. The shoots which then grow bear enormous leaves and the fewer shoots you leave, the bigger the leaves. 'The tree' will then grow up to 2-2.5m (6-8ft) at the highest, acting as a giant foliage plant in the border.
It will expect compensation for so much ill-treatment in the form of nutrients, water and well-drained soil.

Paulownia tomentosa – fruits

Pennisetum alopecuroides 'Hameln'

Pennisetum

 ☀

Pennisetum alopecuroides or Chinese fountain grass has long plumes which bloom with bristles resembling bottlebrushes. The cultivar 'Hameln', 60cm (2ft) has darker bristles and flowers earlier (July into September) and more profusely than the species; 'Little Bunny', 30cm (12in) lives up to its name, flowering with little 'rabbits' tails'.
Pennisetum orientale grows up to 90cm (3ft). It needs fertile soil and full sun.

Pennisetum orientale

Penstemon 'Rich Ruby'

Penstemon digitalis

Penstemon

❀ ⚲ ☼

Penstemons are perennial plants and sub-shrubs, most of which are grown as annuals as they are not fully hardy. Temperature and rainfall are not the only factors in this, they are also dependent on well-drained soil. The cultivars with large flowers in particular will not survive the winter in colder areas. Instead of giving them a protective covering you can take cuttings of shoots in September. The following narrow-leaved penstemons are

Penstemon 'Sour Grapes'

reasonably frost hardy: 'Andenken an Friedrich Hahn', garnet-red; 'Apple Blossom', small, pale pink flowers with pink and white-striped throat; 'Evelyn', lavender pink flowers with white and maroon-striped throat; 'Schoenholzeri', red flowers with pale and deep, pink-striped throat.

Wet winters do not suit penstemons as they are not tolerant of wet feet. Among the broad-leaved penstemons 'Sour Grapes' is a mixture of lovely shades of violet and blue; 'White Bedder' ('Snow Storm') has large flowers; 'Rich Ruby' has thick clusters of dark red flowers.

The species *Penstemon barbatus*, 80cm (32in) high with red flowers is frost hardy, as also *Penstemon digitalis* 'Husker Red', with white flowers and purple foliage. *P. digitalis* has many white or lavender flowers and looks good in the border, over 1m (3ft).

Penstemon is such an extensive genus that nine pages of the *R.H.S. Dictionary of Gardening* are devoted to the species and cultivars and David Way has written a book exclusively on penstemons.

The Hardy Plant Society recently published a foretaste, the booklet *Penstemons* by the same author.

Perovskia

This sub-shrub is 1.5m (5ft) high, resembles perennial plants and combines well with them. It has deeply cut, aromatic grey foliage and grey-white stems bearing profuse spikes of lavender-blue flowers from late summer to mid-autumn.

Perovskia atriplicifolia 'Blue Spire' is the best known; 'Blue Haze', has less deeply cut, slightly greyer foliage and flowers of a deeper blue. They love the sun and well-drained soil and grow best if cut back to the ground every spring.

Persicaria (Polygonum)

KNOTWEED

The names of this plant lead to a great deal of confusion. First called *Polygonum*, then *Persicaria* and now back to *Polygonum* in the big *R.H.S. encyclopedia*. The growers wisely kept the name *Polygonum* in their catalogues. But we must be consistent and *Persicaria affinis (Polygonum affine)* is a beautiful ground cover for a shrub border. The species,

30cm (12in) flowers with deep pink spikelets, the cultivar 'Darjeeling Red', pinkish-red, 'Donald Lowndes', salmon pink and best of all, 'Superba' flowering very freely with pink

Persicaria bistorta

spikes. *Persicaria amplexicaulis (Polygonum amplexicaule)*, 70cm (28in) is a beauty for the border. The various cultivars reflect the popularity of this plant. 'Alba', 1.2m (4ft), has white spikes; 'Speciosa', ('Firetail'), 1.2m, bright red; 'Inverleith', 60cm (2ft), dark red; 'Rosea', 1.2m (4ft), pink. P*ersicaria (Polygonum) bistorta*, or Bistort, 70cm (28in) has a splendid cultivar: 'Superba', with many bright pink spikes. *Persicaria filiformis (Polygonum filiforme)*, 70cm (28in) has lovely dark green foliage flecked with brown when in the shade, and spikes of flowers. *Persicaria (Polygonum) weyrichii* grows up to 1.7m (5¹/₂ft) does not grow rampant and has large, impressive foliage and creamy-white spikes. They all love fertile, moisture-retaining soil and sun or light shade.

Petunia

☽ ☼

The petunia is more suitable for pots, tubs and hanging baskets than for the border. But with some thought and care the petunia can also be used in the border. For instance, a white one with small flowers, combined with the 'Lime Green'- nicotiana and a hosta with a white edge. Surfinias are new petunia cuttings which make good ground covering; some of them can also be sown.

Persicaria weyrichii

Petunia 'Purple Wave'

Petunia 'Mirage Lavender'

Petunia 'Mornclifton'

Phacelia

☽ ☼

Phacelia tanacetifolia, 60cm (2ft) is used as green manure, but its purple-blue flowers are so lovely that it could well be planted in the border. This Phacelia also attracts many insects, like the annual *Phacelia campanularia*, or California bluebell. This is much

Phacaelia tanacetifolia with *Zinnia*

Phacaelia campanularia

lower, 20cm (8in) with deep blue, bell-shaped flowers, white on the outside. *Phacelia parryi* 'Admiral', 50cm (20in) is all blue and *Phacelia purshii*, 40cm (16in) has larger, light blue flowers with a creamy-white centre. This is a modest plant, but useful in an annual border; it can be planted among the perennials as green manure. The plant does not tolerate too much moisture, so a hot summer would be ideal for it.

Philadelphus

⚜ ☼ ○

This is such a common shrub that it is usually forgotten. It flowers briefly, in May/June, sometimes July but it makes up for this with its wonderful fragrance.

It loves full sun and fertile, moist soil. *Philadelphus coronarius*, or Mock orange is the most common and grows anywhere, even in dry, poor soil. The cultivar 'Aureus' has golden-yellow foliage when sprouting, later turning greenish-yellow and it remains

Philadelphus coronarius 'Aureus'

Philadelphus

attractive after flowering is over. 'Variegatus' has white-edged leaves. There are several more lovely cultivars: 'Albâtre', with double but still fragrant flowers, is lower; 'Belle Etoile, 2m (6ft) with fragrant, single white flowers and a lilac-pink centre; 'Miniature Snowflake', 1m (3ft) with strongly-scented white flowers - a low, dense shrub; 'Nuage Rose', low, with fragrant single white flowers and dusty-pink centres; 'Snowdwarf', 1.5m (5ft) with yellowish green foliage and double, fragrant white flowers; 'Snowgoose', 1.5m with small, dark green leaves and double white flowers with a strong scent.

Phlomis tuberosa

Phlomis russeliana

Phlomis

🌸 ⚘ ⚘ ☀

These are familiar, grey-leaved plants with whorls of flowers, still pretty after flowering is over. *Phlomis russeliana* and *phlomis tuberosa* are fairly frost hardy down to -15°C (5°F). This also applies to *Phlomis fruticosa*, or Jerusalem sage as long as the plant has a sheltered position in very well-drained soil. *Phlomis tuberosa*, 1.5m (5ft) has purplish-pink flowers, also attractive after flowering. The cultivar 'Amazone', 1.8m (5¹/₂ft) is a lovely selection with lilac-pink flowers, not so untidy. *Phlomis russeliana*, 80cm (32in) blooms with-soft yellow flowers and grey-green leaves, providing such good ground cover that no weeds can compete with it. *Phlomis fruticosa* has yellow flowers and yellowish, grey-green leaves. These plants need sun and very well-drained soil.

Phlox

🌱 🌸 ☀

Phlox is a very varied genus with colourful annual and perennial, low and high plants - and even creeping rock plants. The annual *Phlox drummondii* is often seen as a mixture of all kinds of showy colours and there are even mixtures like 'Twinkles Mixed Colours', with star-shaped flowers. But they are also available self-coloured and in a more subdued mixture of different pastel shades. 'Phlox of Sheep', 30cm (12in) is a mixture of the loveliest pastel shades, combining very well in an apricot-coloured border.

But the perennial phloxes are the ones which remind us of grandma's garden path. A whiff of their scent is enough to call up the flagstones with the great clumps of phloxes in the border at the side. The faded flowers adorned the path. Do you suppose that those phloxes still exist? The odd strong one perhaps.

Phlox drummondii 'Grandiflora' (Choice Mixed)

Phlox carolina 'Mrs Lingard'

Phlox divaricata 'Chattahoochee'

Phlox paniculata

flowers has some beautiful, low cultivars:'Blue Dreams', 40cm (16in), blue; 'Chattahoochee', 20cm (8in), an unusual shade of blue; 'Clouds of Perfume', 40cm (16in), blue; and 'May Breeze', 40cm, white. Cultivars are not always needed; the species *Phlox paniculata*, 1.5m (5ft) has loose plumes of lilac-blue flowers. But there are also lovely cultivars available for those in search of other colours in the garden: 'Albast', 80cm (32in) with white flowers; 'Blue Evening', 1.2m (4ft), blue and sweet-scented at night; 'Lichtspel', 1.2m with soft pink and lilac flowers; 'Rosa Pastell', with soft-pink flowers.

It is quite impossible to name them all, there are so many. The only piece of advice is to buy

Photinia – the young leaves are bright red

Many of the older cultivars are sensitive to mildew, eelworm and wilt, but there are new varieties free of mildew. 'Hesperis', 1.4m (4^{1}/2ft), with lavender-blue flowers and 'Utopia', 1.8m (5^{1}/2ft), with pale pink flowers are new selections. Good growers propagate their paniculata strains by root cuttings, not by softwood cuttings (this is often done, increasing the risk of eelworm). Their work all goes to promote a high standard of health in phloxes. *Phlox carolina*, the thick-leaved phlox, has some strong cultivars: 'Bill Baker', 60cm (2ft), magenta-pink; 'Magnificence', 90cm (3ft), lilac-pink; 'Mrs. Lingard', slightly higher with snow-white flowers. *Phlox divaricata*, 30cm, (12in) with violet-blue them from a reliable grower, the rest is a matter of taste.

Phlox needs fertile, friable, well-drained soil and sun or light shade. It is suitable for formal and natural borders.

Photinia

⁂ ☼ ○

Photinia x fraseri, an evergreen shrub, has several cultivars grown for the splendid colours of its foliage and hardier than the type. 'Red Robin' needs a sheltered spot as it is not always hardy. The young leaves are brilliant red turning a dark, bronze-green later. 'Birmingham' has oval leaves with blunted tips, a coppery-red colour when young. 'Robusta' has thick, leathery leaves and coppery red shoots, the most hardy evergreen *Photinia*.

It tolerates chalky soil, but deciduous photinias such as *Photinia villosa* var. *laevis* prefer acid soil. This *Photinia* is bigger, growing up to 5m (15ft), with orange-yellow autumn colours.

Phuopsis

⚛ ☼ ○

An unusual perennial plant with long, narrow leaves in whorls, like those of bedstraw. The rounded heads of pink flowers are close together and bloom from June into August.

Phuopsis stylosa 'Purpurea' has darker, purplish-pink flowers and needs to be cut back in spring. The plant needs very well-drained soil without which it will disappear completely.

Phuopsis stylosa 'Purpurea'

Phygelius

⁂ ☼

This plant does not tolerate temperatures lower than -5°C (23°F) so it is more suitable for a tub than for the border. But it is worth planting one in a sheltered spot, with a thick layer of mulch to cover it in winter. The most

Phygelius aequalis 'Yellow Trumpet'

Phygelius × rectus 'Devil's Tears'

Phygelius × *rectus* 'Winchester Fanfare'

Phygelius × *rectus* 'Winchester Fanfare'

familiar is *Phygelius aequalis* 'Yellow Trumpet', with pale yellow flowers. *Phygelius x rectus* has many lovely cultivars also stemming partly from 'Yellow Trumpet'. 'Devil's Tears has pendent, deep pink flowers; 'Salmon Leap' has orange flowers tinged with salmon pink and 'Winchester Fanfare' has pendent, pinkish-red flowers. *Phygelius x rectus* 'African Queen' is fairly hardy with

orange-red flowers. Another possibility is to plant those which are not hardy in large pots in the border and to store them frost-free in winter.

Phyllostachys

乀 ☼ ○

According to Charley Younge, the expert on bamboo, *Phyllostachys* is the most bamboo bamboo of them all. It has everything we associate with bamboo, - rapid growth, something exotic - and it is also evergreen though some of the foliage may be damaged. It may be too high for your border, but it would make a beautiful green backdrop.

Most of these are of medium height, 3.5 - 4m (10^1/2 - 12ft) or higher. *Phyllostachys aurea*, the Fishpole bamboo, 5m (15ft) has small, light green foliage and 'Albovariegata' has striped leaves. *Phyllostachys aureosulcata*, the Golden-groove bamboo has small, olive-green leaves and dark green stems with yellow grooves. This bamboo can grow up to 4-7m (12-21ft) with zigzag stems, later growing erect and perfectly straight.

Phyllostachys nigra, 4-5m (12-15ft) has green stalks turning black later on. *Phyllostachis nigra* var. *henonis* has a more compact habit than the type, with less damage to the foliage. Bamboo needs plenty of water especially

Phyllostachys aurea

Phyllostachys aurea 'Albovariegata'

Physalis alkekengi var. *franchetii*

Physalis – fruits

during the first year after planting and it likes manure once a year.

They are tolerant of any soil, as long as it is well-drained because they dislike wet feet.

Physalis

CHINESE LANTERN

 ☀

Related to the potato, this plant encloses its fruits in little lanterns, the plain or coloured calyxes. *Physalis ixocarpa*, an annual Chinese lantern has several cultivars which produce edible berries. The best-known of these is *Physalis peruviana*, which hides its berries in creamy-yellow lanterns. The ripe berries taste a little like pineapple; it is a perennial plant grown as an annual and it needs a long, hot summer to produce berries. It is suitable for a natural border. The familiar perennial plant *Physalis alkekengi* (var. *franchetii*), the orange Bladder cherry or Winter cherry spreads, so this is also more suitable for a wild border. Chinese lanterns can be dried. The cultivar 'Zwerg', is a lovely dwarf variety with pretty lanterns.

Physostegia

OBEDIENT PLANT

 ☀

The flowers of this plant have hinged stalks that can be turned in any direction, obediently, like the leaves of a rubber plant made of plastic, and very true to its name. It is a strong and healthy plant which grows in any

Physostegia virginiana 'Bouquet Rose'

Physostegia virginiana 'Vivid'

243

good garden soil, the one thing they cannot tolerate is a long period of drought.

The colours of the cultivars range from white and all shades of pink to red. 'Bouquet Rose', 70cm (28in) has pink flowers; 'Red Beauty', 1m (3ft) pinkish-red; 'Summer Snow', 60cm (2ft) pure white and so is 'Javelin', 1m (3ft); 'Summer Spire', (1m) dusty pink; 'Vivid', 40cm (16in) purplish-pink. The obedient plant combines well with other perennial plants.

Phytolacca

❀ ☼ ○

Phytolacca americana, the Red-ink plant or Virginian pokeweed, is the most common species. This large, shrubby perennial plant has clusters of white flowers, later turning pink.

The flowers are followed by poisonous blackish-pink berries which look delicious. Formerly used to colour wine, they are so poisonous that it is better to wait with this plant if you have small children. It needs plenty of room with its height of 1.5m (5ft) and similar spread. The foliage is very decorative. The plant is at home in a border for perennial plants, a mixed border or a shrub border, as long as the soil is fertile and moisture-retentive.

Pieris japonica

Pieris

✿ ○ ●

These are evergreen shrubs varying in height from 50cm-2m (20in-6ft). Most of them flower early in March and April with white, pink or pinkish-red pendent or upright clusters of flowers. Several cultivars are grown for their variegated leaves or brightly coloured young shoots. These plants need acid soil and if yours is not acid you can plant the smaller species in a pot or tub. The most striking and best-known *Pieris* is surely the hybrid-cultivar 'Forest Flame', which eventually grows up to

Phytolacca americana

2.5m (8ft). Young leaves and shoots are bright red, as though the forest is in flames, true to its name.The foliage turns a fresh green later. This cultivar sprouts early and is sensitive to late night frost. 'Flaming Silver' resembles this, with white-edged leaves. 'Mouwsvila' is more variegated and also stems from 'Forest Flame', like the former. *Pieris Japonica* has some splendid cultivars with dense sprays of flowers: 'Purity' is fairly low with large sprays of pure white flowers; 'Rosalinda', 1.2m (4ft) has pale pink flowers, like 'Valley Rose'.

Plantago

✿ ☼

Wild species of plantain may be lovely in the wild, but no one really wants them in the border. The red-leaved *Plantago major* 'Purpurea', 25cm (10in) and 'Karmozijn' are very good border plants. They seed themselves with pleasure and will come up all over the border without being a nuisance as their red leaves go well with anything. *Plantago major* 'Rosularis', 15cm (6in) is a very unusual plantain

Plantago major 'Purpurea'

Plantago major 'Rosularis'

Platycodon grandiflorus 'Perlmutterschale'

because it looks as though it has strange, rose-like flowers which are really dense rosettes of leaves.

This is a beautiful plant for the edge of the border. *Plantago major* 'Giant Form' is indeed a giant plantain with green leaves, resembling a *Hosta*. It grows up to 80cm (32in) not counting the stems, but unfortunately it is not reliably hardy.

Platycodon

BALLOON FLOWER
✿ ☼ ○

It is very obvious that balloon flowers are related to campanulas. There is only one species, *Platycodon grandiflorus* with several lovely cultivars including 'Albus', 'Fuji Blue', 'Fuji Pink', Fuji White' and 'Hakone Blue' with splendid, double, cup-and-saucer-like flowers; 'Mariesii' is light blue; 'Perlmutterschale' is mother-of-pearl-pink. All these balloon flowers are 40 - 50cm (16-20in) high, flowering from June until the end of August. They need light, well-drained soil in the sun or partial shade. The plants are late to sprout so be careful when weeding.

Pleioblastus chino 'Tsuboi'

Pleioblastus

Caution is needed with the dwarf bamboo, *Pleioblastus* as many of them spread, taking up a large area in no time. This may be just what you want, but if not, you must select one without creeping rhizomes. *Pleioblastus viridistriatus* 'Auricoma' has green foliage and is slow-spreading. This bamboo is hardy, but its foliage may be damaged. *Pleioblastus chino* 'Elegantissimus' has green and white-striped foliage, 2-3m (6-9ft) high, no rhizomes as a rule. 'Tsuboi' is a lovely striped cultivar. This dwarf bamboo is mainly used as ground cover in places where it can be allowed to spread. Many types can be cut back to ground level at the end of winter after which they put out fresh green sprouts. They can also be used to form a hedge.

Podophyllum

This is a wonderful plant for the shadow border. It needs moist soil rich in humus so that it is best to dig plenty of compost into the soil before planting. *Podophyllum hexandrum* , 40cm (16in) is the species most often grown, with brown leaves, pink flowers and red fruits in May and June. The cultivar 'Majus' is higher, 70cm (28in). Its foliage

unfurls like a collar with beautiful markings, after flowering is over. *Podophyllum peltatum*, the May apple, has deeply lobed green leaves which hide large white flowers, 5cm (2in) across.

Polemonium

JACOB'S LADDER

Polemonium caeruleum is a splendid jacob's ladder with blue flowers which seeds itself. For those who do not care for this there are cultivars which are not self-seeding. 'Hopleys', 80cm (32in) has pink flowers; 'Lambrook Manor' (Lambrook Mauve'), 50cm (20in) with mauve flowers. 'Album' is a popular white cultivar. *Polemonium carneum* has soft pink flowers, fairly low, 35cm (14in).

Polemonium reptans 'Firmament' is light blue; 'Blue Pearl', bright blue; 'Pink Beauty' also 35cm (14in). *Polemonium pauciflorum*, 50cm (20in) has large yellow flowers. It is a

Polemonium caeruleum 'Lambrook Manor'

Polemonium caeruleum 'Album'

Polemonium carneum

Polygonatum multiflorum

Polygonatum multiflorum

good thing that this plant seeds itself as it is a short-lived perennial plant in colder areas. Both high and low polemoniums are suitable for a cottage border.

Polygonatum

SOLOMON'S SEAL

 ○ ●

Solomon's seal is a wonderful shadow plant which can spread given the right conditions, if it is not disturbed. Solomon's seal prefers fertile, well-drained soil, but also moisture-retentive soil as it does not tolerate heat or dry conditions. These are beautiful, arching plants with decorative foliage and small, pendent often fragrant flowers.

Polygonatum multiflorum, the common Solomon's seal is the only one still seen in the wild. Depending on their position, the plants grow to a height of 30 -90cm (1-3ft) with leaves 5-15 cm (2-6in), the green-edged white flowers are in groups of two to six together, the fruits are blue-black.

Polygonatum multiflorum 'Variegatum' has white-edged foliage. (*P. x hybridum* 'Striatum' is sometimes mentioned separately but is *P. multiflorum* 'Variegatum'). *Polygonatum odoratum*, the fragrant Solomon's seal is an endangered species, only seen in a few places. This sweet-scented Solomon's seal has green-tipped white flowers, singly or in pairs (in rare cases clusters of three to five), a magnificent plant altogether. *Polygonatum verticillatum*, the Whorled Solomon's seal is another endangered species which has almost disappeared in the wild. The plant is the only type to have leaves growing in whorls on upright stems, the berries are red, deep purple

later. *Polygonatum stewartianum*, 90cm (3ft) has narrow leaves and rose-red flowers. *Polygonatum curvistylum*, 40cm (16in), a Solomon's seal from the Himalayas, has arching, purple stems with whorls of dark green leaves and elegant, little mauve flowers clustered on long stems. *Polygonatum falcatum* comes from Korea and Japan and has

Polygonatum multiflorum 'Variegatum'

247

small, white flowers in clusters of two to five. *Polygonatum falcatum* 'Variegatum' has reddish stems and white-edged leaves. *Polygonatum x hybridum* has white flowers with a green edge; the crossing has resulted in several beautiful cultivars. 'Weihenstephan', 1m (3ft) has large white flowers grouped in clusters of four. This cultivar is sterile so there are no berries. No shadow border should be without Solomon's seals. They are also surpisingly good for cutting. Polygonatum multiflorum used to be brought on under glass for this purpose.

Polygonum see Persicaria

Polypodium

✿ ○ ●

This is a low-growing fern which, like all ferns, combines well in a shadow border. *Polypodium vulgare*, 30cm (1ft) the common polypody and *Polypodium interjectum,* 40cm (16in) are native ferns growing in woodland soil, poor sandy soil, dunes and also on old pollard willows and walls.

They feel at home in a shadow border adjoining an old wall. But these excellent evergreen ferns will thrive just as well without old walls, preferably in fairly dry soil. New fronds appear quite late.

Polystichum

✿ ○ ●

An extensive genus of evergreen ferns stemming from the Alps and tropical rain forests, ferns for the garden and ferns only suitable for the living room or for a greenhouse. *Polystichum aculeatum*, the hard shield fern and *polystichum setiferum*, the soft shield fern are both endangered species. Fortunately the shadow border need not do without them as they are grown at the nurseries.

Polystichum aculeatum, 50cm (20in) is a splendid fern with glossy dark green, finely-cut fronds with spiny, pointed pinnae. *Polystichum setiferum*, 50cm (20in) has many cultivars. 'Divisilobum' has finely divided fronds and is more tolerant of a dry position than other ferns. 'Herrenhausen', 40 -60cm ($1^{1}/2$-2ft) high with a spread of 1m (3ft) is a well-known fern used in bouquets. This plant forms bulbils along its stalks enabling it to be propagated true to type; this is not so when it is propagated by spores. That is why it is important to buy plants from a good grower. 'Wollastonii', 40cm (16in) has very finely-cut fronds.

Polystichum acrostichoides and Polystichum munitum both come from America.. *P. acrostichoides*, 50cm (20in) the Christmas fern is used for christmas decorations; it does well in the garden and sprouts fairly early. *P. munitum*, 80cm (32in) grows slowly, forming large, cup-shaped clumps eventually. *Polystichum polyblepharum*, 60cm (2ft) is the most beautiful evergreen fern; it needs a sheltered spot to prevent damage to early-sprouting fronds, from late frost.

All these ferns like very well-drained soil and do not tolerate winter wet. Like most ferns they are very suitable for a shadow border.

Polypodium vulgare

Polystichum setiferum 'Divisilobum'

Potentilla 'Volcan'

Potentilla fruticosa 'Goldfinger'

Potentilla

✦ ⚘ ☼

Some potentillas are perennial plants, some are shrubs. The perennials, with strawberry-like leaves and brightly-coloured flowers, were neglected for a while, but they are back again now. They love the sun and are trouble-free as long as the soil is well-drained. *Potentilla nepalensis* 'Miss Willmott' is the best known, with pink flowers and cherry-red centres. 'Roxana' has red buds and copper-pink flowers. Both grow up to 40cm (16in), flowering from July into September. 'Melton Fire' grows higher with large, apricot-coloured flowers. The following are hybrid-cultivars: 'Gibson's Scarlet' with blood-red flowers;

Potentilla fruticosa 'Blink'

'Volcan', brown-red; 'William Rollison', dark orange, semi-double flowers with a yellow centre; 'Yellow Queen', bright yellow, double flowers. *Potentilla tridentata* 'Nuuk', 20cm (8in) has rosettes of leathery, green leaves and white flowers. Shrub potentillas are all cultivars of *Potentilla fruticosa*, of low or medium height.

They are deciduous and the flowers, very like perennial plant flowers, bloom for a long period, beginning at the end of spring, some continuing into autumn. They prefer to grow in the sun, except for the red, pink or orange-flowered potentillas which fade in the sun. 'Abbotswood' is a familiar cultivar, 1.5m (5ft) high, a white-flowered *potentilla* which blooms throughout the summer and into autumn.

'Blink' ('Princess') is a compact, low shrub with pale pink flowers and a yellow centre; 'Goldfinger' is often grown, a cultivar with big, deep yellow flowers; 'Sommerflor' has blue-green foliage and fairly big flowers; there are many more cultivars to choose from.

Primula

✦ ○

'The' primula does not exist as there are so many variations in the 550 species of primulas that some of them are not even recognizable as primulas. Many of the smaller types are treasured like jewels in rock gardens and greenhouses. Several higher primulas are excellent for a moist border in the shade and we shall concentrate on these. No auriculas or colourful pot plants but candelabra, drum-sticks and other primulas which grace the border, whatever the colour. An odd man out,

Primula vialii

Primula prolifera

not usually recognized as a primula and not always easy to grow, is *Primula vialii*, 40cm (16in). A native of China, this primula flowers in June and July with conical spikes, purplish-violet at the base with scarlet tops. The drumstick primula, *Primula denticulata* has a completely different habit, a little stiff for the border perhaps, but nice along the edge. *Primula denticulata* 'Alba' has white drumsticks. An imposing primula often planted by the waterside in English gardens is *Primula florindae*, the Giant cowslip. These plants bloom in July and August with pendent clusters of sulphur-yellow flowers, a beautiful combination with hostas.

Candelabra primulas bear whorls of flowers in tiers on the stem, like a wedding cake. *Primula beesiana*, 60cm (2ft) has deep pink flowers with an orange eye from May into July.The orange-yellow to red flowers of *Primula bulleyana* appear in the same period, 80cm (32in).

A multi-tiered Candelabra primula is *Primula japonica*; there are cultivars in various colours including 'Alba', 50cm (20in) and 'Miller's Crimson', 60cm (2ft). *Primula pulverulenta*, (60cm) is a Candelabra primula with carmine-purple flowers in June and July, flowering at the same time as the yellow *Primula prolifera (P. helodoxa)*.
Primula elatior, the slender Oxlip is suitable for a natural border, like *Primula veris*, the

Primula pulverulenta (red) with *P. prolifera* (yellow)

Prunella grandiflora 'Loveliness'

Cowslip herself. Both are yellow and it is important to make sure in a natural border. Primulas need fertile soil, rich in humus and cool so that it does not dry out, in a shady spot.

Prunella

SELF-HEAL

❁ ☼ ○

The common native *Prunella vulgaris* grows along woodland paths, in moist meadows and lush valleys. This little plant, 25cm (10in) high with bluish-purple flowers appearing from May into September, is a ground cover which seeds itself with great enthusiasm. For this reason it is not a good bedding plant. *Prunella grandiflora* has larger flowers as its name suggests and it blooms with violet-blue flowers from June into August. There are cultivars in other colours: 'Alba', white, 'Carminea', carmine-pink and 'Loveliness' lilac-pink. *Prunella x webbiana* 'Rosea' is a purplish-pink

Prunella grandiflora 'Alba'

251

Prunella × webbiana 'Rosea'

Prunus subhirtella – a canopy over the border

Prunus spinosa 'Purpurea'

self-heal with bigger flowers. Prunellas are suitable for the edge of the border or as ground-cover in a shrub border. They will grow in any soil and situation.

Prunus

CHERRY

The Portugal laurel, *Prunus lusitanica* is a half hardy evergreen shrub which can grow up to 3m (9ft). Cultivar 'Angustifolia', a pyramidal shrub 2m (6ft) high has narrower leaves and is less frost tender. The shrub flowers in June with upright clusters; it is also evergreen and suitable for clipping and topiary work. *Prunus spinosa*, or Blackthorn or Sloe is a different Prunus altogether, flowering early, in March/April with little white flowers on the bare, spiny wood. These are followed by large

Prunus lusitanica – flower

blue-black fruits from which sloe gin is made. The shrub spreads by means of rhizomes and is more suitable for a woodland setting or a wild garden than for a formal border. *Prunus spinosa* 'Purpurea' is less unruly, with dark, purple-brown foliage and white flowers. 'Rosea' sprouts with bronze-coloured leaves, later turning dark green and flowers in April with salmon-pink flowers. *Prunus subhirtella* 'Autumnalis', the white, semi-double ornamental cherry and 'Autumnalis Rosea', with pink, semi-double flowers grow into robust shrubs or small trees, open enough to lean over the border.

Pulmonaria

Lungwort is one of the loveliest shade- loving plants and among the earliest of them to flower. It forms excellent ground cover and has

Pulmonaria saccharata 'Mrs Moon'

Pulmonaria angustifolia 'Mawson's Variety'

blue, pink, red or white flowers and beautiful foliage, sometimes variegated. It is sensitive to mildew when in dry soil. If you cut the foliage of lungwort back to the ground after flowering need not wait long for fresh foliage to appear. There are numerous species, cultivars and hybrid-cultivars available.

Pulmonaria angustifolia, with red flowers turning violet-blue later is the most common. 'Azurea' has deep-blue flowers, carmine in the bud; 'Blue Ensign' has larger flowers and

Pulmonaria saccharata 'Margery Fish' (*P. vallarsae* 'Margery Fish')

foliage. *P. angustifolia* 'Mawson's Variety' has narrow leaves and blue flowers turning red with age, like that of many pulmonarias. Beth Chatto grew two cultivars of *P. angustifolia*, namely 'Beth's Blue' and 'Beth's Pink', which has lightly spotted leaves. *Pulmonaria longifolia* has very narrow, spotted leaves and bright blue flowers. 'Lewis Palmer' has broader, spotted foliage and soft blue flowers turning pink later.

Pulmonaria officinalis, spotted lungwort is an endangered species, sometimes seen on old estates. 'Alba'', white, 'White Wings' too but with a pink eye. The sky-blue 'Cambridge' ('Cambridge Blue'), which used to be classed with Pulmonaria saccharata turns out to be a cultivar of *P. officinalis*. 'Sissinghurst White' is a well-known, very beautiful white plant, also associated with *P. saccharata*, as is 'Alba', perhaps even lovelier than 'Sissinghurst White'.

'Mies Stam' stems from 'Alba', a sturdy plant with spotted leaves and soft carmine-pink flowers. 'Dora Bielefeld' has pure pink flowers; 'Highdown', silver leaves and vivid blue flowers; 'Mrs.Moon', spotted foliage and lilac-red flowers turning purplish-red; 'Pink Dawn', pink flowers and white-spotted leaves; 'Reginald Kaye', silvery-white spotted leaves with a fine green edge, purple-and-red flowers; 'Margery Fish', pink-and-blue flowers, silvery-green spotted foliage growing lighter gradually - also used to belong with *P. saccharata*, but is now *Pulmonaria vallarsae* 'Margery Fish'.

Pulmonaria rubra syn. *P. montana* has splendid red cultivars: 'Bowles Red', 'David Ward' and 'Redstart'. There are many more pulmonarias and even more to come.

Pulsatilla vulgaris – feathery seed heads

Pulsatilla

Pulsatilla vulgaris, the Pasque flower, used to grow naturally by rivers, but it has completely disappeared in the wild. Formerly known as *Anemone pulsatilla*, these flowers resemble anemones and appear early, in March and April.

Pulsatilla vulgaris

Pyrus salicifolia 'Pendula'

Pulsatilla vulgaris 'Röde Klokke'

They are a violet-purple colour, encircled by a small collar of hairy leaves. Afterwards they are still decorative with their feathery seed heads. 'Alba', a pure white cultivar and 'Rubra', with brownish-red flowers both flower in March and April, like the species. 'Röde Klokke' produces red flowers a month later, in April and May. Some of the hybrids are available with double flowers in white, pink, purple and red. They are not really suitable for the border, but in early spring they can show off at the edge, to be followed by other plants. They like full sun and well-drained soil rich in humus.

Pyrus

PEAR

Pear trees and ornamental pear trees are not border plants at all, but there is one exception, *Pyrus salicifolia* 'Pendula', an elegant little tree with drooping branches and grey,downy foliage which combines very well with other shrubs, especially roses, and with large perennial plants. The grey leaves are a good foil for blue, pink and white flowers. The tree can be kept in check by pruning and in spite of its weeping branches it can also be trimmed for topiary work. It will grow in any soil, but it prefers fertile soil and a place in the sun. Pears and ornamental pears are noted for their tolerance of air pollution, wind and coastal wind.

Pyrus salicifolia 'Pendula'

Ranunculus acris 'Multiplex'

Ranunculus ficaria

Ranunculus

BUTTERCUP

Not many garden enthusiasts would welcome buttercups in their garden. They may look wonderful in a meadow, but they grow rampant in a border and are difficult to wipe out. There are buttercups which make beautiful border plants without becoming invasive. *Ranunculus aconitifolia*, 70cm (28in) is one of them. The plant itself is 60cm (2ft) high with abundant dark green, deeply-cut foliage, from which white buttercups emerge in May and June. A very decorative plant for a moist spot in partial shade. The cultivar 'Pleniflorus' ('Flore Pleno') has double, white flowers and will only grow in very rich soil. *Ranunculus acris* - the Double meadow buttercup - 'Multiplex', 70cm (28in)

Ranunculus acris 'Multiplex'

Reseda odorata

flowers from May into September with small, double yellow flowers. *Ranunculus ficaria*, the lesser celandine, spreads rapidly, but is useful as ground cover in a shrub border where it will cover every inch of open ground. The shiny-yellow stars will make up for this in early spring, so will the fresh young foliage which appears afterwards, only to die off in May - not a ground cover for the whole season but one to use with discretion. *Ranunculus ficaria* has several less invasive cultivars of which 'Brazen Hussy' with dark bronze-brown foliage is the best-known.

Reseda

MIGNONETTE

The annual types of resedas are most often grown. Their relations in the wild, *Reseda*

Reseda luteola

lutea and *Reseda luteola* are sometimes found in herb gardens and wild borders. *Reseda alba*, a white annual, 70cm (28in) high has very fragrant conical clusters of flowers, excellent for cutting.

The mignonette, *Reseda odorata*, 50cm (20in), is sweet-scented with a distinctive aroma which attracts many insects, especially bees. The cultivar 'Red Monarch' is 25cm (10in) high. The plants will grow in any garden soil, but they need a sunny spot.

Rheum

RHUBARB

❀ ☼

This is a decorative foliage plant with plumes of flowers as an added bonus. The most familiar and often planted is *Rheum palmatum* var. tanguticum, with deeply lobed and toothed foliage. The leaves are red when sprouting, the long stems, 2.5m (8ft) are pinkish-red. The species *Rheum palmatum* has green foliage; the plant is only suitable for a really large border and as a specimen. *Rheum australe* is lower and the white clusters of flowers 'only' 1.5m (5ft) high. *Rheum spiciforme*, 1.5m, from central Asia has a rosette of reddish leaves and slender flower spikes. Ornamental rhubarb needs fertile soil -

hardly surprising with such a crop of foliage. The soil must be moist, but not boggy.

Rhododendron

⚘ ○ ☼

The genus *Rhododendron* is so immense that it needs its own books.We will concentrate on the azalea, now also called *Rhododendron*, but still referred to by its common name, azalea. Japanese azaleas are evergreen and flower profusely in spring with colours ranging from white to pink, lilac, red and orange. They are available as house plants and if you are lucky they can be planted outside later. The deep red, double hybrid-cultivar 'Moederkensdag' is often sold as a pot plant. There are so many of these Japanese azaleas, classified as large-flowered and small-flowered varieties. The following are large-flowered: 'Beethoven' - mauve-lilac; 'Fedora' - deep pink; 'Kathleen'- dusty pink; 'Lilac Time' - deep lilac; 'Palestrina' - ivory and 'Vuyk's Scarlet'. Some of the small-flowered include; 'Addy Wery' - deep red; 'Amoena' - lilac; 'Campfire' - deep red; 'Hino-crimson'; 'Purple Splendor'; 'Stewartstown' - orange-red. These azaleas vary in height from 60cm-1.2m (2-4ft). They will grow in the sun as long as the soil is moist, but they prefer a spot in partial shade, sheltered from the wind. They need acid soil (acidity 4.5-5.8) enriched with plenty of good, rotted organic matter. Deciduous azaleas grow up to 1.5m-2.5m (5-8ft) with big trumpet-shaped flowers, in colours ranging from pastel shades to bright red and orange. Several of them are very fragrant and many have beautiful autumn colours.

Rhododendron 'Amoena', evergreen azalea

Azaleas *(Rhododendron)* display their colours in the border

Rhus typhina

The deciduous azaleas are also divided into groups. The Mollis azaleas and the knaphill-Exbury azaleas are not scented; the Occidentalis-hybrids, the Pontica-hybrids and the Rustica-hybrids are fragrant. The following are hybrid-cultivars:

- Mollis azaleas: 'Adriaan Koster' - yellow; 'Apple Blossom' - pink; 'Dr. M. Oosthoek' - orange-red; 'Koningin Emma' - salmon-orange; 'Koster's Brilliant Red' - orange-red; 'Salmon Queen' - yellow-salmon-pink and 'Willem Hardijzer' - deep red
- Occidentale-hybrids: 'Exquisita' - pale pink with a yellow blotch; 'Irene Koster' - pure pink with a yellow blotch and 'Magnifica' - yellowish-pink
- Pontica-hybrids: 'Coccinea Speciosa' - orange; 'Corneille' - pink, double; 'Fanny' - purplish-pink; 'Nancy Waterer' - golden-yellow
- Rustica hybrids: 'Freya' - salmon-yellow, double and 'Norma' - orange, double
- Knaphill-Exbury azaleas: 'Ballerina' - white with a yellow blotch; 'Balzac' - orange; 'Cecile' - deep pink with a yellow blotch; 'Gibraltar' - deep orange; 'Golden Flare' - golden-yellow with a bronze blotch;

'Golden Sunset' - golden-yellow with orange blotch; 'Klondyke' - deep golden-yellow; 'Royal Command' - vermilion and 'Sun Chariot' - deep golden-yellow.

Rhus

SUMACH
🌿 ☼ ○

Rhus glabra is a robust shrub with large, feathered leaves turning a beautiful red in the autumn. The female plants bear green plumes in June and July which later turn red. The leaves of cultivar 'Laciniata' are feathery with deeply-cut leaflets. The best-known is *Rhus typhina* with its familiar, velvety shoots and the lovely red plumes of female plants which they retain all winter. The leaflets of cultivar 'Dissecta' are deeply dissected. It would not be wise to plant *Rhus typhina* in a mixed border as it spreads by means of rhizomes. These are easier to remove in a shrub border where this is not a problem

Ribes

CURRANT
🌿 ☼ ○

Many edible berries such as the blackcurrant, the redcurrant and the gooseberry are species

Ribes sanguineum 'King Edward VII'

Ribes speciosum

of *Ribes*. There are also several ornamental ribes suitable for the shrub border. The most familiar is Ribes sanguineum which became so popular at one time that no one would have it in the garden; but it has lovely flowering cultivars, including 'King Edward VII', which blooms in April and May with deep red clusters of flowers. 'White Icicle' has fresh green foliage and clear white flowers in April. This new cultivar from Canada is considered to be an improvement of the old 'Tydemans White'. 'Pink Rain' has short, pink flowers, rose-red in the bud so that they look bicoloured. 'Pulborough Scarlet' has big clusters of deep red flowers with a white centre; 'Barrie Coate' has deep pink flower clusters in March and April. The flowers of *Ribes alpinum* are not so striking, but it is tolerant of shade. A beautiful plant for the collector is *Ribes speciosum*, the Fuchsia-flowered currant. The young shoots of this 2m (6ft)-high shrub are red, the leaflets glossy green. The fuchsia-like lacquer-red flowers appear in late spring to be followed by round, red fruits. It seems too good to be true and the snag is that this plant is not fully hardy and should be grown against a sunny wall facing south or west.

Ricinus

♀ 🌿 ☼

There are few annuals with such splendid and large foliage. The Castor-oil plant *Ricinus communis* is not really an annual, but a shrub. It is grown as an annual because it comes from the tropics and does not tolerate any frost at all. They are not planted for their unimportant flower heads. The Castor-oil plant has seen some changes over the years. It was a great favourite in Victorian times, after which it was

Ricinus communis

Robinia hispida

neglected until recently and now these imposing plants are making their comeback. At the turn of the century they formed the pompous centrepiece of a colourful Victorian mosaic bed of annuals. Later they were often used as specimen plants, sometimes in tubs. They have now been re-discovered and everyone wants one in the border, especially the dark-leaved types. They will grow up to 2m (6ft) easily, if the soil is fertile enough and they have enough water. Brown-leaved cultivars are 'Impala', 'Carmencita' and 'Gibsonii', 1.2m (4ft), to name but a few of the many cultivars. The seeds are like beans and need soaking overnight before sowing. But be

Ricinus communis 'Carmentica'

careful - the seeds are highly poisonous and ripen even in cold areas. It is better not to have this plant in your garden if there are small children about. Given full sun, fertile soil and plenty of old manure the effect will be fantastic.

Robinia

 ☼

Most Robinias are trees, not suitable for a mixed border or a shrub border. But - there are a few exceptions. *Robinia hispida*, the Rose acacia grows to only 1.5m (5ft) and combines the true, feathered acacia foliage with clusters of pink flowers in June. The shrub forms rhizomes and does not fit easily in a subtle design. *Robinia elliottii* is a low shrub, and thorny, in contrast with the former, bearing large lavender-pink flowers in May and June. Both love the sun and chalky soil.

Rodgersia

 ○ ●

No garden with good, moisture-retentive soil should ever be without rodgersias. These unusually decorative foliage plants are restful among the colourful flowers in the border. They are extremely sturdy, distinctive foliage plants, more like shrubs than perennials. The best-known *Rodgersia* is the chestnut-leaved *Rodgersia aesculifolia*, 1m (3ft) high with creamy plumes of flowers. The leaves resemble those of the horse-chestnut tree, divided and palmate, like a hand. 'Irish Bronze' grows higher with bronze-coloured foliage. *Rodgersia pinnata*, 90cm (3ft) resembles this, but its leaves are partly feathered and the flowers are rose-red. The cultivar 'Elegans',

Rodgersia aesculifolia

Rodgersia sambucifolia

Rodgersia podophylla 'Rotlaub'

fertile, moist soil and an annual dressing of ripe manure. Watering is essential in dry periods.

Romneya

CALIFORNIAN POPPY

It has to be said that *Romneya coulteri*, the Californian poppy from southern California is not fully hardy, (to -10°C, 14°F) but it is well worth trying. It may grow well in a sheltered spot in the full sun, in really well-drained soil and with a protective layer in winter. You will

Romneya coulteri

1m, has glossy leaves with brown-red edges. 'Superba', 1.4m (4½ft) has dark green, glossy foliage with bronze coloured young shoots and pink flowers. *Rodgersia podophylla*, 80cm (32in) from Japan has palmate foliage composed of triangular, finely-lobed leaves It is a distictive plant to remember with white clusters of flowers. The leaves turn a beautiful red in th e autumn. 'Rotlaub' produces red young shoots in spring. *Rodgersia sambucifolia*, 80cm (32in) has feathered leaves - like elderberry leaves - and compact white plumes of flowers. 'Kupferschein', 80cm, has copper-coloured young foliage and 'Rothaut' brownish-red. These foliage plants need

Rosa 'Sally Holmes'

Rosa 'Graham Thomas'

be rewarded with magnificent, single fragrant white flowers with a striking tuft of stamens. The leaves are small, blue-green and the plant responds well to pruning. The californian poppy is a plant for those with green fingers or with a garden in the south of England.

Rosa

ROSE

Roses can be grown quite well in the border. It will depend on the group to which they belong: perennial plants or other shrubs. A rose is a

Roses in a mixed border

remarkable plant and it has been treasured for this reason in special beds with only black earth for company. Now we treat her differently. The modern shrub roses are a valuable asset in the border with their flowers and rose hips later on.The species of botanical roses belong to this group, (the roses which still grow in the wild somewhere on earth) and also any roses which do not belong to the large-flowered bush roses, polyantha, miniature or climbing roses. A shrub rose takes its place among the shrubs in the garden. *Rosa glauca* is such a shrub rose.This rose, 4m (12ft) high, with purple-brown, blue-bloomed leaves, single pink flowers and red rose hips also has an elegant, arching habit and red stems. *Rosa glauca* 'Carminetta' has single pink flowers and a profusion of red rose hips. *Rosa x mariae-graebneriae* grows up to 1.5m (5ft) high with pink, fragrant flowers, red rose hips and a finale of beautiful autumn colours. *Rosa rubiginosa*, the Eglantine or Sweet briar, has fragrant leaves, apple-scented, especially just after the rain. This shrub rose, 3m (9ft) high, has rose-pink flowers and oval, orange-red hips. *Rosa rugosa*, the Hedgehog or Japanese rose familiar in public parks with its coarse foliage and large rose hips, has some splendid cultivars, old and new: 'Roseraie de L'Hay' has semi-double, carmine flowers and a good white rose is 'White Captain'. Many shrub roses flower once, like other flowering shrubs. But we are spoilt with roses, we want to see them flowering the whole season like the large-flowered roses and the floribundas. Added to this, several rose growers wanted to achieve a looser habit than the rather starchy large-flowered Hybrid Tea roses and the polyantha roses. The result is that there are now many shrub roses which combine a natural habit with longer flowering. 'Mozart' is a familiar shrub rose which flowers until the first night frost; 'Lavender Dream' is a low shrub rose with lavender pink flowers; 'Sally Holmes' has single, creamy-white flowers; 'Cappa Magna' is a very strong rose with single red flowers; 'Golden Wings' is a high shrub rose flowering abundantly with pale yellow flowers; 'Ballerina' is a long-flowering shrub rose with bright red flowers and a white centre which goes on flowering until winter steps in. Large-flowered roses and polyanthas are not so big; these roses are usually planted in a rose bed. They can also be combined with annuals or perennial plants, but they must never be hedged in by the other plants. This would lead to their remaining damp too long in wet weather and this could lead to disease. These roses are best combined with lower and looser plants.

English roses or Austin roses developed by the English rosarian David Austin are very suitable for the border.At least three roses should be planted close together, so that they can interweave and look like one shrub. The English roses usually flower throughout the summer, fragrant and the old-fashioned, fully double kind. English roses such as 'Abraham Darby' and the once-flowering 'Constance Spry' grow so high that they need to be trained over an arch or wall or support for climbing roses. The following are English roses: 'Bibi Maizon', pink; 'Emanuel', pink; 'English Garden', pale yellow; 'Evelyn', apricot; 'Gertude Jekyll', blush pink; 'Graham Thomas', yellow; 'Sharifa Asma', pale pink; 'The Pilgrim', pale pink and 'Warwick Castle', pink. Shrub roses are not quite so demanding regarding the soil as the strongly cultivated roses, but both need good, fertile, well-drained soil and sun.

Rosmarinus

This evergreen sub-shrub is not always fully hardy. It needs a sheltered spot, very well-drained soil and full sun - but it may still be frozen in a severe winter.It can withstand -10 to -15°C (14 to 5°F), but a wet or very severe winter could be fatal. *Rosmarinus officinalis*, or Rosemary, 50cm to 1m (20 - 30in) has many cultivars, some of which are hardier.

Rosa 'Abraham Darby'

Rosmarinus

Rubus odoratus

Rubus idaeus 'Aureus' and *Hosta* 'Francee'

Rubus thibetanicus

Rubus

BLACKBERRY   BRAMBLE

 ☼ ○

shrubs which do well in shrub borders or mixed borders. *Rubus idaeus* 'Aureus' is a yellow-leaved, low raspberry.

The following hybrid-cultivars are grown for their flowers: 'Benenden', 2m (6ft) high with a spread of 3m (9ft), is an arching shrub with pure white flowers (5cm - 2in across) in May; 'Margaret Gordon' has reddish-brown stems and large, fringed white flowers in May and June; 'Walberton' flowers in July and August with lavender-pink, very large flowers, red in the bud; *Rubus odoratus*, the Flowering raspberry or Thimbleberry, is a robust shrub flowering in July and August with clusters of carmine-pink flowers. *Rubus thibetanus* is an upright shrub, 2m (6ft) high and 4m (12ft) spread with unusual, bluish-white bloomed shoots, feathered leaves, purplish-lilac flowers in July, followed by bloomed black or red fruits. *Rubus thibetanus* 'Silver Fern' has showy silver-grey, hairy foliage and white-bloomed stems, also very attractive in winter, like those of the species. Rubus, with its fairly scrambling growth, is tolerant of any soil and will grow anywhere.

These shrubs are planted especially for their lovely shoots and they respond well if cut back

Rudbeckia nitida 'Herbstsonne'

Rudbeckia hirta 'Rustic Dwarf's Mixed'

Rudbeckia

CONEFLOWER

❀ ☀

Rudbeckias are cheerful flowers from North America. They used to be planted more often than now, perhaps they are waiting for the multicoloured or yellow border to get the upperhand of the pink, blue or white borders. They are really strong plants for any soil, in the full sun. Most rudbeckias have conical

to the ground every year after flowering. Rubus is a fruity genus comprising all kinds of blackberries, raspberries, Japanese wineberries and several.

Rudbeckia fulgida 'Goldsturm'

Rudbeckia maxima

266

centres surrounded by sunny yellow petals. *Rudbeckia laciniata* 'Goldquelle', 90cm (3ft) which bears fully double, yellow flowers. *Rudbeckia fulgida* var. *deamii*. 80cm (32in) is golden yellow with a black and brown centre *Rudbeckia fulgida* 'Goldsturm' is a well-known yellow one with a black centre. *Rudbeckia maxima* is 2m (6ft) high, has conical centres surrounded by drooping yellow petals and showy blue-green sheaths of foliage around the stems. *Rudbeckia nitida* 'Herbstsonne', 2m (6ft) is an old and trusted cultivar with slightly pendent yellow petals and a dark centre. *Rudbeckia occidentalis*, 1m (3ft) has green petals and a brownish black centre. There are also annual and biennial rudbeckias, or rudbeckias which are grown as such because they are short-lived plants. The short-lived perennial plant *Rudbeckia hirta* has many attractive cultivars grown as annuals.

Ruta

RUE

Rue is better-known as a culinary herb than as a border plant. All the same, *Ruta graveolens* 'Jackman's Blue' is eminently suitable for the border. The colour of the double-feathered foliage is most unusual, blue-green perhaps. The little yellow flowers are a perfect match with the foliage. This small shrub, 30-50cm (12-20in) high prefers a place in full sun, but also tolerates some shade. Take care when weeding near the rue on a sunny day, as the juice of the plant can cause the same blisters as the giant hogweed. There is also a variegated rue, nothing in comparison with the blue-green one. Rue will grow in any soil - preferring dry to wet.

Ruta graveolens

Ruta graveolens

Salpiglossis sinuata

Salpiglossis in de border

Salpiglossis

♀ ☼

Salpiglossis sinuata resembles the petunia but is not a well-known annual and usually considered too garish. The inside of the flower is beautifully marked. It is available in colour mixtures and also self-coloured. 'Gloomy Rival' is cream with brown, yellow and gold markings; 'Kew Blue' is dark blue. These are tropical plants which love humid heat, preferring the greenhouse to the border in bad summers.

Salvia

SAGE

♀ ☊ ۞ ⚬ ⚬ ☼

This is a huge, cosmopolitan genus of plants, many of which are grown in the garden. The salvia is not an easy plant to define, it

Salvia × nemorosa 'Blauhügel'

Salvia coccinea 'Lady in Red'

comprises so many different annual, biennial and perennial plants, sub-shrubs and shrubs. We will deal with the salvias suitable for the border here. *Salvia coccinea* is an annual, red, 1m (3ft) high and good for some lovely cultivars. First the scarlet 'Lady in Red', 50cm (20in), a gold-medal winner of "Fleuroselect"; 'Pink Pearl', 75cm (2^1/2ft) is salmon with white; 'Red Indian', 75cm, scarlet; 'White Dove', 75cm, pure white, like 'Snow Nymph', 40cm (16in). *Salvia farinacea* resembles lavender. 'Strata', 45cm (18in), another prize-winner, has blue-and-white flowers on a grey spike; 'Victoria Blue', 45cm with deep blue flowers and 'Victoria Silver', 45cm with pure white flowers. The annual *Salvia viridis (Salvia horminum)* shows off its large, colourful bracts; those of 'Blue Monday', 60cm (2ft) are violet-blue and of 'Pink

Salvia × nemorosa 'Mainacht'

Salvia × nemorosa 'Rose Queen'

Salvia × nemorosa 'Plumosa'

Sunday', 60cm, pinkish-carmine. 'White Swan', 60cm has green, white-veined bracts. *Salvia argentea*, is a short-lived plant regarded as a biennial. This plant is 1m (3ft) high with silvery, woolly leaves and branched spikes with clusters of white flowers appearing in July and August. The plant seeds itself, like the *Salvia sclarea*, which can grow up to 1.2-1.5m (4-5ft). The broad bracts are white, the flowers pink. There are various forms available of which the Adana is currently the best. 'Alba' is a good white cultivar.

We now come to the perennial salvias of which we will consider the hardy types of interest for the border. Unusual salvias are so often sold as hardy border plants, only to disappear after one winter. *Salvia nemorosa* is always ready to please the gardener. This species has many lovely cultivars including 'Amethyst', 90cm (3ft), lavender-pink and long-flowering, as is 'Blauhügel', 40cm (16in), true blue; 'Mainacht', 40cm, dark blue; 'Rose Queen', 40cm, lavender pink and darker bracts; 'Rögen', 40cm, compact, dark blue; 'Tènzerin', 90cm (3ft), violet; 'Viola Klose', 45cm (18in), a striking deep purple, begins to flower in May.

Salvia nemorosa 'Plumosa' is a sage, 50cm (20in) high which does not flower but keeps its beauty for a long period thanks to its decorative purple bracts. *Salvia officinalis*, the true sage and culinary herb, also has some beautiful cultivars. 'Albiflora', white and 'Berggarten' is grown more for its foliage than its flowers, but this plant with oval, grey-green leaves, 60cm (2ft) high makes excellent

Salvia officinalis 'Albiflora'

Sambucus nigra

ground cover in dry soil. 'Purpurascens', 50cm (20in) is often planted in the border for its dark, purplish -red foliage. These plants need protective covering in winter. *Salvia verticillata* has a familiar cultivar, 'Purple Rain', with lilac-blue flowers which match their mauve-purple bracts perfectly. *Salvia przewalski*, 1m (3ft) has large purple flowers from June until the end of August, with a strong scent of incense.

Salvia azurea, (not fully hardy) needs some support with a height of 1.6m (5¹/₂ft) and it is unusual with bright blue flowers which do not appear until the autumn. *Salvia hians* (not fully hardy) 80cm (32in) has dark blue, very sweet-scented flowers. *Salvia bulleyana*,

Salvia verticillata

60cm (2ft) has big, pale yellow flowers with a purple lip. *Salvia glutinosa*, 1m (3ft), a bushy plant with yellow flowers prefers the shade, in contrast with other salvias. Salvia pratensis 'Indigo', 90cm (3ft) flowers long, from July until the end of September, indigo-blue. Many of the salvias are fragrant and several are used medicinally and for culinary seasoning.

Salvias are very attractive to bees; they love the sun and prefer their soil dry rather than too wet.

Sambucus

ELDER

Sambucus nigra 'Aurea', the Golden elder, has beautiful golden-yellow foliage, especially in spring, later turning a pale lime colour. Sambucus racemosa 'Plumosa Aurea' has deeply cut leaves, bronze at first, later golden-yellow. *Sambucus racemosa* 'Sutherland Gold' is just as lovely but not so sensitive to scorching by the sun.

These golden elders are at their best in partial shade, where there is less risk of scorching. There is a dark-leaved elder *Sambucus nigra* 'Guincho Purple' ('Purpurea'), with dark foliage maturing to a deep purple-brown,

Sambucus nigra 'Guincho Purple'

Sanguisorba obtusa

Sanguisorba tenuifolia var. purpurea

blending well with pink clusters of flowers. Dark-leaved elders do not grow as rapidly as the species and they form an attractive asset to a shrub border or a mixed border. Elders grow in any soil.

Sanguisorba

BURNET

 ☼

Sanguisorba officinalis, the great burnet, 1.5m (5ft) which still grows in the wild by the waterside, in verges and on railway embankments, cuts quite a good figure in the border. This slender plant with a loose habit has finely cut leaves and flowers from June to September with short, dense spikes of reddish-purple flowers. Cultivar 'Tanna', 80cm (32in) has bright red spikes with the same, loose habit. *Sanguisorba canadensis*, 1.5m (5ft), the Canadian burnet from the northeast of North

Sanguisorba officinalis

America, a sturdy, upright plant with light green foliage, has long, narrow spikes of white flowers opening from below upwards in August and September. *Sanguisorba dodecandra*, 1m (3ft) has elegant white flower spikelets and blue-green foliage. Sanguisorba obtusa, 1m, has lovely, arching spikes of bright pink flowers in July and August and interweaves itself sociably among other plants. There is a white cultivar, 'Alba'. *Sanguisorba tenuifolia* var. *alba*, 1.8m (5 1/2ft) is a decorative plant with beautiful foliage and small white flower spikes. Like the above, the *purpurea* variety flowers in August and

September with red spikes.

Sanguisorbas are very suitable for a wild border with their natural habit. They feel at home in moist soil by nature but they also tolerate dry conditions.

Santolina

These low, formal sub-shrubs are often used in the same way as lavender, as a low hedge around a herb garden or along the border. They are grown more for their foliage than the button-like flowers and respond well to clipping. They need light trimming after flowering to promote compact growth. Hard pruning does not agree with them, like lavender. The best-known are the grey-leaved *Santolina chamaecyparissus*, the Cotton lavender, 50cm (20in). 'Lambrook Silver', 35cm (14in) is so intent on its foliage that it does not bloom at all. *Santolina chamaecyparissus* var. *corsica* (*S.c.* var. *nana*) is only 25cm (10in) high. The creamy yellow flowering 'Edward Bowles', 30cm (1ft), a cultivar of *S. chamaecyparissus* according to an official list of perennial plants, belongs with *S. neapolitana* according to the expert, Krüssmann. *Santolina chamaecyparissus* 'Lemon Queen' forms a pleasing mound, 60 x

Santolina chamaecyparissus 'Lemon Queen'

Santolina chamaecyparissus var. *corsica*

Santolina rosmarinifolia

60cm, (2x2ft), with grey foliage and lemon-yellow flowers. There are two forms of *Santolina rosmarinifolia*, the Holy flax; *Santolina rosmarinifolia* subsp. *rosmarinifolia* has hairless, bright green leaves. *S. rosmarinifolia* subsp. *canescens* has completely woolly grey leaves. Holy flax loves the sun and dry conditions.

Saponaria

☀ ✿ ☼

The annual soapwort, *Saponaria calabrica*.

Saponaria ocymoides

30cm (1ft), is an excellent, freely flowering rock plant, as also *Saponaria ocymoides* or Tumbling Ted, 15cm (6in). Both are also suitable for the edge of the border, and the last is often planted as ground cover. The species has bright pink flowers and a white cultivar, 'Alba'. *Saponaria x lempergii* 'Max Frei', 40cm (16in) is planted even more widely; it is a splendid border plant, covered with pink flowers from June into September. *Saponaria officinalis* which grows wild near rivers and embankments, has two cultivars with double flowers: the white 'Alba Plena' and the pink 'Rosa Plena', 70cm (28in) high. The plants need well-drained soil and sun.

Sarcococca

CHRISTMAS BOX   SWEET BOX

❀ ☀ ○

Small evergreen shrubs with long, narrow glossy green foliage. They flower at the end of winter with fragrant little white flowers. They

Sarcococca confusa

Saponaria officinalis

will grow in any fertile soil, preferably chalky. They grow gradually, most of them reaching a height of 80cm-1m (32in-1ft). The shrubs are ideal for their foliage which can be cut for bouquets the whole year round. *Sarcococca confusa*, the highest at 1.8m (5¹/₂ft), has fragrant flowers sometimes followed by black berries. *Sarcococca hookeriana* var. *digyna*, 50cm (20in) has dark green, slightly narrower leaves, flowers tinged with pink and black berries. *Sarcococca hookeriana* var. *humilis*, 40cm (16in) is considered to be the most hardy *Sarcococca*.

Sasa

🌿 ○

Sasa palmata is an evergreen, spreading bamboo with splendid broad leaves, growing up to 2-2.5m (6-8ft) and it may spread in width. *Sasa veitchii*, 1.5m (5ft) is always recognizable as the leaf-edges dry out in winter giving it a variegated look. Both bamboos are fully hardy and only suitable for a natural environment as they take up a great deal of space.

Saxifraga

SAXIFRAGE
❀ ☼ ○

Many saxifrage are so low that they only belong in a rock garden. There are a few exceptions which deserve a place in the border: Saxifraga cortusifolia var. fortunei, 30cm (1ft) which does not flower until September and *Saxifraga cortusifolia* 'Rubrifolia', 30cm, with red-brown foliage. Both bloom with plumes of small white flowers.

Saxifraga cortusifolia var. *fortunei*

Saxifraga pennsylvanica

Saxifraga pennsylvanica, 70cm (28in) has creamy-white plumes with long, narrow leaves. *Saxifraga rotundifolia*, 50cm (20in) has rounded foliage and loose plumes of flowers. The old-fashioned *Saxifraga x urbium*, London pride, (*S. umbrosa x Saxifraga spathularis*) makes a good edging plant, 30cm (1ft) high. This plant forms lovely rosettes from which the long stems emerge bearing pink flowers. 'Elliotts Variety' ('Clarence Elliott') has small leaves, 'Variegata', white-flecked, 'Aureopunctata', yellow-flecked. Saxifragas need some sun and partial shade and well-drained soil without winter wet.

Saxifraga × urbium

Scabiosa

SCABIOUS
♀ ✿ ☼

Scabiosa atropurpurea, 90cm (3ft), the annual scabiosa, is often sold in a mixture of matching shades including white, pink, red, blue and purple, but it is also available self-coloured. 'Blue Cockade' is lavender-blue; 'Oxford Queen', lilac-blue ; 'Salmon Queen' salmon pink. The flowers of these annuals are usually double. *Scabiosa stellata*, 45cm (18in) with unusual, rounded seed heads, good for drying. Their names describe them: 'Drumstick', 30cm (1ft) with blue flowers; 'Paper Moon', 70cm (28in) with blue-white flowers; 'Ping Pong', small white flowers. *Scabiosa columbaria*, the perennial scabious which still grows wild in dry meadows, has a wonderful cultivar - 'Butterfly Blue', 40cm (16in). The bluish-lilac flowers appear in April and the plant continues to bloom well into October. 'Pink Mist', 40cm, also flowers long, from May into September. *Scabiosa caucasica*, a perennial plant, has many lovely cultivars: 'Clive Greaves', lavender-blue, a cultivar from 1929: 'Fama', a strong plant, dark blue ; 'Miss Willmott', creamy-white flowers; 'Stèfa', dark blue flowers. *Scabiosa lucida*, 50cm (20in) with mauve flowers, blooms long, from June into September. *Scabiosa ochroleuca*, 80cm (32in) flowers as long with small, lemon-yellow flowers. *Scabiosa webbiana* (s. *ochroleuca* var. *webbiana*) has creamy-white flowers and is

Scabiosa caucasica 'Miss Willmott'

Scabiosa columbaria 'Butterfly Blue'

Scabiosa columbaria 'Pink Mist'

lower. *Scabious* need full sun and will definitely not grow in acid soil. They make beautiful border plants and are also good flowers for cutting.

Scutellaria

SKULLCAP
✿ ☼

Growers all agree that of all the scutellarias, *Scutellaria incana*, 70cm (28in) is the best and loveliest border plant. This slightly stiff, grey-leaved plant bears spikes of slate-blue flowers in August and September.

Scutellaria altissima, 60cm (2ft) has blue flowers with a white lip.
Scutellaria baicalensis, 30cm (1ft) has blue with violet flowers. *Scutellaria scordiifolia* has violet-blue flowers and dark green, long, narrow leaves. *Scutellaria columnae*, 60cm

Scutellaria altissima

Scutellaria scordiifolia

(2ft) flowers with maroon flowers. These are trouble-free plants which will grow in any good garden soil.

Sedum

STONECROP

❀ ☼

The cultivars of *Sedum spectabile* and *Sedum telephium* and their hybrid-cultivars are the most familiar varieties of stonecrop. Beginning with the last, 'Herbstfreude', 50cm (20in) is the best-known with crimson heads of flowers; 'Joyce Henderson', 70cm (28in) is newer with pinkish-brown flower heads; 'Matrona', 80cm (32in) is a much-loved *Sedum* with red stalks, grey-green foliage and pink heads of flowers; 'Mohrchen' has dark red leaves and reddish-pink flowers; 'Robustum' has carmine flowers and bluish foliage flushed with red. Well-known cultivars of *Sedum spectabile* are: 'Brilliant', 40cm (16in), a dark, deep pink; 'Septemberglut', with large fluffy heads of flowers; 'Star Dust', 40cm, with greenish-white flowers. *Sedum*

telephium subsp. *maximum* has smaller, yellow flower heads. The creamy-white, woolly heads of the flowers of *Sedum* 'White Towers' show off the high red stalks. The added bonus with these plants is that they are extremely attractive to butterflies and bees. They love the sun and well-drained soil.

Sedum 'Mohrchen'

Sedum 'White Towers'

Selinum carvifolium

Selinum wallichianum

Selinum

  ○

A special, upright plant with finely divided, lacy foliage and beautiful, flat heads of white flowers. The flower stalks are reddish-brown. There are six species of which three are more or less familiar: *Selinum carvifolium*, 60cm (2ft); *Selinum tenuifolium*, 1.5m (5ft) with smaller heads of flowers and *Selinum wallichianum*, 1m (3ft) with bigger white flower heads.
The plants flower in July and August, interweaving well as they do so; they need good, moisture-retentive soil.

Sidalcea

The best-known *Sidalcea* is 'Elsie 'Heugh', 80cm-1m (32in-3ft) high, a hybrid-cultivar with pale pink flowers clustered on spikes and recognizable by its frilled petals.

'Mr. Lindbergh' has darker, reddish purple petals. Both flower in July and August. 'Brilliant', a cultivar of *Sidalcea oregana*, has red flowers. Hybrid cultivars are: 'Little Princess', a denser habit, pink, like 'My Love', 'Rose Queen' and 'Sweet Joy'- they flower from July until September. *Sidalcea oregana*

Sidalcea 'Elsie Heugh'

Sidalcea 'Rose Queen'

subsp. spicata has pale pink, delicate clusters of flowers. *Sidalcea candida* has white flowers. *Sidalceas* are quite hardy but they do not tolerate winter wet in the ground and need protective covering when it freezes. They will flower until the first frost if faded flower spikes are removed.

Sidalcea oregana subsp. *spicata*

Sidalcea candida

Silene dioica

Silene

CAMPION CATCHFLY

The campion, *Silene dioica*, which grows wild in broad-leaved woods and on the banks of ditches, may seem too common for a border, but this plant does very well in a wild border. There are also some pleasant annuals in the family suitable for use in beds and borders. *Silene coeli-rosa* 'Cherry Blossom', 60cm (2ft) has pink flowers and a white centre; 'Blue Angel' and 'Rose Angel' are lower, 25cm (10in). They are lovely for cutting.

Silybum

The biennial *Silybum marianum*, Blessed Mary's thistle, is often grown as an annual, but the best foliage appears in the second year - and this dark green, white-marbled foliage is what the plant is grown for. If the pink thistle flower heads get a chance to set seed you could start a nursery.

The plant will flower longer if the deadheads are removed before the seeds ripen. The cultivar 'Adriana' has pure white flowers contrasting well with the foliage. This magnificent

Silybum marianum – blad

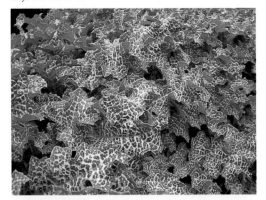

Silybum marianum

plant grows up to 1.5m (5ft) high. Snails and slugs love it so look out for them at first. Mary's thistle will grow in any soil in the full sun.

Sisyrinchium

These plants with grass-like foliage and iris-like flowers are often grown in English gardens. They are not hardy in colder areas. This genus has undergone some name changes so that even the experts are at a loss, but the following should be correct. *Sisyrinchium angustifolium*, 25cm (10in) is just like a small iris, with grassy leaves; it flowers in violet-blue at the tips of its stems from April until the end of June. *Sisyrinchium montanum* , 30cm (1ft) is a lovely, bluish-purple species with star-like flowers and a pale yellow centre.

Sisyrinchium striatum, 50cm (20in) the most familiar, has iris-like leaves and spikes creamy-yellow flowers in June and July. It has such a distinctive outline that it will help to give the border a structured design. This species is one of the strongest, but it needs to be protected in winter and is not long-lived. Fortunately the plant seeds itself.

Sisyrinchium also has a variegated aunt: 'Aunt May', 50cm (20in) with yellow-striped

Sisyrinchium angustifolium

Sisyrinchium striatum

leaves. 'Biscutella' has apricot-coloured flowers. *Sisyrinchiums* are not easy to grow, but they are well worth the effort if you can give them a sunny spot and very well-drained soil.

Skimmia

Some skimmias have berries, others do not, because the male and female flowers are on two different plants.

The buds of these shrubs develop during late summer, early autumn. The buds of male cultivars of *Skimmia japonica* look very good in the winter.

Female shrubs have fewer flower plumes, but they are decorative with their bright red berries. *Skimmia japonica* 'Nymans' is a female form with clusters of scarlet berries which are ripe from mid-October; 'Red Princess' has berries a month earlier; 'Scarlet Queen' is a fairly tall shrub with large clusters of bright red berries; 'Veitchii', 1.5m (5ft) (self-pollinating) has large, red berries. Male

cultivars of *Skimmia japonica* are: 'Fragrant Cloud', a fairly dense, free-flowering shrub; 'Rubella' (*Skimmia x foremanii*), with red leaf stems and veins and large, showy flower plumes, brown-red in the bud. *Skimmia reevesiana* 'Ruby King' is a male cultivar with profuse flowers.

At Christmas the foliage of this plant is often used for decoration. It is best in some areas not to plant it in the front garden in case of theft. Skimmias need soil rich in humus and a cool, shady spot.

Smilacina

These plants love the shade and they grow slowly, eventually becoming beautiful foliage plants, 80cm (32in) high. They flower in May and June with creamy-white plumes of flowers. They turn a pinkish-brown after flowering, still attractive and followed by berries if all goes well. If the plants are grown from seed they will bear many fruits but if they are divided there will be fewer. *Smilacina*

Skimmia japonica 'Rubella'

Smilacina racemosa

Smilacina racemosa

racemosa, or False spikenard is most often grown and it is the most impressive plant. *Smilacina stellata* only has unobtrusive little stars in a loose cluster, instead of showy plumes. These plants need humus-rich and moisture retentive-soil - especially when in leaf - and a shady position, or partial shade.

Smyrnium

☂ ☼ ○

It is as though *Smyrnium perfoliatum*, 60cm-1m (2-3ft) is luminous in the garden. The upper, yellowish-green rounded leaf of this unusual plant grows around the stem.

Above these the small, lacy heads of yellow flowers are like a haze of light. They are biennial plants which seed themselves in fertile, moist, well-drained soil, in a sunny

Smyrnium perfoliatum

position. The garden need never be without smyrniums *Smyrnium olusatrum* though rare, still grows in the wild; it used to be grown in the herb garden as an alternative for celery.

Solidago

GOLDEN ROD
 ☼ ○

Golden rod has the reputation of being rampant and sensitive to mildew. Buying a golden rod without due care can make a gardener rue the day he ever planted the weed. But there are lovely cultivars, lower, which do not fall over, hardly grow rampant, or just slightly, and are resistant to mildew.

'Cloth of Gold', 40cm (16in) flowers early, in July; 'Golden Dwarf' is a low golden rod, 30cm (1ft) with a dense habit and yellow flowers; 'Golden Mosa', 70cm (28in), lime-coloured foliage and deep yellow flowers; 'Laurin', 40cm (16in), golden-yellow flowers; 'Ledsham', 80cm (32in), bright yellow flowers. Finally, 'Praecox', 50cm (20in) and 'Strahlen-krone', 60cm (2ft).

Most golden rods flower in August and September. *Solidago caesia*, 80cm (32in) has elegant yellow flower heads; *Solidago rugosa*, 1.3m (4¹/₂ft), (not rampant, not at all sensitive to mildew) is suitable for a wild border.

All golden rods are good flowers for cutting, easy plants which will grow in any soil and situation - they are at home in light shade or sun.

Solidago 'Laurin'

Solidago 'Ledsham'

Solidago caesia

Solidaster (X)

This cross between *Aster ptarmicoides* and *Solidago canadensis* was already popular at the beginning of the century. The sunny, yellow aster-like flowers are good for cutting, often used in mixed bouquets. *x Solidaster luteus*, 70cm (28in) has branched clusters of pale yellow flowers; its familiar cultivar 'Lemore' has yellow clusters of flowers. Solidasters flower in August and September; they will grow in any soil.

Spartium

The shrub *Spartium junceum* or Spanish broom has green shoots and leaves which soon fall; it is not fully hardy. Scented, golden-yellow pea-like flowers cover its dark green branches from May to September.

It needs well-drained, chalky soil and will tolerate coastal wind which will also give it a bushier look. The shrub can be kept in shape by pruning well in spring, but not down to the old wood.

Spiraea

Spiraea grows in any soil, preferably in the sun. There are various very strong species and cultivars, often grown in public gardens. They are also excellent in perennial, mixed or shrub borders. *Spiraea x arguta*, 1.8m (5½ft), the Bridal wreath or Foam of May is one of the

Spartium junceum

Spiraea × arguta

Spiraea japonica 'Anthony Waterer'

Spiraea nipponica

Spiraea nipponica, 2.5m (8ft) is an upright shrub flowering with white heads of flowers. *Spiraea thunbergii*, 1m (3ft), flowers with white clusters in April and May.

Stachys

♀ ✿ ☼

The familiar grey Lamb's tongue or Bunnies' ears, *Stachys byzantina* is the best-known group of this genus. The plants are grown

Stachys byzantina

best-known with slender, arching branches bearing clusters of pure white flowers at the beginning of May. This shrub will even grow in dry conditions. *Spiraea cantoniensis* 'Lanceata', 1m (3ft) blooms in May and June with clusters of double white flowers on slightly arching branches; frost tender.

Spiraea chamaedryfolia, 1.5m (5ft) has beautiful foliage, fairly large white flowers in clusters - and spreading rhizomes. *Spiraea douglasii*, 2.5m (8ft) bears long, pink plumes along the ends of its branches. The deep pink 'Anthony Waterer' is probably the most familiar cultivar of *Spiraea japonica*. 'Albiflora' produces white posies in July and August; 'Dart's Red' has carmine flowers; 'Golden Princess', 40cm (16in) has yellow leaves and pink flowers; 'Gold Flame', 70cm (28in) has bronze-coloured shoots turning golden-yellow, then lime-coloured with purplish-pink heads of flowers.

Stachys byzantina 'Cotton Boll'

more for their leaves than for the grey spikes which are often removed; Gertrude Jekyll did this, only using lamb's tongues for their effective foliage. 'Big Ears', 50cm (20in) has big leaves, 25cm (10in) long; 'Cotton Boll', 40cm (20in) flowers with little globes; 'Silver Carpet' grows low, does not flower, good ground cover. There is more to *Stachys* than lamb's tongues and bunnies' ears. *Stachys grandiflora*, 60cm (2ft) has ordinary green foliage and big, purplish-pink flowers. The pink cultivar 'Rosea' is lower, 30cm (1ft). 'Superba', 70cm (28in) has lilac-pink flowers and splendid foliage. *Stachys monnieri* has an

Stachys grandiflora 'Rosea'

Stachys grandiflora

Stachys byzantina 'Big Ears'

unusual cultivar, 'Hummelo'. This plant is 90cm (3ft) high with lilac flowers irresistable to bumblebees which pay constant visits. 'Rosea', 90cm (3ft) has pale pink flowers. *Stachys annua* is an annual, woolly plant with white flowers, 30cm (1ft) high, attractive to many insects. These plants are not difficult to grow, as long as they are in the sun.

Stephanandra

This small, deciduous shrub will grow in any situation, in any soil, dry or wet. *Stephanandra incisa*, 1.2m (4ft) has elegant, arching

Stephanadra incisa 'Crispa'

shoots with plumes of little creamy-white flowers in June and July. The cultivar 'Crispa', 50cm (20in has more deeply-cut foliage, forms excellent ground cover, like 'Interzon', which is lower. *Stephanandra tanakae*, 2m (6ft) needs a sheltered, sunny position. The shrub flowers in June and July with cream-coloured flower heads; its leaves turn orange-yellow in the autumn.

Stokesia

This is not a well-known plant - it resembles the cornflower. *Stokesia laevis*, 50cm (20in)

Stokesia laevis

is the only species, with large, lilac-blue flowers. 'Alba' 40cm is a white cultivar, so is 'Träumerei', 40cm (16in), flushed with pink. Stokesias flower from July into September with good cutting flowers. They need well-drained, preferably sandy soil and sun.

Strobilanthes

❀ ☀

This plant is related to *Acanthus. Strobilanthes atropurpureus* is admired for its autumn flowering; it forms a large, shrubby clump 1.5m (5ft) high and needs protective covering in winter.

Symphoricarpos

SNOWBERRY
❀ ☀ ○ ◐

The flowers of this shrub are uninteresting, but we all know the berries from the days when we used to stamp on them, to make them pop loudly. The berries appear in the autumn and the shrub retains them in winter because birds do not eat them. *Symphoricarpos albus* var. *laevigatus*, 1.8m (5¹/₂ft) is

Symphoricarpos albus

the best-known snowberry, retaining its white berries into December. *Symphoricarpos albus* 'Constance Spry' has larger white berries. *Symphoricarpos x chenaultii*, 1m (3ft) has clusters of purplish-pink berries. *Symphoricarpos x doorenbosii* 'Mother of Pearl' is a robust shrub with big, white berries flushed with pink, later turning a uniform pink. *S. orbiculatus* is a low, rounded shrub with small, purplish-red berries which are retained for a long period. Perhaps you associate the shrub with public gardens, but just think how

Symphoricarpos in winter

Symphyandra wanneri

Symphytum officinale 'Azureum'

good the berries are in bouquets; they are only planted in parks because they are strong shrubs which will grow in any soil, in sun or shade.

Symphyandra

❀ ☼

These are little-known plants, clearly related to

Symphytum officinale 'Coccineum'

campanulas. They flower for a long period with large, pendent, bell-shaped flowers. Some are short-lived and better grown as biennials. *Symphyandra armena*, 30-60cm (1-2ft) has lovely white bells and dark green foliage. *Symphyandra pendula*, 50cm (20in) has pendent, creamy-white bells. There is a whiter cultivar, 'Alba'. *Symphyandra wanneri*, 35cm (14in) has violet-coloured flowers. *Symphyandra pendula* (syn. *S. ossetica)*, has a splendid hybrid, thought to be the result of a cross with a *Campanula*. It is a strong plant, 50cm (20in) high, forming green clumps and bearing pendent, ice-blue bells, 4-5cm (1¹/₂-2in) long. It loves full sun and well-drained soil.

Symphytum

COMFREY
❀ ☼ ○

Comfrey is a splendid plant for a wild garden; it grows too rampantly for comfort in a cultivated garden. *Symphytum x rubrum*, 30cm (1ft) is not rampant, with pendent red flowers instead of blue; the plant makes leaf rosettes and sets them off with these flowers. *Symphytum grandiflorum*, 40cm (16in) with yellowish-white flowers makes good ground cover - a nice way of saying that it spreads - a pleasant plant with cultivars in other colours: 'Hidcote Pink' and 'Wisley Blue'. *Symphytum caucasicum*, 1m (3ft) is coarser, but its flowers are a lovely blue and it is less rampant. There are also variegated comfreys, for instance *Symphytum x uplandicum* 'Variegatum', 70cm (28in), green foliage with a broad, creamy margin and lilac-blue flowers. This plant is often grown for its effective foliage

Symphytum × rubrum

alone and the flowers then removed. *Symphytum x uplandicum* itself has pink flowers which turn blue or purple. Fortunately there is also the common comfrey, *Symphytum officinale,* growing wild on the banks of the ditch. This also has the following

cultivars for the garden: *Symphytum officinale* 'Coccineum', red and 'Purpureum', purple. The plants often grow too well in the garden.

Syringa

LILAC
🌿 ☀ ○

Leaving the familiar, large-flowered lilacs which usually grow into big shrubs to one side, there are several smaller-growing lilacs suitable for the border. *Syringa meyeri* 'Palibin' is a slow-growing shrub, 1m (3ft) high, maroon in the bud and with long, lilac-pink plumes in June and July. *Syringa microphylla* 'Superba', 1.8m (5$\frac{1}{2}$ft) has deep pink flowers in loose clusters in May, continuing into September. *Syringa patula* 'Miss Kim', 2m (6ft) flowers in May with long, branched, violet-purple plumes. Lilacs love the sun and need well-drained soil. It stimulates growth to remove faded flower heads for the first few years.

Syringa meyeri 'Palibin'

Tagetes erecta 'Vanilla'

Tagetes erecta 'Safari'

Tagetes

AFRICAN MARIGOLD

African marigolds have a reputation for being very stiff and formal - and so they are. The familiar globes on erect stalks have been trying to improve their image for years, without much success. There is little to be done with the squat plants and their round flower heads, like dwarves with their heads between their shoulders. It is an improvement if they have longer stems, like *Tagetes tenuifolia* which deserves a place in the border. This small-flowered African marigold forms cheerful clumps 20-30cm (8-12in) high and flowering profusely. 'Corina' is orange; 'Lemon Gem' yellow and 'Paprika' brown-red. 'Tessy Gold', a cross between *T. tenuifolia* x *T. erecta* grows higher than the former and golden-yellow. The tall, true African marigold *Tagetes erecta*, 80cm (32in), in many colours varying

Telekia in the border

Tanacetum parthenium 'Butterball'

from cream ('Vanilla', 'Safari') to all shades of yellow and orange, could be used in the border with discretion, but they are better off in a row in the kitchen garden for cutting purposes. African marigolds excrete a substance which keeps eelworms at a distance; they are sometimes planted in combination with roses for this reason. They will have to be sown early for this purpose as the excretion does not take place until four months after sowing.

Tanacetum

The perennial feverfew, *Tanacetum parthenium (Chrysanthemum parthenium)* is grown as an annual; it has some attractive cultivars and the taller of these are suitable for

291

Tanacetum vulgare

Tanacetum vulgare 'Crispum'

Telekia speciosa

the border. 'Roya', single flowers and 'Ball's Ultra Double' and 'Butterball', both double, grow up to 60 - 80 cm (24-32in). 'Rotary' wtih curved petals, resembling a Rotary emblem, 60cm high.

Tanacetum vulgare, the tansy which grows in the wild, has some civilized cultivars: *Tanacetum vulgare* 'Crispum', 80cm (32in) has attractive, fern-like foliage and yellow flower buttons; 'Silver Lace', 1.2m (4ft), has silvery, hairy leaves. *Tanacetum macrophyllum* is a large, fairly coarse plant with grey-white heads of flowers.

Tanacetum cilicium, 1.2m resembles the last, but its foliage is grey and it tolerates more sun. Plants which used to be called *Chrysanthemum coccineum* and before that *Pyrethrum*, are now also known as *Tanacetum*. Most of these are colourful, daisy-like cultivars belonging to the Coccineum group. They combine well in the border with their height of 50 - 80cm (20-32in), preferably in good garden soil and full sun. 'Alfred' is dark red; 'Eileen May Robinson' is pink; 'Red King' is cherry-red; there are also some double-flowered cultivars. The genus *Tanacetum* seems to embrace plants which do not belong together. Feverfew was formerly used to combat fever; tansy was supposed to prolong life.

Telekia

❀ ☼ ○

Telekia speciosa, 1.5m (5ft) is definitely not suitable for a tidy border. But in a wild garden it is an impressive figure, with large, heart-shaped foliage and big, yellow ray flowers

from June into August. The plant prefers moist soil in a sunny spot, but not at midday. The soil must not be too rich.

Tellima

❀ ○ ◓

Tellima grandiflora, or Fringecups is a really strong plant, good ground cover and evergreen all the winter. The stems, 80cm (32in) high are clustered with small green flowers tinged with red.

Remove faded flowers to avoid self-seeding. 'Purpurteppich' and 'Rubra' have reddish foliage and these cultivars are probably the same plant, each other's synonyms. The plants are easy to grow with few needs. They are excellent shadow plants for places where no other plants will grow.

Tellima grandiflora

Teucrium scorodonia

Teucrium

GERMANDER

This may be familiar as a low hedge in the herb garden, but not as a border plant. *Teucrium hircanicum (T. arduini)* is a lovely, bushy plant with grey-green foliage and long spikes of deep purple flowers. It blooms from July into September. *Teucrium scorodonia*, 50cm (20in), grows on sandy regions in the wild; it has a cultivar 'Crispum marginatum', with green, scalloped leaves and a white margin, turning purple in winter, pale green flowers; 'Crispum' has scalloped foliage without the margin. *Teucrum chamaedrys* (the wall germander) 'Nanum', 30cm (1ft) is often used for hedges; *Teucrium x lucidrys*, 50cm (20in) is a sub-shrub with spikes of pink flowers. These plants need a place in the full sun and prefer dry soil.

Thalictrum

MEADOW RUE

These elegant border plants combine well with others because they are not intrusive. The leaves are finely divided and the flower head is a loose plume. *Thalictrum aquilegifolium* 'Album', 1m (3ft) has flowers with striking white stamens; 'Purpureum', 1.3m (4½ft) and

Thalictrum aquilegifolium 'Purpureum'

Thalictrum flavum subsp. *glaucum*

Thalictrum polygamum

'Thundercloud', 1m, both have lilac flower plumes. *Thalictrum delavayi (T. dipterocarpum)* is the best-known. This 1.5m (5ft)-high plant has big clusters of small lilac flowers with yellow stamens, flowering from July into September. 'Hewitt's Double' has double, lilac flowers and 'Sternenhimmel', ('Alba') is covered with a cloud of snow-white flowers. *Thalictrum flavum* subsp. *glaucum*, 1.5m (5ft) has blue-grey foliage and pale yellow plumes.

Thalictrum lucidum can grow up to 2m (6ft), with pale yellow flowers. The 2m-tall stems of *Thalictrum polygamum,* flowering with white clusters, stay in place even in winter. *Thalictrum rochebrunianum*, one of the most beautiful, has dark purple stems and small lilac flowers with yellow stamens. 'Elin' is an unusual Swedish cultivar with grey-blue, later greenish-grey foliage and large, branched, white clusters of flowers. It can grow up to 3m (9ft). Thalictrum likes moist soil rich in humus. A layer of mulch will help if the soil is too dry.

Thermopsis

✿ ☼

This is a rare plant with flowers resembling lupins. *Thermopsis caroliniana (T. villosa)*, 1.2m (4ft) has dense spikes of yellow flowers in June and July, followed by long seed pods and blue-green foliage. *Thermopsis lanceolata (T. lupinoides)* is lower, 70cm (28in), flowering earlier, in May and June. *Thermopsis mollis*, 90cm (3ft) already has sulphur-yellow flowers in April. Experts and growers

Thermopsis caroliniana

cannot agree on the names for this plant, bit it is difficult to come by so we shoud be satisfied with one species, whatever it is. The plant needs a sunny position in dry soil.

Thymus

THYME

Thyme is a herb that generally grows so low that it is only used at the edge of the border, or at the sides of a path, or as ground cover. A low hedge of *Thymus vulgaris* at the front of the border is also a good idea. There are so many different species, cultivars and hybrid-cultivars; the owner of a herb nursery in England already has over 130! There are green-leaved and variegated thyme, creeping, prostrate thyme - white, pink and purple-flowering thyme. *Thymus x citriodorus* 'Silver Queen' has silvery foliage and lilac-pink flowers; 'Variegatum', variegated leaves. The

Thymus × citriodorus 'Variegatus'

Thymus 'Doone Valley'

Thymus serpyllum 'Pink Ripple'

cultivar 'Aureus' has golden leaves. The hybrid-cultivar 'Doone Valley' has grey-green foliage flecked with golden-yellow and lilac flowers. *Thymus serpyllum*, creeping thyme only 5cm (2in) high, has a white cultivar 'Albus', a mauve one 'Coccineus' and 'Pink Ripple'. *Thymus praecox,* (as *Thymus serpyllum* should be called) has the most cultivars. 'Hall's Variety' is lilac and woolly, like the soft 'Pink Chintz'. It is impossible to survey all the different thyme plants; they all need full sun and chalky soil.

Tiarella

FOAMFLOWER

Tiarella cordifolia, 25cm (10in) is the most familiar foamflower, a pleasant plant for soil deficient in lime, flowering from April into June with slender white spikes of flowers. The

Tiarella wherryi

Tiarella cordifolia

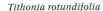
Tithonia rotundifolia

plant will soon spread if it is comfortable. The leaves of cultivar 'Oakleaf' are like those of the oak; it has pinkish-white flowers. *Tiarella polyphylla*, 35cm (14in) has elegant spikes of cream to pink flowers. 'Kew Form' is the improved form. *Tiarella wherryi*, 30cm (1ft) has really beautiful foliage and a pointed spike with small pink or white flowers. Tiarellas make excellent ground cover in the shade.

Tithonia

MEXICAN SUNFLOWER

Tithonia rotundifolia is a tall, sturdy plant, 1.5m (5ft) with large orange flowers resembling zinnias or small sunflowers. They flower from August into October and usually need sticks or neighbouring plants for support. 'Torch' is an orange cultivar and there is also a mixture, New Hybrids, 45cm (18in) high with pale green, divided leaves and yellow flowers. They are good for cutting.

Tolmiea

PICKABACK PLANT...YOUTH-ON-AGE

Not many people know that this house plant

will grow very well in the garden, able to withstand a temperature of -17°C (3°F). The name illustrates the way in which young plantlets develop from brood buds on the leaves. Roots are formed where the plantlets touch the ground and the pickaback plant is on its way. It spreads without growing rampantly, making good ground cover or edging. The leaves of *Tolmiea menziesii* are light green, the stems emerging from them are like those of *Tellima*. The cultivar 'Taff's Gold' has light green, yellow-marbled foliage. Youth-on-age requires fairly moist soil in a shady spot.

Tolmiea menziesii in the border

Trachymene coerulea

BLUE LACE FLOWER
♀ ☼

Trachymene coerulea is still to be found in many catalogues under *Didiscus caeruleus*. It is a lace flower with lilac-blue flower heads and finely divided leaves - often called *Scabious* by those who are not familiar with the plant. It grows to 60cm (2ft), flowers for a long period, from June into October and is excellent for cutting. It needs fertile soil and a sheltered, sunny situation.

Trachymene coerulea

Tradescantia virginiana 'Zwanenburg Blue'

Tradescantia 'Innocence'

Tradescantia

SPIDERWORT
❀ ☼ ○

One of the species has a much nicer name - Moses-in-the-cradle, which describes the way the small flowers are tucked away in the grassy leaves. The genus is called after John Tradescant (1608-1662), a gardener, botanist and plant hunter. He was the first English botanist to visit Russia, bringing back many plants, also from other expeditions. One of the plants which he introduced from North America was *Tradescantia virginiana*. Many hybrid-cultivars were developed from this plant, varying from white to all shades of blue, even red.

The colour of the species varies from blue to pink and - rarely - white. 'Zwanenburg Blue' has large, dark blue flowers; 'Charlotte' is bright pink; 'Innocence' is a pure white; 'Osprey', white with violet stamens; 'Rubra', maroon.
All tradescantias flower from June into September and although the flowers bloom for one day only, there are so many new ones every day that this does not show. They will grow in any soil if not too dry and in a sunny position, or partial shade.

Tradescantia 'Osprey'

Tricyrtis

TOAD LILY

❀ ○ ◐

The toad lily flowers quite late and looks so exotic that it does not seem hardy. Fortunately appearances are deceptive, the plant is hardy and its subtle colours blend well with other perennial plants in the border. *Tricyrtis*

Trifolium incarnatum

formosana, 60cm (2ft) flowers in September and October with lilac-purple spots on a lighter background. *Tricyrtis hirta* is white flushed with pink and with red spots. 'Alba' has white flowers, sometimes purple-spotted; 'Miyazaki' has white flowers with many lilac spots; 'White Towers' is a bushy plant with white flowers. *Tricyrtis latifolia*, 70cm (28in) flowers early in June with brown-spotted, soft yellow flowers. These plants like moist soil rich in humus and a spot in the shade. If the soil is sufficiently moist they will grow in the sun and flower earlier.

Trifolium

CLOVER

♀ ☼

Even the clover family is not above bedding down in the border, but not all species are suitable. The annual *Trifolium incarnatum*, 50cm (20in) with beautiful crimson flowers, very attractive to insects, is often used as green manure - but it also looks good in the border. *Trifolium pannonicum*, Hungarian clover, 70cm (28in), a perennial plant with creamy-white flowers good for cutting. *Trifolium repens* is a creeping clover, very useful as

Trifolium rubens

ground cover. 'Pentaphyllum' has brown leaves with a green edge; 'Susan Smith' has yellow-variegated foliage; 'Wheatfen' has

Trillium chloropetalum var. *giganteum*

purple foliage and red flowers. *Trifolium rubens*, 40cm (16in) has long, pinkish-red little heads of flowers, blooming from below upwards, still attractive when faded. This clover, which flowers from June to August, tends to fall over but grows up again. Clovers prefer full sun and well-drained soil.

Trillium

TRINITY FLOWER   WOOD LILY

These are woodland plants which feel at home in a shadow border and also look good in a shrub border. The soil must be moist and rich in humus. These are unusual plants with thick rootstocks which produce shoots with three leaves in a whorl, from which the flowers emerge. They grow slowly, but if they are comfortable they will spread a little further every year. They go underground in summer to

Trillium luteum

Trollius chinensis 'Golden Queen'

prepare themselves for the following year, flowering early, from April until June. *Trillium erectum*, Birthroot or Squawroot, 50cm (20in) has dark green foliage and chestnut-maroon flowers. The cultivar 'Album' is even lovelier with whitish-green flowers.

Trillium grandiflorum

Trillium chloropetalum var. giganteum has marbled leaves and dark red or white flowers. Trillium grandiflorum, 40cm (16in) or Wake-robin is the best-known, most striking species and the easiest to grow. Big, pure white flowers later turning pink match the collar of light green leaves. *Trillium luteum*, 30cm (1ft) has yellowish -green flowers and lightly spotted leaves. *Trillium recurvatum*, 35cm (14in) has marbled foliage and chestnut-brown, recurved petals. *Trillium sessile*, only 25cm (10in) has beautifully marked leaves and chestnut-brown flowers. *Trillium undulatum*, 30cm (1ft) has white to pale pink flowers and is difficult to grow because the soil has to be acid and really well-drained. Once you have seen trilliums you will want to start a shadow border for them. *Trillium erectum* and *Trillium grandiflorum* can grow in the sun, as long as they have good, moist soil and shade in the heat of the day.

Trollius

GLOBEFLOWER

It is obvious that globeflowers are related to

Trollius europaeus 'Superbus'

buttercups. They have larger flowers and do not grow rampant, like many species of buttercups. A dry border on sandy soil will not do for these plants because they need moist, more substantial soil and are often planted by streams and in marshland gardens. *Trollius chinensis* 'Golden Queen', 80cm (32in) blooms from May into July with orange-yellow flowers. *Trollius europaeus* 'Superbus', 60cm (2ft) has large sulphur-yellow flowers.

Most of the globeflowers are hybrid-cultivars in all shades of yellow and orange. 'Cheddar' and 'Taleggio are both 60cm high and pale yellow. 'Earliest of All', 50cm (20in) has golden-yellow flowers; 'Etna', 60cm, dark orange; 'Lemon Queen', 60cm, lemon-yellow; 'Orange Princess', 50cm, large orange-golden flowers; 'Prichard's Giant', 90cm (3ft), dark orange-yellow; 'T. Smith', yellow. Trollius likes cool, moist, fertile soil and sun or light shade.

Trollius 'Lemon Queen'

Ursinia anethoides

Ursinia

Ursinia anthemoides is an annual, South African plant; its orange flowers with a dark ray and centre remain open when the sun is not shining. The cultivar 'Annegreet' has ochre-yellow flowers with a dark ray. They love full sun and well-drained soil; good flowers for cutting.

Uvularia

This is an unusual, almost unknown plant for a shadow border. It is a woodland plant resembling Solomon's seal but with larger, yellow flowers. *Uvularia grandiflora*, the Bellwort or Merry-bells flowers from April into June with lemon-yellow, lily-like flowers on arching stems. *Uvularia perfoliata*, 60cm (2ft) is like the former, but it is lower with greenish-yellow flowers; The cultivar 'Citrina' has creamy-yellow flowers. These natives of fertile woodlands require light or partial shade in the garden, and soil rich in humus.

Valeriana

VALERIAN

The true *Valeriana officinalis*, 1.2m (4ft) which grows in the wild by the waterside and in moist, deciduous woods, is also suitable for a wild border. The colour of the flowers is pink; cultivar 'Alba' is white. *Valerian phu* 'Aurea', 80cm (32in) has lovely, golden-yellow young foliage, turning green in summer. It has

Veronica austriaca 'Knallblau'

Uvularia grandiflora

the same pale-pink flowers as *Valeriana officinalis*. *Valeriana allariifolia*, 90cm (3ft) has pink flowers. These are easy plants that will grow in any soil.

Valeriana alliariifolia

Veratrum californicum

Veratrum album

Vancouveria

 ○ ◐

This smaller relation of the *Epimedium* is useful for ground cover in a shadow border of perennial plants or shrubs. *Vancouveria chrysantha* is evergreen with leathery leaves which flowers in April and May with small, lemon-yellow flowers. *Vanvouveria hexandra* is deciduous and much like an *Epimedium*. It is 30cm (1ft) high, with white flowers and was in fact formerly called *Epimedium hexandrum*. Both species like soil rich in humus.

Venidium

♀ ☼

Venidium fastuosum is a true sun-loving plant which never opens to reveal its centre in bad weather, while it is the centre which is so stunning about this plant.
'Zulu Prince' has white petals with a contrasting dark ring around a black centre. 'Orange Prince' has orange petals with a black

Venidium fastuosum 'Zulu Prince'

ring encircling a black heart. They are good flowers for cutting, opening up indoors whatever the weather.

Veratrum

 ○ ◐

This is an impressive plant with ribbed leaves resembling those of hostas and just as attractive to slugs and snails. It is not readily available and if you find one it will not be cheap. This is understandable as it grows at a snail's pace. It could take seven years to flower and then only in very rich, deeply-dug soil. A border plant for persevering gardeners only. *Veratrum album*, 1.5m (5ft), or White false hellebore has long, white-to-green spiraea-like plumes of flowers and finely ribbed foliage. *Veratrum nigrum*, 1.2m (4ft), or Black false hellebore is slightly more common with splendid ribbed leaves and long stems bearing reddish-brown flowers.

Veratrum califoricum, 2m (6ft) is a stately, robust plant with long stems and spikes of brown-black flowers. *Veratrum* should be planted and then left where it is for years. It does not like to be moved about and needs a spot in fertile, moist soil in the shade or partial shade.

Verbascum

MULLEIN

Many species of mullein are biennial or short-lived perennial plants, but they usually seed themselves freely. Most of them like the sun and prefer dry soil, except *Verbascum blattaria*, the moth mullein. They are most decorative with tall spikes set with flowers. Some mullein is grown mainly for its leaf rosettes, such as *Verbascum olympicum* which forms a silvery-white rosette 1m (3ft) across. *Verbascum chaixii* 'Album', 80cm

Verbascum in the border

(32in) is one of the most popular mulleins. This is partly due to the beauty of this plant as it weaves its way through the borders in the garden of Ton ter Linden in the Netherlands. The flowers are white, the stamens purple. *Verbascum bombiciferum*, a biennial, has leaves covered with white down and yellow flowers. To name a few of the many hybrid-cultivars: 'Cotswold Queen', 1.2m (4ft), dark apricot; 'Densiflorum', yellow; 'Pink Domino', 90cm (3ft, pink); 'Royal Highland', 1.2m, apricot.

Verbascum chaixii 'Album'

Verbascum 'Cotswold Queen'

Verbena × hybrida met *Persicaria affinis*

Verbena × hybrida 'Romance Apricot'

Verbena

♀ ❀ ☼

The common verbena of gardens sold as a colourful bedding plant has various hybrid-cultivars in pleasant colours suitable for the self-coloured border. Neither 'Peaches & Cream' in apricot, cream, pale orange and yellow nor 'Romance Apricot' will look out of place in an apricot-coloured border. 'Romance Lavender' and 'Lilacina' (a cultivar of *Verbena rigida*) have lavender-coloured flowers. These low verbenas are useful for the

Verbena bonariensis

edge of the border, but there are also higher varieties. *Verbena bonariensis*, 1.4m (4¹/₂ft) high, is a plant with lilac-purple flowers and such a loose, thin habit that it never intrudes The plants will disappear after a winter with temperatures lower than -10 C (14 F), but they will have seeded themselves amply. *Verbena hastata* 1.2m (4ft) has violet-blue flowers in erect, tubular spikelets. The species and the cultivars 'Alba' and 'Rosea' flower from July into September and the faded flowers still look quite good in the border. *Verbena macdougalii*, 1m (3ft) has lilac-purple, upright, unbranched spikes of flowers and coarsely-toothed foliage, altogether coarser than Verbena hastata. *Verbena canadensis* 'Homestead Purple' is fully hardy with beautiful, dark purple heads of flowers and only 30cm (1ft) ,high, contrasting with the higher varieties. Verbenas love the sun and well-drained soil.

Veronica

❀ ☼ ○

The true *Veronica* is as blue as can be, but there are also pink and white varieties. They vary in height from very low creepers, 5cm (2in) to the tall ones almost 1m (3ft) high. It should not be difficult to find a *Veronica* to suit every border. *Veronica austriaca* has cultivars 30-40cm (1-1¹/₂ft) high, excellent for the border: 'Ionian Skies', sky-blue; 'Kapitèn', deep blue; 'Knallblau', vivid blue; 'Shirley Blue', lilac-blue; 'True Blue'.and 'Royal Blue', true to their names. *Veronica austriaca* subsp. *teucrium* is bright blue with small leaves while those of the species can be oval or oblong.

Veronica spicata 'Pink Damask'

Veronica gentianoides

'Rosenrot, 40cm, deep pink; 'Pink Damask', 40cm, pink; 'Spitzentraum', 60cm (2ft), light blue. *Veronica sibirica* is now called *Veronicastrum sibiricum* and *Veronica virginica* is now *Veronicastrum virginicum*. Veronicas prefer good garden soil and sun, but they will also grow in light shade.

Veronicastrum

Veronicastrums are tall, stately border plants which used to belong with the veronicas, with a few exceptions. *Veronicastrum sibiricum*,

Veronicastrum sibiricum 'Apollo'

Veronicastrum sibiricum

Veronica gentianoides, 40cm (16in) is an especially decorative, light blue Veronica with leaf rosettes, flowering in May and June. 'Alba' has dark green foliage and white flowers; 'Pallida' has porcelain-blue flowers. *Veronica longifolia*, 80cm (32in) has blue spikes of flowers. 'Blauriesin' is bright blue, 'Schnee-riesin' is white. Unfortunately the species and its cultivars are susceptible to mildew. *Veronica spicata*, the Spiked speedwell, has green foliage and blue flowers, growing to 50cm (20in). Some of its many cultivars are: 'Alba', white, 40cm (16in); 'Erika', 30cm (12in), pink; 'Romiley Purple', dark violet;

Veronicastrum virginicum in de herfst

Viburnum carlcephalum

1.8m (5¹/₂ft), has leaves in whorls on the stems which are topped by spires of flowers.

'Apollo' has long, twisted lilac spikes of flowers and 'Spring Dew' is white, both flowering in July and August. *Veronicastrum virginicum*, 1.2m (4ft) is a distinctive figure with long, blue spikes. 'Alboroseum', 1.2m, is pinkish; 'Album', 1.2m, white; 'Diana', 1.4m (4¹/₂ft), white; 'Fascination', 1.8m (5¹/₂ft), lilac-coloured, from Ton ter Linden's gardens; 'Lavendelturm', 1.8m, lavender-blue; 'Pink Glow',1.2m, pale pink. These plants are lovely even in winter and they should stay in place for as long as possible. *Veronicastrum* needs the same growing conditions as the higher veronicas; good soil and light or partial shade.

Viburnum

🌿 ☼ ○

The lower viburnums are known for their foliage, flowers or berries. *Deciduous viburnums* are generally hardier than the evergreens. There is one exceptional *viburnum* which treats us to flowers at a time when there is nothing else to be seen outside, and that is *Viburnum x bodnantense*. This shrub flowers from late autumn well into the winter and its flowers stand up to the frost. 'Charles Lamont' has pure pink flowers; 'Dawn' is strongly-scented and 'Deben' has pink buds

and white flowers from autumn into spring. *Viburnum x burkwoodii* 1.8m (5¹/₂ft) is another lovely one with white flowers from the autumn until the end of spring. 'Anne Russell' has sweet-scented flowers; 'Chenaultii' flowers two weeks earlier; 'Park Farm Hybrid' has larger flowers. *Viburnum x carlcephalum* has fragrant flowers, pink in the bud, white when open. *Viburnum plicatum* resembles a hydrangea; 'Mariesii' is a well-known white cultivar and 'Pink Beauty' an unusual one, first white, then pink. Both have splendid autumn colours. *Viburnum*

Viburnum plicatum 'Mariesii'

Viburnum rhytidophyllum

carlesii 1.5m (5ft) flowers in April and May with brownish-pink buds and white flowers. *Viburnum davidii*, 40cm-1m (16in-3ft)) is an evergreen shrub with narrow, three-veined, glossy green foliage, heads of white flowers in early summer and bright blue berries in autumn and winter. *Viburnum farreri*, 2.5m

Viburnum plicatum 'Pink Beauty'

(8ft) flowers from February into April with fragrant pinkish-white flowers. *Viburnum rhytidophyllum* has large, evergreen leaves and cream-coloured flowers. *Viburnum opulus* 'Park Harvest', 1.5m (5ft) is a Guelder rose with golden-yellow foliage, white flowers and red berries. *Viburnums* do not like chalk and prefer a place in the sun in fertile, moist soil. They will not thrive in poor soil.

Vinca

PERIWINKLE

☼ ⸎ ○ ◗

The Greater periwinkle (*Vinca major*) and the Lesser periwinkle (*Vinca minor*) have many cultivars. They form an excellent, evergreen ground cover. The lesser periwinkle is fully hardy, the greater is not reliable. *Vinca major* has large leaves and purple-blue flowers like its cultivar 'Variegata', and leaves with a creamy edge; 'Reticulata' has blue flowers and large, green and yellow-veined leaves. *Vinca minor* has small leaves. 'Alba', white flowers; 'Atropurpurea', purple flowers; 'Argenteo-

Vinca major 'Reticulata'

variegata', silver -and 'Aureo-variegata' gold variegated leaves; 'Bowles' Variety' ('La Grave') has large, lavender-blue flowers; 'Gertrude Jekyll' flowers freely with starry white flowers. Vincas usually flower from March/April through to June/July. They grow on any humus-rich soil.

Viola

VIOLET

The perennial violet, *Viola cornuta* 25cm (10in), or Horned violet is an excellent border plant, flowering early in May with lovely small blue flowers continuing into September. 'Alba' has smaller, white flowers, also suitable for the border along with other hybrid-cultivars of the Cornuta group. Not all of them are long-lived, but the following are strong varieties: 'Ardross Gem', purple flowers with a yellow centre; 'Blue Splash', white splashed with blue; 'Boughton Blue', a very strong plant with light blue flowers; 'Eastgrove Blue' ('Eastgrove Blue Scented'), with long stems; 'Fiona', fragrant

Vinca minor 'Gertrude Jekyll'

white flowers, the edges flushed with mauve.; 'Hazelmere' ('Nellie Britten'), mauve; 'Ivory White', with larger flowers; 'Milkmaid', light blue flowers turning milk white; 'Molly Sanderson', almost black - needs a light background to set off the flowers; 'Victoria Cawthorne', lilac-pink flowers. *Viola labradorica* has small, violet-blue flowers and

Viola 'Ardross Gem'

Viola odorata

deep purple foliage. *Viola gracilis*, a purple-blue violet, flowers from March until the end of September! *Viola odorata*, the friendly Sweet violet, flowers very early in March and April with small, sweet-scented flowers. When the flowers have faded the leaves start to grow and the violet becomes a foliage plant. 'Red Charm' has reddish-purple flowers, 'Königin Charlotte' violet-blue. *Viola sororia* 'Albiflora' blooms in April and May with pure white flowers, but its cultivar 'Freckles', white spotted with lilac, is more widely-known. Violets love moisture-retentive soil and a spot in sun or shade.

Viola labradorica

Waldsteinia ternata

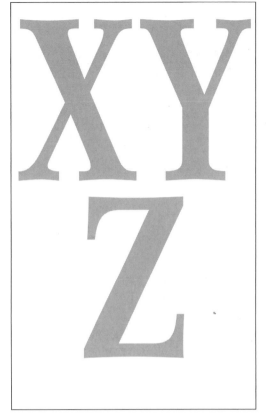

Waldsteinia

 ○ ●

Waldsteinia ternata makes good ground cover with runners forming a spreading mat - not desirable in the border, but useful for ground cover under shrubs. It is a cheerful, fresh-looking plant with three-parted leaves and yellow flowers. *Waldsteinia geoides* forms dense clumps without runners. It has clusters of yellow flowers and blooms in April and May. This plant could well be used for ground cover in the border. It is uncomplicated and will grow in any normal garden soil.

Yucca

 ☼

The formal rosettes of these striking plants were used as focal points by Gertrude Jekyll in her borders. Her favourites were *Yucca filamentosa*, or Adam's needle, *Yucca flaccida (Y. filifera)*, *Yucca gloriosa*, or Spanish dagger and *Yucca recurvifolia*. They are usually planted as a specimen. *Yucca filamentosa*, 1.2m (4ft) has stiff, grey-green rosettes and a tall stem with white, pendent bells. 'Variegata', 1m (3ft) is a yucca with narrow leaves edged with cream-white. 'Schneetanne', 1.5m (5ft) has cream-white flowers and foliage with a silvery-green sheen. *Yucca flaccida*, 1.5m forms upward-growing rosettes bearing creamy bell-shaped flowers. 'Golden Sword' has yellow-striped foliage; 'Ivory' has white-striped foliage. *Yucca recurvifolia* and *Yucca gloriosa* are not fully hardy in cold areas. They need full sun and good soil.

Yucca in the border

Yucca

Zinnia elegans

Zinnia

Zinnia

⚥ ☼

Self-coloured zinnias can be planted in the border with discretion. The following are tall, giant-flowered zinnias: the canary-yellow 'Canary Bird'; the lilac 'Dream'; the green 'Envy Double'; the carmine-pink 'Illumination'; the white 'Polar Bear'; the red 'Scarlet Fame' and the 'Yoga' series in golden-yellow. 'Yoga Gold', the lilac 'Yoga Mauve' and the soft yellow 'Yoga Primrose' are exceptionally tall and they also have large flowers. The cultivars of *Zinnia pauciflora* are less stiff; they are now called *Zinnia peruviana,* but fortunately the cultivars have not been changed. These zinnias are 75cm (2^1/$_2$ft) high, more branched, with smaller flowers and a

Zinnia 'Caramel'

more natural habit. Red cultivars are 'Bonita Red', 'Red Spider' and 'Indian Red'. There are also 'Bonita Yellow' and the apricot-coloured 'Caramel'. Zinnias flower in July and August and thrive in sun and fertile soil.

Zinnias in various colours

Index

Bibliography

Marlene Ahlburg, Helleborus, Nieswurz, Schneerosen, Lenzrosen, Verlag Eugen Ulmer

Andreas Bärtels, Zwerggehölze, Verlag Eugen Ulmer

Trevor Bath, Joy Jones, The Gardeners Guide to growing Hardy Geraniums, David & Charles

John Bergmans, Vaste planten en rotsheesters (uitgave 1924) Voorheen de erven Loosjes

John Bergmans, Vaste planten en rotsheesters (tweede druk 1939), J.H. Faassen-Hekkens

Peter Beales, Klassische Rosen, Dumont

Alan & Adrian Bloom, Blooms of Bressingham Garden Plants, Harper Collins Publishers

B.K. Boom, Flora der gekweekte kruidachtige gewassen, Veenman en Zonen

B.K. Boom Flora van Kamer- en kasplanten, Veenman en Zonen

B.K. Boom Nederlandse Dendrologie, Veenman en Zonen

Darthuizer Vademecum 1994

Brian Davis, The Gardener's Illustrated Encyclopedia of Trees & Shrubs, Viking

Lothar Denkewitz, Farmgärten, Verlag Eugen Ulmer

Rudolf Dirr, Hamamelis und andere Zaubernussgewächse Verlag Eugen Ulmer

Colin Edwards, Delphiniums, The Complete Guide, Crowood

Walter Ehrhardt, Hemerocallis Daylillies, Batsford

Alfred Fessler, Der Staudengarten, Verlag Eugen Ulmer

Karl Foerster, Einzug der Gräser und Farne in die Gärten, Verlag Eugen Ulmer

Reinhilde Frank, Päonien, Pfingsrosen, Verlag Eugen Ulmer

Hermann Fuchs, Phlox, Verlag Eugen Ulmer

Het Nieuwe Fuchsia Handboek, Groenboekerij

Rodney Fuller, The Complet Guide of Pansies, Violas and Violettas, Crowood

Alfred B. Graf, Tropica (vierde druk) Roehrs

Alfred B. Graf, Hortica (eerste druk) Roehrs

Christopher Grey-Wilson, Poppies, Batsford

Mark Griffiths, Index of Garden Plants, Macmillan Press

Mabel G. Harkness, The Bernard E. Harkness Seedlist Handboek (tweede druk), Batsford

Sarah Hart, Plantenvinder voor de Lage Landen (Editie 95-96, Terra

James C. Hickman e.a., The Jepson Manual of Higher Plants of Califonia, University of California Press

The Hillier Manual of Trees and Shrubs, David & Charles

The Hilliers Gardener's Guide to Trees & Shrubs, David & Charles

Anthony Huxley e.a. The New Royal Horticultural Society Dictionary of Gardening, Vier delen, The Macmillan Press Ltd

Clive Innes, The World of Iridaceae, Holly Gates International

International Checklist for Hyacinths and Miscellaneous Bulbs KAVB 1991

Helmut Jantra, Siergrassen, Groenboekerij

Leo Jellito e.a., Die Freiland Schmuckstauden, Verlag Eugen Ulmer

Klaus Kaiser, Anemonen, Verlag Eugen Ulmer

Fritz Köhlein, Hosta (Funkien), Verlag Eugen Ulmer

Fritz Köhlein, Freiland sukkulenten, Verlag Eugen Ulmer

Fritz Köhlein, Iris, Verlag Eugen Ulmer

Fritz Köhlein, Nelken, Verlag Eugen Ulmer

Fritz Köhlein, Primeln, Verlag Eugen Ulmer

Fritz Köhlein, Riddersporen, Gottmer

Fritz Köhlein, Saxifragen, Verlag Eugen Ulmer

Gerd Krüssmann, Manual of Cultivated Broadleaved Trees and Shrubs Vol I, II en III, Timber Press

Mineke Kurpershoek, Bloembollen in de tuin, Hollandia

H.J. van de Laar e.a. Naamlijst van vaste planten (derde druk), Proefstation voor de Boomkwekerij 1995

H.J. van de Laar e.a. Naamlijst van houtige gewassen (vijfde druk) Proefstation voor de Boomkwekerij 1995

Christopher Lloyd, Clematis, Viking

Tony Lord, The RHS Plant Finder 1996/97 RHS

Corinne & Robert Mallet, Harry van Trier, Hortensien, Verlag Eugen Ulmer

Brian Mathew, Hellebores, Alpine Garden Society

Brian Mathew, The Smaller Bulbs, Batsford

Currier McEwen, The Siberian Iris, Timber Press

Ruud van der Meijden, Heukels' Flora van Nederland (22ste druk), Wolters-Noordhoff

Erhard Moser, Rhododendron, Wildarten & Hybriden, Neumann Verlag

Wiert Nieuman, Rotsplanten, Groenboekerij

Jisaburo Ohwi, Flora of Japan, Smithsonian

Piet Oudolf, Henk Gerritsen, Droomplanten, Terra

Kristo Pienaar, Inheemse Plante vir die tuin, Struik Timmins Uitgewers

Roger Phillips, Martyn Rix, Bloeiende heesters, Spectrum

Roger Phillips en Martyn Rix, Bol- en knolgewassen (tweede druk), Spectrum

Roger Phillips en Th.F. Burgers, Bomen van de gematigde streken, Spectrum

Roger Phillips, Grassen, varens, mossen en korstmossen, Spectrum

Roger Phillips en Nicky Foy, Kruiden, Spectrum

Roger Phillips en Martyn Rix, Rozen, Spectrum

Roger Phillips en Martyn Rix, Vaste planten, Spectrum

Graham Rice, Elizabeth Strangman, The Gardeners Guide to growing Hellebores, David & Charles

Christine Recht, Bambus, Verlag Eugen Ulmer

Alan Rogers, Peonies, Timber Press

Mien Ruys, Het Vaste Plantenboek (derde druk) Moussault's Uitgeverij

Georg Schmid, The Genus Hosta, Timber Press

Werner Schöllkopf, Astern, Verlag Eugen Ulmer

Roger Turner, Euphorbias a Gardeners Guide, Batsford

T.G. Tutin e.a. Flora Europaea, Cambridge University Press

Helga & Claus Urban, Camellia's, Gottmer

Julia Voskuil, Een tuinboeket Eenjarigen, Terra

David Way, Penstemons, The Hardy Plant Society

Peter F. Yeo, Geranium, Verlag Eugen Ulmer

Zander, Handwörterbuch der Pflanzennamen, Verlag Eugen Ulmer

Various magazines and periodicals:
Gartenpraxis, Groei en Bloei, The Garden, Dendroflora, Succulenta, Alpine Garden Society, Scottish Rock Garden Club, Gesellschaft der Staudenfreunde, Hardy Plant Society.

Nursery catalogues:
Kwekerij de Bloemenhoek, Vaste plantenkwekerij Rob de Boer, De dikke zadenlijst van de Cruydt-hoeck, De Hessenhof, Coen Jansen, Kwekerij Kabbes, Eleonore de Koning, Peter Nijssen en Piet Oudolf.

Photography credits

The photographs in this book are by George M. Otter, with the exception of the following which are by Mineke Kurpershoek: (l-lerft r=right)

p39 top r, 55 centre r, 82, 87 bottom r, 97 top r, 102 bottom r, 110 top and bottom l, 111 top l, 125 bottom l, 138 bottom, 144 top r, 145 bottom r, 166 top l, 176, 182 centre r, 183 bottom l, 185 top l, 199 top r, 210 top, 236 bottom l, 240 bottom l, 242 bottom r, 247 top r, 257 bottom, 261 bottom r, 263 top r, 267 top l, 276 centre r, 285 bottom r, 289 top r, 295 top l and top r.

Photolocation

Belgium
Arboretum Kalmthout
Herkenrode
Villa Julienne

Great Britain
Arley Hall, Cheshire; Barnsley House, Gloucestershire; Bernwode Plants, Buckinghamshire; Bicton Park, Devon; Blickling Hall, Norfolk; Bosvigo House, Cornwall; Bressingham Gardens, Norfolk; Calderstones Park, Merseyside; Capesthorne Hall, Cheshire; Castle Kennedy, Schotland; Catforth Gardens, Lancashire; Cawdor Castle, Schotland; Chatsworth, Derbyshire; Chenies Manor, Buckinghamshire; Cholmondeley Castle, Cheshire; Crathes Castle, Schotland; The Crossing House, Cambridgeshire; Culzean Castle, Schotland; Dalemain, Cumbria; East Lambrook Manor, Somerset; The Garden House, Devon; Greencombe, Somerset; Hadspen Garden, Somerset; Helmingham Hall, Suffolk; Hestercombe, Somerset; Hexham Herbs, Northumberland; Hidcote Manor, Gloucestershire; Hill of Tarvit, Schotland; Holehird Gardens, Cumbria; Holker Hall, Cumbria; Houghall College Gardens, Durham; House of Pitmuies, Schotland; Kinross House, Schotland; Levens Hall, Cumbria; Mertoun Gardens, Schotland; Ness Botanic Garden, Cheshire; Newby Hall, North Yorkshire;
The Old Rectory, Northamptonshire; Poyntzfield Herb Nursery, Schotland; Rodmarton Manor, Gloucestershire; Royal Botanic Garden Edinburgh, Schotland; Savill Garden, Surrey; Stapeley Water Gardens, Cheshire; Tatton Park, Cheshire; Threave Garden, Schotland; Trengwainton Garden, Cornwall; Wallington, Northumberland; Yorkshire Garden World, North Yorkshire

Finland
Botanic Garden Helsinki

The Netherlands
Arboretum Trompenburg, Rotterdam; Bamboepark, Schellinkhout; De Blommenhof, Rockanje; Jan Boomkamp Gardens, Borne; Botanische Tuin D'n Hof, Overloon; Botanische Tuinen Universiteit Utrecht; Botanische Vijvertuin Ada Hofman, Loozen; CBN-showtuin, Heemstede; Marijke van Dijk, Heerle (NB); De Drie Wilgen, Harkstede; De Dwaaltuin, Rockanje; Berna van Essen, IJsselstein; Geesterhof, Bergen (NH); De Hagenhof, Angeren; 't Hof Overwellingen, Wemeldinge; Hoveling Plant BV, Berkenwoude; Huis Bingerden, Angerlo; Juust Wa'k Wou, Schoondijke; Kasteel de Haar, Haarzuylens; Kasteel Middachten, De Steeg; Kasteel Warmelo, Diepenheim; Kasteeltuinen Arcen; Kijktuinen Irène Jansen, Gieten; Koelemeijer Tuinen De Hof van Heden, Z.O.Beemster; De Kooihof, Ankeveen; Kwekerij de Beemd, Warffum; Kwekerij Rob de Boer, Frederiksoord; Kwekerij de Border, Delden; Kwekerij de Boschhoeve, Wolfheze; Kwekerij Coen Jansen, Dalfsen; Kwekerij Eleonore de Koning, Oudelande; Kwekerij de Heliant, Appelscha; Kwekerij Ida Hartog, Peize; Kwekerij Kabbes, Suameer (Fr.); Kwekerij de Kleine Plantage, Eenrum; Kwekerij Matthijs Smaal, Ruinen; Kwekerij Piet Oudolf, Hummelo; Kwekerij Overhagen, Velp; Kwekerij Ploeger, De Bilt; Kwekerij de Zandhoogte, Tolbert; Kwekerij Pieter Zwijnenburg Jr., Boskoop; De Lange Kroft, Angeren; De Mattemburgh, Woensdrecht; Modeltuinen Harrie Boerhof, Dwingelo; Priona-tuinen, Schuinesloot; De Rhulenhof, Ottersum; De Rozentuin, Oostvoorne; Herman Simons, Wouw; Sophora Natuurtuinen, Lelystad; Sortimentstuin Boomteeltpraktijkonderzoek, Boskoop; Summer Garden, Enkhuizen; Tuinen Mien Ruys, Dedemsvaart; Tuinen Ton ter Linden, Ruinen

Sweden
Botanische tuin Uppsala